Solo to the Top of the World

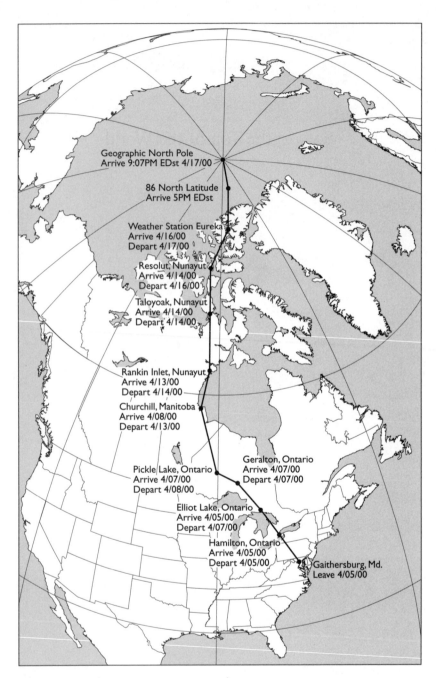

Gus McLeod's flight to the Geographic North Pole

SOLO

to the

TOP

of the

WORLD

Gus McLeod's
Daring Record Flight

Gustavus A. McLeod

Smithsonian Books

Washington and London

Production editor: Robert A. Poarch
Proofreader: Laura Starrett
Designer: Brian Barth

Library of Congress Cataloging-in-Publication Data
McLeod, Gustavus.
   Solo to the top of the world : Gus McLeod's daring record
flight / Gustavus McLeod.
      p. cm.
   ISBN 1-58834-102-X
   1. McLeod, Gus—Journeys—Arctic regions. 2. Pilots—
United States—Biography. 3. Arctic regions—Description and
travel. 4. North Pole—Description and travel. I. Title.

G635.M39 A3 2003
910'.9163'2—dc21
[B]   2002035970
British Library Cataloguing-in-Publication Data is available

Manufactured in the United States of America
10 09 08 07 06 05 04 03   5 4 3 2 1

⊛The paper used in this publication meets the minimum re-
quirements of the American National Standard for Information
Sciences—Permanence of Paper for Printed Library Materials
ANSI Z39.48-1984.

Contents

Acknowledgments

▼

I would like to dedicate this book to my grandmother, Annie Easterling Gray. Her guidance and inspiration was the moving force that gave me the need to seek the test.

But hers was not the only influence in my life. My parents, Reverend John R. McLeod and Jonell Gray McLeod, held me to high standards. But no matter what course I would have taken, I knew my parents were on my side. My grandfather, Areather McLeod, gave me the connection to my name and its history. My great grandmother, Lara Hollaway Gray, gave me the stubbornness of a mule. Grandfather Daniel Gray, Aunt Seabia McLeod Hughes, Uncle Charlie, R. L., Clyde, Great-great Uncle Martin Luther Gray, Great Uncle Garrett Gray, Great Uncle Martin Gray, Great Aunt Dorothy Gray, sisters Ann McLeod Piper and Jovonsia McLeod Taylor, brother Daniel McLeod, Aunt Debora Gray Fleder, Uncle Booker Felder, Aunt Doris Gray Perkins, Aunt Calpurnia Gray Weathersby, Uncle Dock, Uncle L., Uncle M. C., Fay Weathersby, Herman McLeod, Garland Gray, Ben Alvin Gray, Bennard Herbert Gray, Cynthia Gray Scales, Joe Gray, Martin L., Martin Gray Jr., Harry Gray, Ronald Weathersby, La Barbara Weathersby, Selvanus Powell Weathersby III, Paul Gray Pope, Great Aunt Deborah Gray Pope, Great Uncle Clemmens Easterling, and all my relations both near and far, the most diverse group of humanity every to call itself related, you are in me and with me always.

The famed Tuskegee Airmen have always been my heroes. I am proud to call some of them my friends. Charles Magee, Bill Broadwater, Sam Rhodes, Leo Gray, Harry Shepard, Ira O'Neal, Elmer Jones, J. T. Valentine, Woody Crockett, Hamp Johnson, Walter McCreary, Ted Robinson, Spann Watson, Lee Archer, Roscoe Brown, Gus Palmer, Dr. Florence Parrish St. John, and Ms. Theophia Lee, just to name a few.

Roscoe Tuner, that great bear of a man from my hometown, left his mark on me and Corinth, Mississippi.

But no mention of my life influences would be complete without the mention of Corinth and the people there who made a difference in my life: Louise Collins, the Lumpkin family, Mrs. Shannon, E. S. Bishop, James R. Boyd, Mrs. Allen, Ronald Westmoreland, Do Do, Johnny Johnson, Lee Lee, Mr. Patterson, Harry Crayton, Paulett Agnew, the Long family, Nepolian Lusk, Mrs. Dillworth, Telford Norman, Paul Durr, and Mrs. Pickford.

And then there is Steve Weathers, my high school buddy, best man, and life-long friend to whom I must admit, "You were right."

There were lots of friends who gave their time and labor to this project. Bruce and Valerie Kendall supported and worked tirelessly on my first flight. Randy Smith gave me the front cowling. Lenny Charles helped me hang an engine in a field. The Baughers family, Ali Telipore, Capital Area Light Flyers, Tull Morgan, Robbie Vajdos, Don Sanders, Paul Thommesen, Stephen Shechtel, Joe Hunt, Jerry Lewis, Rick Galvin, Greg Thailmus, Louis, Daryl Governale, Frank Johnson, Ross Merry, Harry Jackson, Ed and Linda Primozic, Joe Groverow, Walt Starling, Bill Rickman, Dave Wojnarawski, Jim Lanning, Jay Rosenburg and Steve Rosenburg, are just some of the individuals who helped me. There are many more, but memory and names sometimes fail me.

To my flying buddy, Doug Duff, "We will miss you."

The friends I met along the journey were special, like Lynn and Bernie Cox who helped me with fuel and friendship, Tim Cameron and Cameron Dole who never let a dull moment spoil a good time, my Inuit friends, Johnny and "Studley" Thomas, who taught me the ways of the North and the Jig, Mayor Denise Lyales of Taloyoak, Terry in Resolute, Jobie, Dave, and Rai in Eureka, Steve and the good people of Keywaten Air, the gang at First Air, and the whole town of Churchill, Manitoba, did their best to make my expedition successful.

I'd like to thank the troops based at Canadian Forces Station Alert and the 400 squadron for their help. I will always remember the monster house that made me a member during my stay there. Digger, Digger, Digger Do, the roof is on fire.

My team that came with me to the Pole was a good bunch. Steve Pearce, you are the best friend a guy could have. Robert Thommesen was always there when I needed him. Thanks, Robert. Lorie Butterfield, thanks for your belief in me and support of me. Dwyne Empy, you are not that funny, but the best damn cameraman I have ever seen.

Thanks to the people at the Smithsonian National Air and Space Museum, Don Lopez and Tom Allison, for helping retrieve the Stearman. Many thanks to the New York Air National Guard, the United States Air Force, and the Naval Reserve out of Andrews for transporting the Stearman. And thanks to Cathy Allen and her staff at the College Park Aviation Museum. To all those I forgot, please forgive me.

My son, Gustavus, helped me write this book. Without him, I could not have written this book. His questions and insights brought out the best and worst of my nature. Between Gustavus and my editor at the Smithsonian Institution Press, Mark Gatlin, they were bound and determined to see the book reflect my soul. Mark Gatlin, what can I say, without you there would not be a book. It was painful at times. But in the process father and son learned a lot more about each other.

Michelle, your work on this book was key. You are a gifted editor.

To my children, Gustavus, Hera, and Lara, never try anything like this. Daddy loves you.

And the biggest thanks of all goes to my wife, Mary Alice Lockmuller McLeod. Yours was the burden of carrying the heaviest load. You stayed behind with the worry of a husband in harm's way while maintaining the details of day-to-day life. I could not have asked for a better wife. We often write what we find difficult to say. For the record, I love you with all that I am.

It is said, "No man is an island." Indeed, mine is a wonderful world. Thank you all.

Introduction

The Corinthian Legion of Pilots

From my schoolyard in Corinth, Mississippi, I saw the Air Force jets—chalk-white streaks strewing from their tails—and heard the roaring power of their engines. It was 1961. I was six years old and I wanted to be a pilot. That spring, I talked my father into taking me to the air show at the Air Force base in Columbus, Mississippi, one hundred miles from Corinth, a long trip at that time. I can still feel my father standing next to me as we looked with awe at a B-52 bomber.

"Look at that!" said my father. "The tire is almost as tall as I am! And this thing flies!"

The wonder of it, I thought to myself. It flies!

As we were leaving the show my father bought me a ten-cent balloon with COLUMBUS AIR SHOW emblazoned boldly on its side. It was huge, as grand as the day had been for me. That balloon managed to stay aloft for almost six months. Even after it was nothing more than a limp rubber shell, I kept it—a little kid running around with his dreams tied to a deflated balloon hanging from his back pocket. The trip to the air show was a turning point in a personal odyssey that began at the age of two when my Choctaw grandmother told me my spirit-animal is the hawk and that would come full circle over the North Pole more than forty years later.

I talked about the air show to anyone who would take my bait: "You know what I saw in Columbus?" or "You wouldn't believe how big those airplanes were!" I even told the old checkers players at J.C.'s Barbershop.

In Corinth, J.C.'s was the unofficial meeting place for the exchange of local information, rumors, and general knowledge. It was also the place where the town's elders—wise men with long memories and stories to tell—played their exclusive games of checkers. Even my father, who was the local preacher, did not have the seniority to join the game. At J.C.'s one could count on catching up on all the gossip and news of any importance. For my father, as for most male Corinthians, a haircut at J.C.'s was a central part of his social life. Every Tuesday afternoon my father would take me to J.C.'s for my haircut; then on Friday night he would go for his. That way he would get the weekend update on Tuesday, and on Friday—"adults only" night—he would get a more detailed wrap-up of the week.

One of those Tuesday afternoons, I told my story of the magnificent Columbus Air Show to the barbers and the checkers players, who listened with great interest. Because there was nothing worth knowing in Corinth if it did not relate in some way to Corinth, at the end of my tale the elders then felt obliged to set me straight on the history of aviation as it related to our town.

"Son, them fly boys in Columbus ain't nothing. Now Roscoe, there's a pilot. That boy was landing them things out on the edge of town 'fore them boys today was even born. They didn't even have airports back then. They could just land them things anywhere. I think Roscoe may have even helped invent them damn things."

"Didn't he have something to do with them boys down in Tuskegee?" another checkers player asked.

"Jimmy, you don't know what you talking about. Them boys in Tuskegee fought in WWII. Roscoe's older than that. He's damn near as old as me, and I'm seventy!"

"Yep," another one chimed in, "now them boys down there in Tuskegee, them boys could fly. But it was old Roscoe put Corinth on the map. He even made some movies."

"Who's Roscoe?" I asked.

"He's one of them Turners from over in north Corinth. He still comes around every once in a while. I saw him less than a year ago over in town."

"I ain't seen him since they named that airport after him over there near Rienze," said another.

"Yeah, old Roscoe even knows Lindbergh and such. You sure he didn't have anything to do with them Tuskegee boys?"

Roscoe Turner was a hero right out of the golden age of aviation. In the 1920s and 1930s, he won numerous closed-course and cross-country races, including the coveted Bendix Trophy, which is now in the National Air and Space Museum in Washington, D.C. Roscoe Turner was also a daredevil, a bigger than life showman who was the first to do the stunt of flying a plane into a house. A large flashy man, who sported a handlebar mustache and wore a diamond-encrusted set of wings on the chest of his flight jacket, Roscoe would do just about anything to attract attention. For one of his sponsors—Gilmore Fuel, whose mascot was a lion—Roscoe bought a lion cub, named him Gilmore, and flew with the cub until he grew too large to fit in the airplane. Upon the lion's retirement, Roscoe paid to have Gilmore cared for until his death. (Gilmore is currently at the Smithsonian Institution's restoration facility in Suitland, Maryland.) Roscoe was the pilot of movie stars and kings, the doer of great deeds, and to me at six years old, the emperor and champion checkers player of all pilots.

In Corinth, there were only two things about aviation that really counted for anything: Roscoe Turner and the boys from Tuskegee. The Tuskegee Airmen were a group of black aviators formed in the early 1940s by the U.S. government as an experiment to see if Negroes were capable of mastering the complexities of modern aviation. And fly they surely could. They flew bomber escort missions in Europe during the Second World War and never lost a plane to enemy aircraft, the only fighter group in the war able to make that claim.

None of the Tuskegee Airmen were from Corinth, and at six years old, I thought that was a fact that bordered on gross negligence. Still, my community was proud of the airmen, and every time pilots were mentioned at J.C.'s, someone was always ready to talk about them and Roscoe Turner.

"Rev," they addressed my father, "take that boy by the airport next time old Roscoe's in town."

One afternoon, two years later, while I was in my room intently working on a model airplane, I heard my father's voice instruct me to put on my good clothes and come with him: "We're going to the airport."

The airfield named after Roscoe was small, a few planes here and there—not anything like the huge Columbus Air Force Base, which, to this day, is the standard by which I judge all other airports. There were no planes flying in or out as my father and I pulled up to a small tin-plated hangar, the only building on the field, almost brazen in its solitude. I was so nervous I could hardly open the car door. Walking dutifully behind my father, as was the custom for children in Mississippi in those days, I stopped in the doorway of the tiny hangar, pausing to take in the scene and prepare my entrance. With my back straight, my chin held high—my bearing was as stately, almost regal, as I could muster—I slowly proceeded in. Attached to the hangar there was a small office and in the office was an old sofa, some tools strewn about, the sweet smell of oil, and a man who got up from a the sofa and greeted my father, "Hi, Rev!"

"Mr. Norman, how are you today? I appreciate you letting me come out like this. I hope we're not too late."

"Rev, Roscoe'll be along here in a bit," Mr. Norman said. "I didn't know you were interested in flying."

"I'm not. It's my son. He's head over heels about it. It's all that boy can talk about. He's driving me crazy!"

Mr. Norman looked to me and smiled. It was the first time my presence in the room had been acknowledged. I remember puffing out my chest to show this mere mortal that I was destined to be a great pilot.

"Son, you want to be a pilot?"

"Yes, sir," was all I managed to squeak out.

"Well, son, maybe I'll take you flying sometime. Think you would like that?"

I felt faint. This guy was a pilot, the first one I had ever met! I was so embarrassed that I hadn't realized his importance that I could not respond.

Gruff and annoyed, my father said, "Say something, boy. The man is talking to you. I don't understand it. At home you can't shut him up. Maybe I should leave him here with you, and then I can get some peace."

"Sure, I'd keep him. He's been looking at nothing but these airplanes since he walked in. I think deep down he's a pilot."

That was my introduction to Telford Norman, the man who would become the most influential person in my life in aviation. Mr. Norman, a white man, and my father already knew each other. My father had a weekly Sunday morning radio show in Corinth, and Mr. Norman was a listener. I am not sure exactly how they met, but it was not uncommon for whites to listen to my father's show or call up to talk to him. At the time I thought it was odd that they did not attend his church service to hear the long version of his sermon, but I guessed they preferred their religion in condensed, radio form. I could not blame them.

While Mr. Norman and my father chatted, I wandered outside to await the coming of the great Roscoe Turner. Without warning an airplane came out of the horizon, circled the field, and landed.

As the plane taxied toward the hangar, rolling down the strip in my direction, I heard my father's voice behind me: "Get out of the way, boy! That thing can kill you!"

But I was transfixed, unable to move. Suddenly my father grabbed the back of my collar and yanked me out of the path of the oncoming plane.

"He's all right, Rev," Mr. Norman calmly interjected, "just a little excited."

As Mr. Norman walked toward the plane, I followed him. He seemed amused by my quick attachment to him, but said nothing as I trailed along. As we reached the aircraft, two men got out. One of the men, the taller of the two, looked at me standing next to Mr. Norman.

With the biggest grin I had ever seen on anyone he gestured toward me and said, "What's this, Telford, a past dalliance of yours?"

The men shook hands, laughing at the tall man's joke and, with me in tow, strolled over to where my father was standing.

"This is Reverend McLeod, the preacher over at City Road Church," said Mr. Telford. "He's got a pretty good radio sermon Sundays on WCMA." (WCMA— "Watch Corinth Move Ahead"—was the only local radio station.)

The tall man spoke. "Oh, yes. Roscoe Turner is my name. Is old Bill Keys still around?"

"J. R. McLeod is mine. And yeah, old Keys is still raising hell." They all laughed at that.

"Me and that boy go way back," Roscoe said. "We used to play together."

I was confused by their conversation and wondered if Roscoe Turner was black. While he appeared to be a white man, my Choctaw granny had told me that if "someone hangs around black folks long enough people assume they are black." I realize now that she was speaking about her own experience.

"Mr. Turner, this is my son, Gustavus McLeod. He's been begging to meet you."

I froze, awaiting the parting of the clouds or the falling-out fit of a person "catching the spirit." But all I felt was an intense urge to go to the bathroom. Roscoe extended his hand to me. I stared straight ahead, a blank expression on my face.

Embarrassed and suddenly perturbed, my father spoke. "I don't know what's wrong with that boy today. He's acting odd. Shake the man's hand, son. We've come all the way out here to meet him."

I was scared, humiliated, and sure my bladder was about to burst. I remember with shame looking up at Roscoe Turner and telling him, between gulping sobs, that "I got to go to the bathroom." My father's face turned beet red as Roscoe doubled over with an explosive laugh and Telford Norman pointed the way to the facilities, on the far side of the hangar.

When I returned, Mr. Norman came up to me: "You all right, son?"

"Yes, sir." My eyes were still teary, but I was no longer sobbing.

"That's the first thing you learn as a pilot, boy," Roscoe said. "Go to the bathroom before you fly." Then Roscoe turned to my father and Mr. Norman and said, "I think he may be a pilot. He's got the trots. Just like we had in the old days."

Everyone laughed, everyone, that is, but me. Years later I learned the meaning behind the joke. In the early days of aviation, the engines were lubricated with castor oil, a strong laxative, and pilots in open cockpits often got sick from the fumes.

A car pulled up and Roscoe Turner got in. The great one was gone almost as quickly as he had come. I was stunned by the abruptness of the departure.

Mr. Norman glanced at me and shrugged, "We're just going to have to get you back out here to make you a pilot. What do you think about that?"

I wiped away the tears and beamed proudly, "Yes sir, yes sir, yes sir."

I did not forgot Mr. Norman's promise to take me flying. I saw him now and again in town or said hello to him when he called my father. But four years would pass before I found my way back to the airport. It was eight miles out of town and getting there would take some luck, pluck, and a particularly lousy day at school.

I had not planned to go to the airport on a particular day. In fact, beyond wishful thinking, I had not made real plans to go the airport on any day. But one fateful afternoon with a bad day of school behind me and a long band practice and a late walk home ahead of me, I decided to go the airport. My plan was as spontaneous as it was simple—so simple that I was surprised I had not thought of it before. All I had to do was get to the airport and back home before my father returned from work. Time was not a major concern since in addition to his preaching, my father worked as a teacher in Tishimengo, Mississippi, and during the school week he would leave Corinth early and not return until late in the evening. Logistics, however, were a problem, but one that was also solved by the Department of Education. Because there was only one school in Alcorn County for people of color, we were bussed to school from every town in the area. The bus going in the direction of Rienze ran alongside of the airport. All that I had to do was to get on that bus, get off at the right stop, walk into the airport, and find Mr. Norman—which is exactly what I did.

Everything was the same as I had remembered it—the small hangar straddling the airstrip on which a small group of planes stood. The growing fear and doubt that had traveled with me on the ride from school suddenly gave way to joy.

"I don't believe I just did this," I said in triumph, as I headed toward the hangar.

As I neared the door it swung open and Mr. Norman stepped out and walked toward one of the airplanes near the strip. He did not notice me.

"Hey, Mr. Norman!" I called, running to catch up with him.

He turned around at the sound of his name. By the time I reached him I was breathing heavily, worn out from the excitement and the dash.

"Hi, Mr. Norman." I said again, just in case he had not heard me clearly the first time. "Remember me? I'm Gustavus McLeod. Remember, I came here with my father to meet Roscoe Turner awhile back?"

I beamed proudly, though most of my memories of that day were anything but proud. He smiled, obviously recalling the day.

"Rev. McLeod's boy. Sure, I remember you. Is your father here?"

When I told him the whole story of how I got there he turned red with laughter.

"You did all that just to come here to the airport? I'll tell you what, anyone who tries that hard to come here deserves to go for a flight. What'd you think about that?"

I was caught off guard by the swiftness of the offer. Mr. Norman wanted to take me up in an airplane. Oh, great day. A gift from the gods of flight; the moment of my redemption was at hand. Mr. Norman told me to get into the airplane, an old J2 Cub. He showed me how to hold my feet down on the brakes so that the plane would not roll while he hand-propped it. The plane did not have a starter, so you had to turn the prop by hand to get it going. A puff of smoke blew back into my face as the engine caught and sputtered to a start. The smell was exhilarating: a heady mix of oil and fuel and propwash, air blasting back from the propeller. One of the oldest jokes in flying is to ask a pilot trainee on his first day at an airport to go out and get a bucket full of propwash. To this day whenever I start an aircraft I remember my first moment in a plane.

We taxied down to the end of the runway. Mr. Norman pushed the throttle, the airplane bolted forward, the sudden rush of power driving me back in my seat. The wheels still spinning, the plane left the ground gently but forcefully. It was a strange sensation, as though the ground was falling away from the plane rather than the plane rising. During the flight, Mr. Norman explained what he was doing and even let me take the controls for a short time. I was in heaven. That first flight was absolutely amazing. As we turned back toward the airport, I knew without question the direction my life would take.

I helped bring in the airplane, thanked Mr. Norman, and collected my things quickly. I was reeling between the joy of the flight and the fear of how I was going to keep it secret.

"Bye, Mr. Norman, I've got to walk, and fast."

"Not so fast," he said and then offered me a ride back to school.

In the car we talked about flying and I told him that I would be a pilot.

"You can come on out to the airport anytime and work for me," he offered. "In exchange, I'll give you flying lessons. But you got to ask your father."

"Sure, Mr. Norman, thanks," I said, although I knew my father would never allow it. After I had embarrassed him in front of Mr. Norman and the great Roscoe Turner, he had made it clear that there would be no more talk of airplanes.

But destiny cannot be thwarted. Once again my father's teaching schedule opened a window of opportunity. He had taken on a job in another town and came home only on weekends or late at night. My mother had started working in the Head Start program, so my sister, Annie, and I were left with a sitter, whose only interests were gossip, men, more men, and food, in any order they came. Since I did not fall into any of those categories, she was never particularly concerned about my whereabouts. Every day I could, I turned up at the airport to work. Mostly I washed airplanes—which I did not mind one bit—and washed each with enthusiastic pride.

I was fourteen by then and I spent every minute I could at the airport. I listened to the pilots talk about flying; listened to them tell stories of things they had done, things they had heard others do. And I dreamed of the things I would do. Sometimes when I was standing around looking like a lost dog, Mr. Norman or another pilot would take me up for a ride. Sometimes they would even let me take the controls. Soon Mr. Norman allowed me to taxi his Cub around by myself. But no one would let me solo.

One secret Saturday, I watched some crop dusters take off, land, and speed-taxi their tail-draggers around the field. Unlike the more familiar tricycle-gear airplane that has one wheel under each wing and a nose gear wheel, a tail-dragger's third wheel is under the tail. Tail-draggers lift tail first from the ground and take off when the rear of the airplane is level with the front. The great fun is to watch the better pilots speed-taxi around the field, front wheels on the ground and the tail in the air, like chickens running in a barnyard.

One day I was alone at the airport, preparing to wash a tail-dragger that was on the other side of the tie-downs, far from the water hose. I decided to taxi it over to the water. When I took over the controls I was overtaken by an irresistible desire to speed-taxi down the taxiway. I pushed the throttle forward for more speed until I was really hauling down the taxiway. I felt the rear of the plane rise and knew that the tail had lifted. I was looking out at the taxiway ahead of me, smiling triumphantly.

What a breeze, I thought.

I decided to drop the tail down and get back to the business of washing the plane when I felt the plane lift up beneath me. In a panic, I looked down the side toward the ground, and sure enough, I had taken off. Paralyzed with fear, I held the stick for dear life. I had no idea how to fly the thing and there I was heading straight for the wild blue yonder.

There was nothing else to do but circle the field and attempt to land. Reluctantly, I took the airplane higher and turned toward the runway, drawing a wide arc in the sky. I was flying more on instinct than real learning. Lining up with the strip on the ground, I slowly descended, fear pounding through my body.

"Please don't mess this up," I said to something deep inside me.

Perhaps I should have been worrying more about my life than the plane, but dying was the last thing on my mind. At the time I felt dying would have been preferable to damaging the plane and having to explain how it happened.

The wheels slammed onto the ground hard and bounced the plane back into the air. I cut the power and the engine slowed to an idle. I froze, holding on to the stick for dear life. The plane drifted back down, hit the ground, and bounced back into the air and down again. Finally the wheels held, rolling fast. I had no control of the airplane. It was rocking back and forth. As it rolled down the pavement, the plane started to career to the right, circling toward the edge of the runway. It crossed onto the grass, back on then off the taxiway, skidding hard into the grass near the fence, where it jostled and turned violently to the left. Then it stopped. Badly shaken, I got out of the plane and calmed myself, relieved that both the plane and I were still in one piece. A few minutes later I climbed back into the cockpit and taxied over to the washing place. My misadventure had left a few marks on the aircraft and a large black skid mark on the runway. I spent the rest of the day trying to rub out the errors of my ways.

I was working on the final touches when Mr. Norman showed up. He gave my work a nod of approval and, grinning broadly, asked me if I thought I could fly the plane as well as I washed it.

"Yes sir," I said, keeping my own smile to myself, "I think I can."

I was in high school when we moved to Washington, D.C., where my father had been assigned to a new church. My flying suffered during those years. On summer trips back to Corinth to visit my grandparents, I saw Mr. Norman occasionally and did a little flying. But that was pretty much it. I spent my senior year in high school in Europe as an exchange student and did not fly that year at all. When I returned from Europe, I enrolled at Catholic University of America in Washington because my parents wanted me to be at home for a while and because CU offered me a good financial package to study chemistry.

Over the summers, I took various jobs ferrying airplanes that no one else wanted to fly to someplace else to be worked on, dusting, or whatever I could get. I flew junk while I waited for something bigger and better to come along. In the meantime, I joined the Marine Corps Platoon Leaders Class, a program designed to turn out commissioned officers upon graduation. I took the Marine aviator's test, scored high, and made plans to become a Marine pilot. But in 1976, when I graduated from college, I was informed that no aviator positions were available. To add injury to that insult, in my senior year the military doctor told me that I would need to wear glasses in a few years, scuttling any hope I had of gaining a flying slot with the Marines. Since I was on a school scholarship and had not taken any money for school from the Marine program, I decided not to take a commission. I graduated from college and the next day married my college sweetheart, Mary Alice Lockmuller.

If 1976 was not a good year for neophyte pilots, neither was it good year for newly hatched chemists. So I did what I knew how to do: I flew part time and went back to school, taking graduate courses in engineering and education at the University of Maryland, College Park. I thought perhaps I could become a pilot in one of the other military branches, but the Vietnam War had ended and pilots were being laid off for peacetime. No slots were available, no matter how much flight time I had.

It was around that time that I learned that if I wanted to get any job piloting I would need my instrument license. So while my new bride worked to support us, I continued at school, worked part time as a security guard, putting whatever money I made, and fair chunk of what my wife made, into a instrument certification course at the College Park Airpark. The comings and goings made for an unusual married life. I worked as a security guard from midnight until eight in the morning, rushed to College Park for classes, and then to the Airpark for flying. I was back at the apartment by four, where I slept until Mary would wake me at eleven to begin the process all over again. Romantic love may be blind, but true love sees everything—Mary deserves to be canonized for putting up with me during that difficult time.

The instructor at College Park was a real airman, a man's man—and the ladies loved him for it. He was one of the nicest fellows I ever met, but he had pretty expensive tastes, which he paid for at his students' expense. As long as he dangled the prospect of getting a license rating, I, for one, kept giving him money.

One day when I was at work on my instrument license, I met Walt Starling, an area traffic reporter and sort of a celebrity at the airport. When Walt went up for his daily report, his fans would crowd around to see him take off. Back then being a traffic reporter really meant something to us hangar rats. I thought he was terrific because he had found a way to make his living as a pilot, and I had not.

Three mornings a week I came into the airport to do my instrument work. On one of those mornings I saw Walt getting ready to go off on his rounds.

He approached me and said, "Hey kid, I see you out here all the time. What are you doing?"

"I'm trying to get my instrument ticket."

Walt laughed heavily. "You're trying to get it here? Well, good luck to you. I hope you've got lots of money."

"I've been flying for a while," I said. "I think I can get my ticket pretty easily."

"It doesn't matter if you've been flying as long as God. You're not going to get your instrument ticket here until you run out of money."

I thanked him for the tip. Walt Starling and I are still friends, and to this day if Walt tells me something I believe it without question.

During the time I was working on my instrument license, I managed to get an interview with a commercial airline. I felt so good about the prospect that I walked into the interview certain I would land the job. I figured my time had finally come to fly for the pros.

"How much jet time did you have?" the interviewer asked, as soon as I sat down.

Jet time? Nobody had told me anything about needing jet time. How the hell did he think I was going to get jet time? I could not even afford time in a twin-propeller airplane, let alone a jet. The military did not have any open slots, and nobody would ever let me ferry a jet.

After telling the interviewer something along these lines, he said, "Sorry, but you need jet time in order to fly for a commercial airline. There are lots of pilots with jet time coming out of the service now. We can't use you."

Desperate for any chance to qualify, I half considered stealing a jet and flying it around for seven or eight hours until it ran out of fuel, then landing the thing, going back to the airlines, and saying, "See. I can fly a jet." But I figured I would probably get about twenty to thirty years in prison for doing such a thing, and by the time I got out my jet time would no longer be current. Anyway, a long time ago I had promised Mr. Norman my airplane borrowing days were over.

My options and my money had run out and I needed more time to spend with my new wife, so I took a job as a science teacher in the D.C. public schools. After that, things really changed for the better: the Central Intelligence Agency (CIA) recruited me for an undercover position. What red-blooded American boy would not jump at the offer to work for the CIA? My four years with the agency are the proudest of my career. While I do not talk about what I did for them, I wholeheartedly recommend the agency to any high-spirited individual looking for challenges and adventure. On a visit to CIA headquarters in McLean, Virginia, I told Director George Tenet that I would always have a special place in my heart for the agency that never sleeps.

After leaving the CIA and spending some time working for others, I decided to go out on my own. I bought a medical supply company and went into business for myself. The pay was better, and Mary and I had two young ones by then. I still flew every chance I could. I bought and sold small planes, flying them in between the buying and the selling to build up time, all the while hoping to find a place for myself in aviation. I could not shake a longing for adventure and continued to search for a way to satisfy the itch to be like my hero, the great Roscoe Turner.

1. Flying Nomads

In the golden age of aviation there was a group of nomadic adventurers called barnstormers, maverick aviators who, with little more than an airplane, hope, guts, and enough fuel to get to the next town, lived the lives legends are made of. Once that "next town" was in sight, the barnstormer would buzz the area a few times, head to a nearby field, land, and wait for the excited townsfolk to come running. It was the 1930s, the hard, dreary, demoralizing years when jobs were as scarce as a good laugh. The arrival of a barnstormer was guaranteed to be a wonderful distraction from the worries of the day. In the carnival-like atmosphere, the pilot would amaze the onlookers with derring-do and follow it up with an offer (for a modest fee) to take any would-be aviators up for the ride of their life in his flying machine. By the end of the day the barnstormer had earned enough for a hearty meal and fuel to get to the next town. The sun would set to the sound of adventures told around a campfire and a satisfied sleep beneath of blanket of stars and a wing of the plane.

It was the life Roscoe Turner had once lived. The life every pilot I know wishes he had a chance to experience: the history pilots all want to be a part of; the story pilots all want to tell.

The flying I was doing in the late 1980s was about as far from barnstorming as one could get. I owned a Beechcraft Baron, a twin-engine piston aircraft that was fast, comfortable, and easy, but as dull as dirt to fly. I was forty years old. My youth and most of my dreams were behind me. I would never be a fighter pilot, an astronaut, or an airline pilot. With a wife and children to care for, and business to run, I knew that taking up a life like the itinerant barnstormer's would have been not only unrealistic but also irresponsible. If nothing else, though, I would have an aircraft reminiscent of the golden days. So I set out to buy a Stearman.

The Boeing Stearman is a tail-dragger, two-seater, open-cockpit biplane, designed in the late 1920s by Lloyd Stearman. In the mid-1930s, the Boeing Aircraft Company purchased the Stearman design to fill the U.S. military's need for a primary trainer. Boeing made substantial modifications and improvements to the design, and named their version the Kadet. But the Stearman name stuck. These days most aircraft referred to as Stearman are, in fact, Boeing Kadets. The top speed of the Stearman is ninety-five miles an hour, which, for its time, was unbelievably fast. The first automobile my grandmother rode in reached a staggering speed of thirty miles an hour. As she put it, "I got dizzy from the speed." The Stearman was a product of those times. Because of the surface area of the four wings, bracing, landing gear, and drag created by the open-cockpit the plane cannot exceed 180 miles an hour, even in a full-power dive straight toward the ground. From the 1930s through to the end of the Second World War, the U.S. Army and Navy used it as a primary training vehicle. It was finally retired from service in 1947. So many Stearmans were available at the time of its decommissioning that one could be bought for less than $200. Private operators picked up most of them. Because its rugged build prevented it from coming apart in the air, most were transferred into service as crop dusters or airshow performers. It would be difficult to find a pilot or an aviation enthusiast who does not feel a sweet tug of nostalgia when watching the charismatic bird with its large biwings land and taxi into an airport.

I bought my 1939 Stearman in 1994. I was able to find one that needed some work from a guy I knew back in Mississippi who specialized in rebuilding Stearmans. I was not in the market for a museum piece. I wanted one I could fix up, ride hard, and put away wet. The sturdy old plane I purchased was sound—meant for the fight, not for the show. I took delivery of the craft at the Montgomery Airpark in Gaithersburg, Maryland. I did not have the time to travel to Mississippi to pick it up, and even if I had, the sorry truth is that I had become soft flying modern airplanes and needed some time on the Stearman before I would feel confident taking it for a long flight.

The day the Stearman was delivered I gave everyone at work time off to come to the airport to welcome her in. I also arranged for my daughter Lara's kindergarten class to see the arrival. I wanted the day to be like a barnstorming day of old, with a magnificent old flying machine making a grand entrance for the crowd. A crop-duster pilot from Mississippi flew the plane up, and as he taxied it in I was surprised to see that he looked to be about seventy years old. I had expected to see a grinning nineteen-year-old taking the job to build flying time, the way I had done when I was that age.

As soon as the majestic yellow and blue bird came roaring up the runway, I jogged out to its side and, as it slowed, jumped into the front seat. The engine still lit, the propeller cutting through the air, I yelled through the noise, "Come on! Let's go!"

In my excitement I forgot to let the airplane taxi near enough to the children to let them get a good look. Nor did I think to give the poor old pilot a chance to stretch out the kinks from hours in the cramped cockpit. Without skipping a beat, the pilot and I were off on a short loop around the airport pattern. I knew others, including my wife and secretary, also wanted a ride, so after the inaugural loop, I persuaded the ferry pilot—who by that time must have been exhausted—to take out seven people, one at a time, for short flights. Beaten and weary, he still managed to wear a wide smile as he peeled himself out of the rear seat of the plane.

Together we put the Stearman into my hangar. The Baron, now relegated to second string, was shoved to the rear, while the Stearman, front and center, stood triumphant. I stayed in the hangar all night looking at her, amazed by my good fortune. I was so taken with the plane that even after I discovered it needed a massive amount of work I was unfazed.

The next morning my son, Gustavus, drove out to the airport for a ride in the Stearman. The winds were heavy but I was confident I could handle them. I was proficient enough in tail-draggers for a quick spin around the pattern. Or so I believed. I revved the throttle all the way. The front wheels were rolling and everything was going perfectly. But when the tail lifted from the ground, a blast of crosswind caught the plane directly across the left side, forcing us off to the side of the runway. In a frantic attempt to correct, I overdid it, swinging the large bird too far to the right. The plane dragged a wing tip and came to rest beside the runway. That first ride was the last my son took with me in the Stearman and to my lasting shame and regret he still does not like flying a tail-dragger. I could almost see Telford Norman shaking his head in disapproval.

I spent the next four days gaining a feel for the plane. I took it on a couple of whirls with Jim Lanning of Gaithersburg, Maryland, one of the best ferry pilots I know. Whenever I needed a quick refresher in any facet of flying or aviation knowledge, Jim was the guy I called. After a couple of takeoffs and landings, as well as a few trips around the traffic pattern, Jim told me I was competent to fly the Stearman. Proud of my renewed biplane skills, I asked Joe Goverrow, a good friend and a great tail-dragger pilot, to fly with me. After the flight, Joe also gave me "thumbs up." With the best two pilots I know saying I was good to go, I took the Stearman up whenever the weather allowed.

One day, during the first winter I owned the Stearman, I was resting in the hangar after some work on the Baron. The temperature outside was 14 degrees Fahrenheit. Though the air was cold, the cloudless day beckoned me to take the Stearman out for a loop. Without questioning whether the rugged plane could handle the cold, I rolled her out, jumped in, and took off on a long excursion. It was dusk when I returned.

As I was lugging the plane back to its central position in my hangar, Alie Talipore (who wears a coat in warm weather and cold) came up to me.

"Gus, it's too damn cold to be flying that thing. You'll to freeze to death flying an open-cockpit in this weather."

We both laughed as I fired back, "I could take that plane anywhere anytime. Hell, I could even take it to the North Pole."

"Oh, yeah?" he chuckled, finding my joke original, at best.

"Oh, yeah," said I.

At the end of a long hot summer day of flying, I would return to home base, pull the grand yellow bird into the hangar, round up a few of the airport guys, and settle in for a session of serious "hangar flying."

"Hangar flying" is the telling of tales about flying. It is akin to fish stories told around a campfire after a long day on the river. For a memorable session of hangar flying all that is needed is the right setting and good airplane stories. My favorite place for hangar flying is my open hangar, with its heady smell of oil rags, tools scattered about, some folding-chairs pulled together, and my blue-and-yellow biplane beauty nearby. One afternoon, while enjoying the ritual with friends, Bruce Kendall, the owner of a local recycling company, came by the hangar. He stopped to listen as I launched into a series of stories that went on for more than an hour. Later Bruce asked if I knew of anyone with a general aviation aircraft who could make it in and out of an airstrip only 800 feet long. It was a direct challenge.

"Of course I know someone—me! Me and this old girl can go anywhere," I boasted shamelessly. "I could stop on a dime and give change!"

He completed his setup by offering to pay for the gas if I would fly him to an ultralight fly-in the coming week. An "ultralight fly-in" is a gathering for ultralight pilots to share their commitment to the sport and to see different types of aircraft. Ultralights are aircraft that do not exceed 254 pounds and sixty-three miles an hour. A pilot's license is not needed to fly an ultralight, as they fly under a different set of rules and are not considered registered aircraft.

"Done deal," I said. "Yes, indeed. I can go just about anywhere with this airplane. I've even been thinking about taking it to the North Pole!"

"Tell me about it," Bruce said—his curiosity tweaked.

I went into a long dissertation on how I had been thinking of flying the Stearman to the pole, explaining at length all the things I thought I would have to do to actually pull it off.

"Could I help you with it?" Bruce asked seriously. "I've got a little money put aside, and this might be fun."

I could certainly use whatever help I could get, I thought—financial and otherwise. "All right," I replied, "let's do it!"

I was stunned that I had actually admitted publicly that I had the crazy idea of taking a sixty-year-old airplane to the North Pole.

"Shake on it," I said, determined to seal the deal, knowing that once I had given my word the stubbornness of my nature would keep me from backing down.

Crazy as the idea seemed, I saw it as the opportunity to snatch hold of the glory and adventure I had always dreamed of. This, I thought, was my chance to capture the spirit of a golden age for myself and for all those who would take part in the adventure with me. No one would ever accuse me of making small plans.

The next weekend, I was working on the plane when Bruce came by to see if I wanted to take a look at one of those truncated airstrips he wanted to fly into.

"It's a private orchard near Westminster, Maryland."

Excited to test my short field landing skills, I closed my toolbox and grabbed a couple pairs of headsets.

"Let's do it," I said.

He questioned whether I could find the strip without a GPS (Global Positioning System), which uses satellites launched by the United States to provide location data anywhere on the planet. I boasted that I could find anyplace with just a map. The truth is, I flew the Stearman around the region so often that I knew the area better from the air than from the ground.

Forty-five minutes later we were circling Baughers Orchard. Bruce was impressed at the ease with which I had located the strip. As we approached the field, Bruce waved frantically toward the ground trying to get the Baugherses' attention.

"Don't worry," I said to him through the microphone on my headset, laughing slightly at his display. "I think they'll hear us."

As I neared the tiny grass strip it dawned on me the tight spot I had gotten myself into. The field may have been 800 feet long, but only 600 feet were usable. Not only were the first 200 feet of the strip far too steep to land on, the field itself was bordered by a pond on one side and an orchard on the other (both of which I wanted to steer clear of). In addition, the plane was over-loaded—Bruce and I are big guys. We were going to need all the braking room we could get: the heavier the mass the more energy it takes to stop it.

On my first try, I attempted to land on the hilly part of the runway since I knew I would need more room than the 600 feet offered. It turned out to be too steep. When the wheels hit, they smashed down hard and bounced us back into the air, forcing me to do a go-around and make another attempt at the landing. I pushed the throttle to full power, barely clearing the trees at the end of the runway, then circled back up and around to take another shot. Bruce, sitting in the front seat, seemed to be enjoying himself. He would have been a bit more concerned, I thought, had he known that hangar flying had gotten more pilots into trouble or killed than engine failure ever did. In the backseat, I was beginning to worry that my mouth had taken in more than I could chew.

On the next touchdown, I planted the tires hard at the top of the grassy incline. They held and the plane did not bounce. I braced myself, knowing we had only 600 feet. I could feel the plane leaning toward the trees, so I applied as much brake as I dared: too much brake and the Stearman would flip over onto its back. With 200 feet to go we were still rolling too fast, but it was too late for another go-around. All I could see was the back of Bruce's head, but he still appeared so calm. One hundred feet from the end of the runway the Stearman started to slow. I had no choice but to brake hard again, causing the plane to skid before it came to a stop, twenty feet short of the trees. As I released my death grip on the stick and took a deep breath, Bruce turned back to me, smiling.

"That was perfect."

My blood pressure was too high to respond to the compliment. I just nodded and taxied the plane toward a small group of people awaiting our arrival.

As I shut down the engine, Bruce hopped out of the plane, as giddy as a school-boy at recess. Rather than follow Bruce's lead, I pretended to be doing something in the plane. My legs were shaky, still in shock over the closeness of the call. I sat there for a few minutes turning radios on, then shutting them off, doing anything I could to gain my composure. As I gathered myself together and climbed out of the plane, one of the Baugherses said, "We've never had an airplane land here before. I didn't think this place was big enough for a real one. That first time when you hit that hill yonder, you sure bounced that thing high."

"It wasn't that bad," I replied, knowing all the while that the hard part was yet to come. "These airplanes are built to take that kind of stuff, sir." How in the hell was I going to get out of there?

After some research, I found that no one had ever flown successfully to the North Pole in an open-cockpit aircraft. There had been a few attempts, the most notable of which was made by the Norwegian explorer, Roald Amundsen, the discoverer of the South Pole. In 1928, with a crew of five, he flew from Spitsbergen, Norway, toward the North Pole in a Latham open-cockpit aircraft in search of the Italian explorer, Umberto Nobile, whose airship, *Italia,* went down on the Arctic ice pack. While Nobile and his team were subsequently rescued, Amundsen and his crew were killed when their plane crashed into the Arctic Ocean. Most of the other ventures to the North Pole in open aircraft ended the same way. Although this frightened me, I still believed I could make it.

The initial planning for the trip centered on the search for a chase plane to follow me to the pole for the purpose of carrying reserve fuel and rescuing me in case I went down on the ice. Bruce and I considered many different types of planes, among them a Helio Courier, a de Haviland Beaver or Otter, a Cessna Sky Wagon, a Cessna Caravan, and a Beech 18. Ultimately, we both agreed that the Beech 18 would be the best machine for the job.

A Beech 18 is a twin radial engine aircraft designed in the 1930s. It is a tail-dragger like the Stearman, and like the Stearman also had a military career. It was used as a bomber trainer and VIP transport during the Second World War. Produced until 1968, the Beech 18 had the longest run of any production aircraft. There are a lot of 18s still around and, although they can be expensive to operate, they are not expensive to buy. We chose it because it was cheap, as tough as the Stearman, could handle high payloads, and had the capacity to carry a sizeable load. And, well, I loved flying them. Like the Stearman, the Beach 18 is a classic aircraft, from the golden days of aviation. It was the perfect choice, the same caliber of plane as the Stearman.

Doug Duff, a friend, had expressed interest in flying the chase plane. Pilots need a special endorsement in their log to fly a tail-dragger because it is more difficult to take off and land than a tricycle gear-aircraft. If Doug were going to fly the chase plane he would need to get his tail-dragger sign-off.

Doug was my best flying buddy. He was the kind of guy I always get along with. He had a way of knowing what I was thinking before I said it. Though he was the same age as me, he reminded me a lot of Telford Norman. We used to say we were aviators first and it did not matter what was second. He had never married, was easygoing, and was an accountant by trade. I could never understand why someone would want to be an accountant, and he could never understand why someone would want to own a medical supply company. Doug was thin as a stick but could outeat any two people I know. I can remember hearing the owner of the local all-you-can-eat restaurant swear as Doug went back for his fifth helping. My daughter, Lara, called him an eating phenomenon.

One afternoon, while Bruce and I were discussing the trip, Doug asked if he could go along.

"Of course you're going," I said. "Who else is going to fly the damn chase plane?"

Doug was such a good friend that it was preposterous to think that I would fly all the way to the North Pole without him. It shocked me that he felt he had to ask.

"I thought," he said, "that you might have had someone else in mind for the job. I haven't got a plane."

"We'll find a plane," I assured him. "And I'll teach you to fly it."

Doug was trying to get his hours up to fly for the airlines. He told me that he was going to start flying traffic reporters over Washington for Monty at Congressional Aviation, a local charter service that leased planes for anything from VIP trips to traffic reporters.

"Don't you have a job already?" I said.

"Yeah, but I can do that at night, and fly for Monty in the day."

I chuckled. "You're going to work your fool self to death."

"UPS is looking for pilots," he stated, a glint of hope in his eyes. "I think if I get enough hours, they'll hire me as a pilot."

"Doug, you're as old as I am. Who's going to hire a forty-five-year-old rookie pilot?"

"Man, they need pilots bad," he responded with determination.

I was sorry that I had tried to bring him back to earth. Doug was just like me. He had not been able to get a job flying during the 1970s; now he was going to take one last shot to do what he had always wanted to do.

"I'm going to fly for a living if it kills me," he said.

He knew he was too old, but nothing was going to hold him back. I respected him for that. It was the mark of a true pilot: we fly because we cannot live any other way.

"Well, good luck. If you get a job with the big boys, maybe there's still hope for me. But I'll be damned if I'll fly traffic, too much sitting on your backside for me. Besides, I've got almost 6,000 hours. How many more do you need to fly for the big boys?"

"I ain't got that many, so I'm going to fly traffic. Besides, I don't care. It's flying, and I can't think of anything else I'd rather be doing." His voice was more forlorn than defiant. "You really think we can do this pole thing?"

"It's a done deal. I'll either make it or perish in the attempt. Either way, as you said, 'it's flying.'"

Bruce and I traveled the country in search of the perfect chase plane for the polar trip. One evening, I was loading a plane for a trip the next day to Atlanta with Bruce, and his wife, Valerie, when Doug arrived to go out on his daily round of traffic flying.

"Can I go to Atlanta too?" Doug asked, anxious to see one of the possible chase planes for the expedition.

I told him that the small airplane, a Mooney, that I had rented for the trip would not support four of us. He did not seem disappointed.

"That's okay," he said. "I'll stay here and fly traffic tomorrow, build up my hours a bit. You mind if I file the flight plan for you?"

I knew we had to file an IFR (instrument flight rules) flight plan because poor weather had been forecast for the route. It is necessary to file an IFR flight plan when a trip cannot be made using VFR (visual flight rules), which require a plane to fly below the clouds and have at least three miles of visibility. When we flew together, Doug would often file my flight plan. He had recently received his instrument rating and needed practice filing plans. I probably should have filed it myself, but I was tired so I agreed and thanked him. Doug told me he would not return from morning traffic until 9:00 A.M., but would leave the flight plan in Monty's office in case I had to take off before he got back.

"Try to wait though, 'cause I'd like to show you Monty's new flight weather computer."

The next morning, when I got to the airport, I went into Monty's office to see if Doug was back. A bunch of employees were sitting around the main desk talking.

I walked in and asked, "Where's Doug?"

Kris, who flew for Monty and also knew Doug well, looked at me with a sad half-smile and answered, "He's never coming in here again."

I was as stunned as I was angry. I assumed that Monty had fired Doug for filing a flight plan for me on company property. What had I done? It was my fault that Doug had filed the plan. Quickly I ran to find Monty and explain. When I caught up with him I blurted out, "Monty, I want to apologize for Doug. It's my fault. I was the one who made him—"

Cutting me off mid-sentence, Monty, stone-faced, said, "Doug's dead. . . . He crashed over at Freeway Airport that morning doing a traffic run. He was landing in instrument flying conditions, hit a house, and he's dead."

For a long time, I felt guilty about Doug's death. In my earlier days of romping around and showing off at the airport, I had a signature takeoff, something left over from my childhood shenanigans. My technique was to take off, keeping the plane right above the runway until the plane accelerates, then pull up hard into a spectacular climbing right turn. Doug liked to mimic my style, which—for a guy with not many flight hours—he pulled off rather well.

Doug enjoyed trying out new tricks. When he started flying for traffic, he learned a stunt called a "traffic reporter's landing." Just before coming in for a landing, he would slow the plane down to a little below stall speed, keeping it in the air by applying a lot of power. With a high nose attitude and almost full power, the propeller helps hold the plane in the air. If executed properly, by the time the wheels touch down the plane is traveling so slowly that it comes to a quick stop. But if the plane loses power or the nose bolts up too high, the plane will stall, causing it to torque roll violently to the right. Because the engine in a small aircraft is not strong enough to accelerate in the nose-up attitude, to abort the landing the pilot has to lower the nose of the plane to gain flying speed, usually with fatal results.

I yelled at Doug when he showed me the landing on one of our outings.

"What, are you jealous?" he said with a laugh.

"It'll kill you, doing that!" I yelled. "One day it'll bite you."

It was a dangerous game, but I have to admit that Doug did the maneuver better than anyone I have seen. Perhaps I was a bit envious of Doug for performing it so well. The truth is I did not have the guts to try a landing like that. There is an old saying, "Here lies smoking Joe, he likes to fly too low and too slow."

The last time Doug and I flew together we flew in the plane that killed him. It was five days before he died. I had planned a short trip to Olean, New York, to pick up Gustavus from his school, Saint Bonaventure University. Doug heard I was planning to fly in the bad weather and immediately volunteered to join me. He could use the instrument time, he said, as he needed more proficiency flying in nonvisual conditions.

Our plan was for one of us to take the controls for the approach to a runway while the other looked out of the window toward the ground. As soon as the second man spotted the airport below, he would take the controls, steering the plane down to the ground and settling it in. This was a good instrument flying technique, used by commercial pilots and others when possible.

Almost as soon as we had taken off from Gaithersburg, we entered into clouds, where, with the exception of a few clear spots, we remained for the entire journey. In mid-Pennsylvania, we broke out of the soup for a moment to the most spectacular vision I have ever witnessed. The sun was cutting through the clouds the way it is often pictured on church programs. The clouds hid the sun, but the beams of sunlight came from behind the clouds like a radiant halo made of a thousand lasers. The ground below was covered with a light fog that made the town below look like it was floating. Rainbows were where the sunbeams were not. The beauty stunned us.

"Is instrument flying always like this?" he asked.

"No," I answered. "You don't see something this nice too often."

"Looks just like heaven," Doug said.

"Think heaven looks this good?" I asked, amused.

"It kind of makes you want to go now, doesn't it?"

The remark scared me. "I don't know, Doug. I'm not quite ready yet. I can wait on that one."

We both laughed. A few minutes later we barreled right back into the soup.

On preparation to land in Olean, I flew approach. I handed the plane over to Doug when he spotted the ground. Immediately, he pulled up the nose of the plane, preparing for a "traffic reporter's landing."

"No!" I yelled. "We're in instrument conditions!"

As the plane began to drift off the centerline of the runway, I grabbed the controls, put us back on course, and made the landing.

"Damn it, Doug! That is going to kill you!" I shouted.

Doug chuckled gleefully. "Still jealous, huh?"

Not wanting an argument, I let it pass. But now I wish I had sat Doug down and really lectured him. If I had, perhaps he would still be alive today.

We picked up my son in Olean and headed back into the same weather system we had come through. This time, we fought quite a headwind the entire way. I looked at the gas gauges, and they seemed low to me. I brought it to Doug's attention. He said we had plenty. Since he flew this crate eight hours a day I figured he knew it better than I did. Near Harrisburg, Pennsylvania, Doug said we needed gas.

"No argument with me," I said. "Let's do it."

I radioed in, "Washington approach, this is N736KL. We request permission to land at Harrisburg."

The controller approved, setting us in the sequence for landing behind three other aircraft. With a worried look on his face, Doug chimed in over the radio.

"Uh, Washington approach, this is N736KL, we can't wait. We've got to come in now."

We were granted a quick landing and I put the plane on the deck at full speed, flying it in all the way to the ground, in case the engine stopped. I wanted as much speed as I could get.

Turning to Doug, I said, "*That's* how you should land IFR."

When we filled the plane, we discovered that we had less than one gallon left in the tank, which means that we had less than five minutes of flying time left—it was about the closest I had ever seen it cut. I was on the verge of yelling again at Doug for taking too many chances, but I decided to go easy. We had made it in, at least.

As we took off from Harrisburg, Doug, in much higher spirits, laughed and turned to me, saying, "It's always an adventure with you."

2. The Quest Begins

Bruce was not a pilot. But he had agreed to share the cost of the chase plane, so it seemed only fair that if he were going to put up half-interest in an aircraft he had no hope of piloting, he should at least get the plane of his choice. After searching far and wide for a Beech 18 we narrowed the search to two; one was in Louisiana, and the other was in Canada. I favored the one in Louisiana—a later model built with a tricycle gear instead of a tail-dragger (which I generally prefer)—because it had less flying time on it and, from the condition of the plane, I could tell the pilot had taken good care of it. Bruce, on the other hand, liked the Canadian plane, a classic looking twin-engine tail-dragger with the panache of the 1930s, owned by a transport company that had beaten the hell out of it. But I had already given Bruce the choice and he was stuck on the Canadian Beech. It was a sweet-looking plane, no question about it, and I grew to enjoy flying it almost as much as the Stearman.

It was going to be a challenge to find someone able (and willing) to fly the chase plane to the North Pole. There were not a lot of tail-dragger pilots around, and even fewer that could fly twin-engine tail-draggers. But with the polar trip still a year off I did not give that problem much thought and simply enjoyed flying around in the Beech 18.

With the chase plane purchased, planning for the polar attempt really took off. My original plan for the test flight was to fly the Beech 18—a larger, better protected plane than the open-cockpit Stearman—to Resolute, a small town in the Canadian Arctic, to scout out fuel stops on the route and to get a feel for the severity of Arctic conditions. Bruce and his wife, Valerie, also talked about joining me on the scouting expedition. My spirits heightened as the plans took shape. We had set the day of departure for April 1, 1999. But just before the first, Bruce's mother, already gravely ill, took a turn for the worse, so he and Valerie decided to stay behind.

With Bruce and Valerie out of the mix, the larger Beech 18 was no longer needed for the test flight, so I decided to make the trip in the Stearman. Since I had not been able to find data on operating a Stearman in the extreme cold, my plan was to take it as far north as possible to see how it would respond. The way I saw it, the Stearman needed the test every bit as much as I did. But my wife disagreed and made no bones about telling me so.

"You don't know anything about the Arctic," Mary argued. "The Beech 18 is a much bigger and safer airplane."

She was right, I knew next to nothing about Arctic travel. But that was the very reason I had to go in the Stearman. The data I would gather on the trip would show me whether or not the polar attempt was even possible in the plane.

"What about the cold?" she persisted. "You could freeze to death in that thing. Remember last year when the engine died and we had to land in that field?"

Mary had a point with that one. The Stearman's engine was the big question mark of the trip. And she knew it from firsthand experience.

One afternoon, two years before, Mary said she wanted to go on one of my afternoon joyrides. Generally she did not like the heavy acrobatics I favor so I went out alone on most of my late afternoon flights. The best times for "turning and burning" are in the early morning and evening, when the air is normally stable. Since I am not an early riser, I more often went out on most calm, and not-so-calm, days to turn and burn in the clear evening air.

"Okay," I said. "But you better know that today I'm in the mood for some serious fun."

"I can handle it," she said. "Let's give it a whirl."

That afternoon Mary sat up front, having the time of her life. I was pulling out all the stops—even flying upside down—secretly trying to make her uncomfortable because I preferred being alone on those evening fun flights. We were flying upside down when the engine blew, sending oil over the front windshield. I yelled to her to get a napkin from under her seat to clean the windshield. While she was bending over to reach for the napkins, the engine let go of another gusher. The oil pressure went to zero and the oil temperature went off the scale. As she was coming up with the napkins, I yelled for her to put her head down because I was going to land in the field below. Less than thirty seconds later, we were safely on the ground.

"I didn't want you to land," Mary said.

When I told her that this was the end of the flight, she responded by saying that she did not like "this muddy field."

Walt Starling was flying traffic reporters that afternoon. Good old Walt had seen me go down in the field. He circled a couple of times and waved. Later I asked him why he did not call the police.

"If it had been someone else, I would have. I knew it was you, so no big deal."

The engine's rear bearing had disintegrated, a common problem with the Continental R670 engine. The Stearman stayed in that field for three months while I took off the engine, had it rebuilt, and reinstalled it with the help of two very good friends, Lenny Charles and Tull Morgan. I called my mother the night the engine died. She wanted to come up and help me with it.

"I'll have it worked out before you get here. But come on up anyway."

My mother loved tinkering, and watching me tinker, with anything mechanical. My father, on the other hand, thought it was improper for a woman to do anything mechanical, much less, hunt, dance, or have an opinion—all of which he saw as fitting behavior for men only. My father had died three years before, so now my mother could tinker to her heart's content. My mother got sick the day after she called me and died within three weeks on her sixty-fifth birthday, before we got the Stearman out of the field. The day we hung the engine, I flew the Stearman out over the Potomac River and dropped a rose for my mother.

Mary's concerns about the inherent weakness of the engine and my safety were reasonable. But if any R670 had any chance of making it to the Arctic and back it was this one. It had only 380 hours on it since it had been rebuilt by one of the best engine men in the business, Don Sanders, of Mustang, Oklahoma. I told Mary that for the test flight I intended to cover the front cockpit and find a canopy to put over the pilot's cockpit, so I would not have to take the full bite of the cold.

The trip to the pole presented two separate engineering problems. The first was how to keep a sixty-year-old plane running in the Arctic. The second was how to keep a forty-five-year-old pilot from freezing to death in an open airplane. Since the test flight was primarily for the plane, I decided to use the canopy for the initial flight to protect myself. If the Stearman survived the test, I could always refine my body gear later in a freezer at home. I had assured Mary that this trip was nothing more, and nothing less, than a test run to find fuel stops, get a feel for Arctic flying, and to see how the plane would respond to the cold. I also promised that I would take off the protective canopy only when I was testing my short-flight ability in an open-cockpit and that I would travel only as far north as I felt it was safe to go.

"I could find out," I said, "that I won't be able to endure the cold."

"Not likely," she sighed. "If you go now, you'll find a way to get back up there." Then, after swearing to her that I would be cautious and wise, I told her that I was going regardless of what she said. After twenty-four years of marriage, I should have learned to listen to Mary. As things turned out, she was, as usual, right.

Not long before the test flight, Bruce mentioned to a local reporter who often showed up at the airport looking for a story that I would probably reach the magnetic North Pole. The magnetic North Pole is the spot where all compasses point. James Clark Ross, an Englishman, discovered it on June 1, 1831, at Cape Adelaide. Since its discovery, the magnetic North Pole has been moving north by northwest and now lies roughly 900 nautical miles south of the geographic

North Pole, the northernmost point on the earth's axis—the very top, where all the longitudinal lines and time zones converge.

During the summer months, the sun at the North Pole remains at approximately the same distance above the horizon twenty-four hours a day. It takes three months to reach its high point and three months to set, after which the area is plunged into darkness for six months. When the sun is up, it appears to circle the horizon, but in fact it slowly spirals up for three months and down for three months.

Later the reporter came to me and asked if I thought I could reach the magnetic pole on the upcoming trip. I really did not know—reaching the magnetic Pole was not one of the main objectives of the trip. But once word got around of the possibility of making the magnetic pole, people wanted to know how had I become mixed up in such a thing in the first place. Why was I doing this? Was I was willing to risk my life on what seemed to be a harebrained scheme? The questions did not surprise me at all. What did surprise me was that I had not thought more deeply about my answers.

At Montgomery Airpark, there is a group of old pilots who on most Saturdays can be found hanging out at one of the nicer hangars. They sit right at the end of the runway side of the hangar so they can take in everything that is going on at the airport while they talk about flying. They remind me of the old checkers players in J.C.'s Barbershop back in Corinth. The guys are critical, to say the least, of each pilot's performance and most of us who have been flying for a long time think highly of these guys' opinion of us as pilots. The thrill of an invitation to hang out with these veterans of air and space is like being asked to join a pilots' hall of fame. At any one time the group might include retired airline pilots, an old Luftwaffe pilot, retired corporate pilots, current airline pilots, an airshow pilot, you name it, but Ralph and Richie Butler are its unofficial leaders. So when Ralph asked me if I truly planned to go to the magnetic North Pole, the respect I saw in his eyes gave me any added incentive I may have needed.

"Is it true about your attempt on the magnetic pole?" Ralph asked.

"Sure. And I'll make it there too. No problem."

In that flash of unguarded pride—my ego has always gotten the better of me—I had reconfigured the trip's objectives to include the magnetic pole. I had transformed the mission from a relatively simple test-push north into a complex and decidedly more dangerous attempt to fly over the magnetic North Pole. Bruce may have hung the idea out for airing, but he could not be blamed for making me reach for it.

Bruce found a protective canopy for the pilot's seat that we could get on and off with ease. It was a Plexiglas bubble that hinged to the windshield. The bubble could be removed by taking out the pin that connected it to the windshield and disengaging a hook of our own design that attached the bubble to the rear of the cockpit. Bruce had persuaded one of the mechanics from his auto junkyard to help outfit the Stearman for the trip. But as we worked together, I quickly found out that three heads were not necessarily better than one.

"I don't like the way this bolt looks," Bruce would complain.

"Yeah, but it's supposed to go that way," his mechanic shot back.

"I don't think so. You need to tighten it from the reverse side, or the grip won't hold," Bruce challenged.

"The wider part of the bolt faces inward."

"It's better to do it my way."

This back and forth went on at such a pace that they spent much of our precious time arguing over who was right and who was wrong, often without resolution.

During this time, we converted the Stearman from a two-control, two-place plane that could be flown from either of two seats, to a one-seat, one-control plane. The front seat was taken out, covered over, and made into a fuel tank and a storage compartment. To accomplish this, we removed the front control stick, replacing it with a one-man crop duster stick, complete with Federal Aviation Authority (FAA) paperwork to undertake installation, which a friend gave me.

As the official mechanic for the job, I took charge of the removal of the old stick and installation of the new one. A licensed aircraft mechanic would check the work. It was a simple task, one that should have taken us three hours to accomplish. Instead, it ended up taking a week.

If I had any hope of making the North Pole by the end of spring, I would have to take full responsibility for the trip. It was my behind that was on the line. If I were going to die because of a bad decision, it would be my bad decision. So after one too many senseless delays, I told Bruce and his mechanic that I no longer needed their assistance and asked an airplane mechanic friend of mine to help me. In one night we redid much of the work and completed the job. By then, April 1, the planned departure date, had come and gone without ceremony, and departure was scheduled for April 16.

A few days before the takeoff, I realized that there were still serious problems without solutions. We had spent so much time on silly carping over insignificant details that major parts of the plane, particularly the engine, had not been given the attention they required. Compounding that concern were the hundreds of pounds of unnecessary gear that had been stored in the front baggage compartment without my knowledge. The way things were going I would soon be flying solo into some of the Earth's most forbidding terrain in an overloaded, undertested airplane, with a temperamental engine.

The night before I took off for parts as yet unknown to me, Mary gave me her parting salvoes on why I should not be traveling alone. I had to reassure her that I was not suicidal and was up to the challenge. We had been in college the first time I took Mary flying. She had never flown before and was understandably apprehensive.

I remembered taking her by the hand and saying, "Don't worry, this is *my* thing. No airplane is ever going to kill me."

I must have said it convincingly, because to this day she has never been afraid to fly with me, even when I fly upside down. I reminded her of that first flight and we both had a good laugh about it. We talked about how hard I had tried to get into aviation, all my hopes and expectations, some realized, most not. She knew, as I knew, that I looked to this flight as a way to prove to myself that I was made of the same stuff as my childhood heroes.

She smiled and said, "I guess if anybody can pull this off, you can. But please, promise me that you'll come back."

"You can count on it," I said, and with that the issue was closed.

I first met Mary Alice Lockmuller when we were both attending Catholic University. Our meeting was, quite literally, due to an accident. My parents gave me a car as a gift in my sophomore year. I think it was my mother's idea. Like many American males, especially ones as aggressive as I was, I wrecked it. To give my mother time to tell my father, and my father time to cool down, I thought it would be a good idea not to be around the house for a couple of days. Once a month, the campus ministry ran a retreat for students in the Shenandoah Mountains. A friend, Peter Andrews, had been after me to attend. I wrecked the car on Friday morning; the bus for the retreat left Friday afternoon. I usually avoided religious gatherings like a plague. The son of a minister, I had had all the churching a body needed for a lifetime. But the retreat sounded like the ideal place to lay low for a while, so I went home to tell my mother what had happened, where the car was, and that I was going away for the weekend on a religious retreat.

"*You're* going on a religious retreat?" she said, a trace of alarm in her voice. "It must have been one hell of an accident. Was anybody hurt?"

"No," I said, "but I thought it would be best not to be here when Daddy hears about it. The car is in petty bad shape."

"Good idea," she replied in her knowing way. "I'll calm him down while you're away."

When pushed—which I often did—my father was overpowering and opinionated. Restraint was what he preached, not what he practiced. Had it not been for my mother's pleadings and my imposing six-foot, one-inch build, he would have probably given me a good thrashing. As it went, no blood was shed but the people in China must have heard the lecture I received when I got back from the retreat. Two months after the incident, my father took a church in Oklahoma City, Oklahoma, and gave the car to my sister. The family moved with him and I stayed in Washington. For the rest of my college years I walked or took the bus.

While the four-day retreat did little for my soul and even less to temper my father's wrath, it did a great deal for my love life. I met Mary at that retreat. We found that we both had a rebellious spirit and over the next few months fell deeply in love. I am not a poetic man. Words of love do not come easily or often. But after twenty-five years with Mary, I can say that the magic is still there.

On the morning of April 17, a crowd of nearly two hundred gathered at the Airpark to see me off. Bruce managed to get most of the area's ultralight flying clubs to be there. A couple of local radio station reporters also showed up. I did not ask anyone to attend, not because I did not want anyone there but because I did not have the time to think about a send-off, and really did not think the test flight merited one. Bruce arranged for a Second World War Jeep to tow the Stearman from my hangar to the terminal. I rode on the back of the Jeep and did an impression of Chuck Yeager in the movie, *The Right Stuff*. It was fun clowning around with the crowd and mugging for photos. There was even a piper to send me off in fine Scottish tradition.

At takeoff, a hail of cheers and clicking cameras sent me on my journey. The atmosphere was circuslike and festive, yet slightly surreal. I suppose that not many watching took seriously my quest to go to the North Pole in that old plane. I did not wonder at their doubts. I had some of my own. I knew I was not as prepared as I should have been. We had done little to equip the engine for the cold and we had not even taken a test flight fully loaded. But I was certain I could figure out things as I went along. I have confidence in my mechanical skills and was used to solving problems on the fly.

The takeoff went off without incident, but I had been up only a few minutes when I noticed that the plane was burning too much fuel and that the battery was weak. I headed for Clearview Airport, about eight miles north.

Clearview is a tiny field owned by a bunch of old-timer pilots, a throwback to the early years of aviation and the type of airport pilots dream of calling home. I thought it was a fitting detour. I bought and installed a new battery and then continued to Frederick, Maryland, where Mary was waiting to drive me home to get some sleep for the real start of the flight that I hoped would begin the next day. There was still much work to be done.

Bruce met me in Frederick the next morning to help put the canopy over the pilot's seat. We also worked on the storage compartment and checked the fifty-gallon fuel tank for leaks. I would carry ninety-eight gallons in all: forty-eight in the main wing tank and fifty gallons in a tank in the front seat. I always got a chuckle out of having that much gas between my legs. I joked about it, saying that if I crashed I would not have to worry about being warm. I tinkered with the aircraft while Bruce put more supplies in the nose of the plane. I did not discover until much later that he had added another thirty-six candy bars, an extra battery, six rolls of duct tape, two rolls of twine, and a GPS communicator to send e-mails via satellite (which I was unable to use).

Late in the morning of April 18, 1999, I said goodbye to my family and Bruce, and took off, once again, on my first Arctic adventure. It took 4,000 feet of runway to rise into the air when normally only 600 feet were needed. Unaware of the immense amount of gear I was carrying, I attributed the discrepancy to the additional tank and fifty gallons of fuel.

Flying north from Washington, D.C., one invariably runs smack into weather over the middle of the Allegheny Mountains. That day was no different. I had been flying for less than three hours when I realized that the fuel continued to burn too quickly. The Stearman usually burned about twelve gallons an hour, but that day it was drinking eighteen to twenty gallons as it struggled against the weather over the mountains.

Looking down on what had become a solid layer of clouds, I noticed a small hole, a lucky break in the floor of gray. Stalling the airplane and putting it into a spin, I went through the hole and entered a clear, deep mountain valley. I urgently needed gas and in quick order spotted Clearfield Airport, just outside of Clearfield, Pennsylvania. When I landed, I fielded the usual questions of where I was going and why. I had been asked similar questions so often that my responses were beginning to sound rote: "The magnetic North Pole this year, the geographic pole next year."

"It'll never happen," I heard back. It was the same response I had heard from almost every pilot I had spoken to about the trip. "It'll never happen."

After the questions and usual amenities, I turned my attention to the more pressing matter of the consumption of gasoline. The gauge was reading almost on empty, and still the plane was heavy. Obviously, it was not the fuel weighing it down. I had begun the morning with ninety-eight gallons. In little more than four hours, I had used up seventy-four gallons just to reach that tiny airport. I also purchased some extra oil at the airport; although, unbeknownst to me the plane was already carrying fourteen extra gallons of oil, adding to the weight. One final problem needed to be solved before I could leave the little field: How would I get out of there?

Soon after I had landed, the skies closed in and it started raining, never a favorable condition for a fair-weather vehicle such as the Stearman. To my relief, an old-timer told me what I needed to know.

"Those mountains are always covered in clouds," he droned, his voice unaffected and steady, as though it was advice he offered often.

"What you've got to do," he continued, "is follow a road a little ways out. It'll take you on a path through the hills. It's a bit windy, but it'll bring you out the other side of those ridges."

"Which road?" I asked, looking toward the opaque horizon.

"Take off heading north, and about two miles from here you'll see two roads going through the mountains. The one on the left goes to the top. You want the one going off to the right. Follow it and you should have about two to three hundred feet of ceiling through the whole pass."

I smiled and thought aloud, "If not, it is going to be ugly when I hit the ridge tops."

"Yeah, and if you take the wrong road, you've messed up pretty bad. But you can get out of there with a wing-over."

A "wing-over" is a maneuver in which a plane is pulled into a steep climb. At the top of the climb the pilot puts one of the rudders full to the bottom (pedal to the metal, if you will), causing the plane to pivot on its own axis and swivel down the other side, completing a 180-degree turn, somewhat like an about-face. A wing-over is the easiest way to escape a boxed canyon.

The conversation filled me with excitement. I imagined myself as a pilot in the 1930s, listening to the seasoned advice of a fellow pilot on the rugged conditions and terrain around them. So off I went, and soon located the recommended path. The old pilot was right: I could not see the mountaintops and had about 300 to 400 feet in the pass to play with. Ten miles later I broke through the ridges and out of the weather. The clouds hung out in the hills, clearing as I flew on.

In the 1920s, when airmail pilots flew in this area, negotiating the Allegheny Mountains was the most dangerous part of the trip. At the Alleghenies, Canadian weather coming down from the north runs head on into upcoming systems from the south, making the mountains extremely hazardous for air travel. I have read many stories about airmail pilots forced to choose between bailing out of their airplane or hitting the ridges below. I was proud of myself for successfully coming through the mountains unscathed.

My quest had begun, I thought to myself, giving new meaning both to the challenge and the accompanying exhilaration and fear. When I was a child, my grandmother, who practiced the ways of the Choctaw, told me that every man must perform his test, a test that brings his consciousness, fortitude, and courage to bear.

The test is a Native American ritual in which a warrior submits himself to physical pain beyond his capacity to endure. Once the terrible threshold of pain is crossed, the mind and the soul are released from the warrior's body to take a demanding spiritual journey, at the completion of which the warrior's vision is purified. No longer clouded and corrupted by earthly things, the warrior's perception of the world and of himself is clarified and a higher state of consciousness and self-knowledge is achieved. The ritual is similar to the "sun dance," because warriors of some western tribes invoked the sun dance by piercing their nipples and hanging themselves in the sun, where they would remain until their vision was complete. For some, death came first.

"Through this ordeal," she cautioned, "a man will discover who he is and will see the true nature of his soul."

I winged on north into the clear and crossed Lake Erie to Hamilton, Ontario, Canada, where I was required to clear Canadian customs. The sky was turning dark by the time I arrived at Hamilton. I had spent the entire day in my Stearman, dodging storm after storm, burning gas, and making too little headway. I was exhausted when I set down. I did not have much gas left and decided to fill the tank before settling down for the evening. The fuel cap on a Stearman is in the center of the top wing, ten feet above the ground. It is reached by climbing to the top of the engine, grabbing hold of whatever you can find, and hanging on for dear life. The lineman was afraid to climb up, so I climbed up, tired and wasted as I was. As I pumped the fuel, I did not notice the reporter approaching the plane.

"What type of plane is that?" he asked eagerly.

Surprised, I turned around quickly to answer him, lost my footing and plummeted eight feet to the concrete, landing on my back. The lineman asked me if I was all right. I said, "I'm okay," even though I hurt like hell. The reporter and a couple of airport workers helped me up. I ached so badly that I decided to ask one of the guys to finish fueling the plane and the other to help me to the hotel where Mary had made arrangements for me to stay. Once at the hotel, I crawled into bed. Still in pain, I lay there until the next morning. Although I had not broken anything, my back was intensely sore for the rest of the day. I hurt so badly I could barely walk and limped for a week.

For the remainder of the trip I filled the tank from the ground and used the fuel pump to transfer fuel to the top tank. I even had a port added on the side of the plane so that the front-seat tank could be filled while standing on the ground.

It was a wet, muggy morning in late April. The runway at Hamilton was 7,000 feet long; I needed 6,500 feet to take off. Once safely into the air, I began to wonder if the wooden propeller could be the cause of the problem. I should have been able to take off easily with full fuel. I was beginning to think that the Stearman's wooden prop could not handle the load. In cruise, a wooden prop performs almost as well as a metal one. But on takeoff, the wood propeller has a tendency to flex a bit, causing it to lose some pull efficiency. A prop is a spinning wing. It actually sucks the plane along. An area of low pressure is created on the forward edge of the prop as it spins. When the wood flexes, the shape of the wing changes and loses lift. The low pressure on the forward edge is not as great; thus there is not as much sucking action. I was reminded of flying Telford Norman's old Piper Cub. Fifty gallons, I figured, must be all the fuel this old tail-dragger of mine can handle.

That morning, I flew to Elliot Lake, Ontario—only 285 miles from Hamilton and I had already burned two-thirds of my fuel. Quickly refueling and spending less than the usual time I like to set aside for bantering with the locals, I left to begin the 340-mile leg to Nakina, Ontario. Twenty miles out of Elliot Lake, I saw the first frozen lake of the trip. I could feel the excitement building in my gut.

It was dusk when I arrived in Nakina; the sun was disappearing into the west, leaving me just enough time to use the last light to locate the landing strip. I had barely made it, having pushed the airplane and myself well beyond capacity. Nakina is a very small town, and after a quick search I discovered that there were no available hotel rooms. There was, though, a schoolteacher who ran a small bed-and-breakfast.

When I arrived at the B&B to meet the owner, the first words out of her mouth were, "I hate this town. I've been here six years, and I've always hated it."

I was taken back, but intrigued. "How did you get here?" I asked.

"My husband came with the lumber mill, then he left me, and I stayed here."

"Well," I said, unsure of how to reply, looking out at the dismal, barren town, "I don't like it either."

The woman told me that there was going to be a party that evening and everyone in town would be there. She asked me if I wanted to go. Normally, I would have jumped at the opportunity, but my back still throbbed from my ungainly fall in Hamilton.

One of the local pilots took me to restaurant where I had my first taste of northern Canadian fare. I do not eat meat. But I do eat fish. The only things on the menu I could eat were the trout and the char.

"I'll have the trout," I said

"Sorry," the waiter answered. "We're out."

"Then I'll have the char."

"Sold out of that too."

"Hmmm. Well, just give me the vegetable plate."

"The only vegetables we have now are mashed potatoes and chips."

"Okay, give me the mashed potatoes."

"You can't order the potatoes by itself. You have to get an entrée."

"What nonmeat dishes do you have in stock?"

"We've got a grilled cheese sandwich."

"Okay, I'll have a grilled cheese sandwich with mashed potatoes."

Ten minutes later, a grilled cheese sandwich showed up with a large slice of ham on top of the cheese. I looked in dismay from the plate to the waiter and back to the plate.

"I don't eat red meat," I said.

"That's the way grilled cheese sandwiches come in Nakina."

I ordered a coke and a slice of pie, and left it at that.

When I look back on the night in Nakina, I realize I owe that schoolteacher a lot of thanks. That night I found out what it means to be cold, really cold. When I went to bed, I noticed a single sheet was the only bedding.

"Oh well," I thought, "this won't be too bad, the house is probably well heated."

That night the temperature dropped to 18 degrees Fahrenheit, and snow began to fall. It was impossible to sleep and I could not find the schoolteacher, who, still at the party, was probably well-warmed by drink, dance, or habit. Meanwhile I was shivering cold. There was no heat, no way to make a fire, and I found no relief in rubbing my hands together, or moving around beneath the solitary sheet. At about 10:00 P.M. I called Mary.

"I'm in this B&B and it's 18 degrees and there's no heat. I only have a thin sheet for covers, and I left my baggage in the airplane. I don't know which way to the airport and I can't find the heat. I hate this, I can't believe I'm this—"

Mary cut me off mid-sentence. "You call me to complain when you're in a house, not in some ditch bleeding to death with an airplane part stuck in you, on a trip I didn't want you to go on, but a trip you needed to make to prove your testosterone levels are adequate, while you leave me to run the business and take care of the family. You tell me you can handle whatever comes. Well, it's coming."

Like a dog, I tucked my tail between my legs, and said the only honorable thing.

"Just joking, honey. How was your day?"

I never called Mary again to complain.

When I woke the next morning, I was frozen almost stiff. Later in the trip, I understood how that night had helped me to acclimatize to the terrible conditions I encountered farther north.

I called Don Sanders, who had built the engine for my Stearman, and told him about the problems with takeoff and gas.

"How much is it burning?" he asked.

"As much as twenty-gallons an hour," I replied.

"Damn, I don't know what's wrong," he answered. "But the thing shouldn't be burning gas like that. How much load is in it?"

"About fifty gallons of extra fuel and eighty pounds of other stuff. I think the takeoff problem is because of the wood prop. We should get metal next time. What should I do about the fuel burn?" I was getting really concerned about this problem.

"Don't know. How's the speed?"

"Speed's fine," I said. "Takeoff performance is terrible, though."

Don told me to keep the distances between my stops down until we could sort out the fuel burn problem. I told him I had 314 miles ahead of me that day and thought I could make that.

3. Becoming a Bush Pilot

▼

Churchill, Manitoba, is 600 miles north of Nakina. Pickle Lake, the next stop on route to Churchill, is 250 miles northwest of Nakina. After falling on my backside in Hamilton and almost freezing it off in Nakina, my body was so stiff I could barely move. The runway at Nakina stretches 4,000 feet, with a frozen lake just beyond the end of the strip. I needed the entire runway to get airborne and a lot of the lake to climb above the trees.

I should have had enough fuel for 600 miles, but the tank was less than half full when I landed in Pickle Lake. I was now certain that the Stearman would not be able to make the 350 miles to Churchill without a stop for fuel. I checked the map but could not find anywhere along the route to stop, so I asked around for suggestions on what I should do. One of the Pickle Lake locals recommended that I talk to Bernie Cox, an outfitter who owned a company that flew goods to the northern villages. Bernie's company, I was told, owned their own aviation fuel caches all around the north.

Bernie Cox is the owner of North Star Aviation. He is a great guy. He not only agreed to let me stop and fuel up at one of his caches, but he offered to donate the fuel to the trip. He told me I could land at a small place called Bearskin Lake, where he stored thirty drums of fuel, and take a drum for the Stearman.

Since I was on my own with nothing to do in Pickle Lake, Bernie asked if I wanted to go fishing. He also offered to try to collect all the pilots in the area for a party that night. I begged off on the fishing, but told him I would enjoy a party.

Pickle Lake is literally at the end of the road in Ontario. From Pickle Lake north, aircraft and trucks traveling winter roads (roads that are navigable only in the hard-freeze months of February and March) supply all the villages in northern Ontario. Most of the pilots in Pickle Lake are transport pilots flying everything from big four-engine turboprops to small ski-equipped four-passenger aircraft. They are the real bush pilots, a rough-and-tumble, independent lot, gutsy enough to pit their piloting skills against the unforgiving north. They are my kind of girls and guys.

While Bernie made arrangements for the party, I went to check out the Stearman. The airplane canopy had started to crack from the cold and vibrations. At some point I knew I would either have to fix it or remove it, but figured I could put that choice off for a while. More important, I had decided to take inventory of all the gear and supplies I was carrying and remove anything I did not absolutely need. My hope was that a lightened load would make it easier for the Stearman to get off the ground. To my surprise and embarrassment, it turned out that what I thought was eighty pounds of gear weighed closer to 400 pounds. I gasped at the amount of stuff I was hauling. I was carrying more supplies to survive comfortably if I crashed than I was carrying to make the trip itself safe. A ridiculous number of unnecessary so-called rescue items were stored in the plane, including lead batteries that did not fit anything I was carrying. I had a shotgun with three boxes of shells and two insulated water bottles that froze after an hour in freezing temperatures. I also had two funnels for filling gas and oil, jumper cables, rain suits, an ax, and a hatchet with an all-purpose tool and sharpener. I had enough stuff to build a cabin and live comfortably in the woods. You can kill yourself trying to equip for failure.

How the additional supplies made it into the plane is still a mystery to me. I suspect that whenever Bruce checked the front storage compartment he added whatever he thought I would need. As long as there was space, things kept being added. We discussed what we thought I needed to bring and kept, I thought, an accurate list of what we loaded. While what we discussed made it into the plane, not everything loaded had been on the list. According to my list, the essential eighty pounds of gear consisted of the sixty-five pounds of survival gear that I packed in the front compartment four days before takeoff (and did not recheck) and a fifteen-pound daypack in the small compartment behind my seat.

Right then and there I started giving away things. All the batteries were donated to townsfolk. I gave Bernie's wife the satellite communicator I had not been able to get to work. The compact discs and tapes were left with the airport manager, along with 252 power bars. I gave away anything I did not need; anything not needed but belonging to someone at home I left to pick up on my return trip.

I called Mary and told her about the excess gear. The six ready-to-eat dinners I found were her contribution and the added CDs were from Lara's collection. It seems Bruce was not the only one adding extra emergency provisions.

I felt bad about leaving Mary with two businesses to run and a child to take care of. But somehow, she manages to take our life together in stride. Before we married, Mary promised that she would always support me in my flying. She has never broken that promise, but I am fairly certain that she did not have times like these in mind when she made it. I said that to her.

She laughed and said back, "I bet you didn't think it would be like this either."

"No," I said. "But if I had known and could have afforded it, I would have done it before we married and saved you all this trouble."

That night, Bernie, true to his word, pulled together a party with every pilot in Pickle Lake in attendance. The menu for the event was hot dogs and beer. That left me with a few beers. After thirty years of flying, I have a few exciting aviation stories to tell. But none of my stories could hold a candle to those of the Pickle Lake pilots. That night's hangar flying was filled with amazing tales of bush pilots in action. By the end of the party, we all agreed on the three best stories—none of my stories gained even an honorable mention.

Bernie Cox himself told the third best story of the night. It went like this: Late in the season, a couple of pilots landed on a lake. The plane broke through the ice and sat in the water on its belly. Bernie was called in for the rescue, requiring him to get the plane off the ice quickly before the whole thing sank. He commandeered a helicopter, lifted the plane to a firm piece of ice, and flew it back to the base for repairs.

Bernie also told the runner-up story of the night. In an attempt to deliver supplies to a remote village, he landed a small single-engine aircraft, a Cessna 172, on a frozen lakebed, again late in the season. He made the difficult landing on wheels. He had been nervous about the landing because there are periods in the Canadian north when the lakes are not frozen deeply enough to support a hard landing but not yet thawed enough for floats. While on rollout, Bernie thought he had found a good lake spot. But as he was rolling, one of the wheels broke through the ice. He jammed the throttle full forward, tilted the plane toward the good wheel, and popped out of the ice after bending back the landing gear. He flew home, landing with one gear bent behind the other, causing the aircraft to roll sideways down the runway.

The winning story of the night was told by another bush pilot. He had been carrying some hunters in his Otter, their canoes tied onto the plane's floats. During the flight, one of the canoes came loose from the float and turned sideways into the slipstream—the air that flows over the aircraft—causing the plane to make a hard right turn. The canoe was such a large impediment in the slipstream that the pilot could not stop the plane's turn to the right. So he circled down from 3,000 feet, turning right the entire time, and landed in a right turn with the canoe still dangling.

We all had a toast and crowned him "hangar flyer" of the night.

I stayed at Bernie's house that night. Before I left the next morning, Bernie told me he did not have a fuel pump for the gas at Bearskin Lake, but that I could borrow one from the villagers. I wondered aloud what I would do if no one were at the airport when I arrived. He told me not to worry—"Just circle the village once in the Stearman and everyone in town would come out." Someone was bound to have a pump I could use.

With thanks and farewells made, I was on my way to Bearskin Lake. After having dumped or given away most of the junk I had been carrying, the plane was off in less than 1,200 feet.

Typical northern Canadian weather plagued me on the way to Bearskin. I flew around and through snow showers most of the way. Snow showers in the northern woods are very pretty and light. It was not very cold, but cold enough to have to worry about ice on the wings. I did not have on my warmest gear but I was comfortable. At times I would fly twenty or thirty feet above the trees, mesmerized by the shadows and hues created by the scattered squalls. I would often fly down to the lakes, just above the ice, and almost giggle at the sheer joy of it all. I remembered Robert Frost's poem, "Stopping by a Woods on a Snowy Evening," and wondered how many more miles I would go before I could sleep. That was flying at its best. I was free as a bird and flying an airplane that was not much faster than a bird. From there on, as I headed deeper into the north, I would run into storms every day. But that day out of Pickle Lake was special.

Ironically, some of stories the bush pilots had told the night before helped me in determining which storms would be the least difficult to negotiate. Some of the most experienced bush pilots flew without instrument rating, which accounted for their expertise at avoiding storms.

The Stearman has a small cockpit with an instrument panel about the size of a large pizza. The instrument panel is comprised of an airspeed indicator, altimeter, oil temperature and pressure gauge, and a cylinder head temperature gauge that I installed. With the seat in cruise position, the sides of the cockpit come to about two inches below my shoulders and in the landing position, about two inches above my elbows. Most pilots (and that includes me) normally do not bother to mess with the seat for landing, because more often than not the seat falls all the way to the bottom of the cockpit, taking the pilot with it.

On the way to Bearskin Lake all of the equipment, except the tachometer, worked well. I later discovered that the "tach" cable had a little oil in it. In the colder temperatures the oil had thickened, preventing the cable from turning, at which point the tachometer stopped. That proved to be a minor problem, as I knew how to tune the engine by ear. After years of flying this bird almost every day, I could listen to the hum of the engine and figure out exactly how fast it was turning. I decided to take a look at the problem in Churchill.

When I arrived in the air over Bearskin Lake, I started in to circle the village, just as Bernie Cox had instructed. Just as in the days of the barnstormers, the townsfolk heard the plane as it approached. The northern sky is clear and quiet, so a plane is heard long before it is seen. Everyone came outside, jumped into their trucks, and headed to the airport even before I finished the circle. It should not have surprised me. For those who live in remote villages, the sound of an airplane means supplies, mail, visitors, and a change from the routine pace of the day. Here, the coming of an airplane was a major event. It was as though I had gone back to a time when, as the old pilots used to say, "men were men and the women liked it."

As I landed on the airport's mile-long runway, I noticed two helicopters sitting on the ground, part of a forestry study underway in the area. As soon as I stepped out of the airplane, an elderly woman came up to me and asked if I had any alcohol on board. I told her that I did not. Since most of the native villages in the north are dry, she wanted to make sure that I was not carrying any alcohol. After witnessing the amount of drinking done in Pickle Lake, I would have said no to her even if I had been carrying booze.

There were a lot of trucks parked at the airport. I wondered why people living deep in a wilderness with only a half-mile of road between the village and the airport needed trucks. The village, which sat at the end of a peninsula, was only 100 yards long and was surrounded by a lake. With the hundred yards of the village, the half-mile to the runway, and the mile of runway, the total driving distance of the whole area was no more than a mile and three quarters. Yet by the time I landed, there was a sizable fleet of trucks parked at the airport.

When I asked why someone needed a truck to drive a mile and a half, I was told that the villagers go back to town when the winter roads are open. The winter roads are constructed between the lakes. When the lakes freeze, the roads meet the lakes connecting the villages. When the lakes thaw, the reverse happens and the villages are cut off from each other and remain that way until the winter returns.

After locating someone with a fuel pump, I found Bernie's gas supply, pulled out a barrel, and started pumping fuel into the plane. Bearskin Lake was the first native village I had visited. Some of the villagers asked me to stay the night, but I did not have the time: Churchill was the day's goal, and I had to make it.

Churchill is 314 miles from Bearskin Lake, which translates into four to five hours in the Stearman, depending on the weather. It was on the flight to Churchill that I felt I truly became a bush pilot. I perfected the technique of using the landscape to my advantage. When slowed by a headwind, I would gain ground speed by dropping down to the lakes and valleys, pulling up right before reaching the trees. The trees blocked the headwinds. If I had a tailwind, I would stay in it, allowing it to push me along. Beyond the fun of it, the maneuver added an average of five to ten miles an hour to my ground speed. I was also pleased at how well I was taking the cold. I had put on forty pounds for the trip, certain that the extra body fat would come in handy. The temperatures here were only in the low teens. It would be much colder later, testing my conditioning as much as my resolve.

About fifty miles south of Churchill, I reached the end of the tree line. It was the first time I had seen tundra. The landscape was treeless, flat, and covered by pools of blue-green water, sometimes with an orange or red hue made by the algae and moss. There was nothing but the endless treeless plain for as far as I could see. The alien terrain reminded me of homemade quilts from my childhood with their odd-shaped patterns and vivid colors—the blue-greens, the oranges, and the reds highlighting the irregular shapes of the tapestry. And there I was, thirty years and a lifetime away from Corinth, flying over the countryside dreaming I was lying on a homemade quilt. I smiled to myself and thought of the saying, "Am I a man dreaming I'm a butterfly, or am I a butterfly dreaming I'm a man?"

I still had thirty gallons of gas in the tanks. The sun radiated brightly and the blue skies lured me on. I had a ball that day soaring, rolling, diving, and buzzing the tundra. When I look back on the thousands of miles I have flown over thirty years, I enjoyed none more than that final fifty miles to Churchill. In an odd way, the experience matured me as a pilot and at the same time let me regain my youth. I had gained self-confidence by flying alone in a plane I loved over one of the most breathtakingly beautiful but isolated spots on the planet. I was overwhelmed by the pure joy of it. Finally, I knew that I had the skills to take the Stearman anywhere. What I did not know—and would not find out until much later—was if I had the will to go anywhere. But on that day, the Stearman and I were one—two parts of the same being, each part an extension of the other. The Stearman was my clothing, my arms and legs. Through the Stearman, I willed myself onward through the pain, the loneliness, and the fear. When I talked to the Stearman, I was speaking, not to something outside of me, but to my inner being, my spiritual self and the hawk within me.

As I approached Churchill it looked like a rocky outcrop nestled on the edge of the frozen Hudson Bay. It was late in the season and the rocks were already showing through the snow.

I radioed the airport, "Churchill tower, this is November 29743. Where should I land?"

"Come in on the dirt runway. It's into the wind and easy to spot."

I followed another plane into the airport, easily finding the runway. But the airplane in front of me kicked up a hell of a dust storm when he landed and I was forced to wait until the dust settled to land.

Once on the ground, I pulled up to a small prefabricated building with a gas truck parked in front owned by a fellow named Cameron Doll, whom I had called weeks before about my trip.

"I've been expecting you," Cameron said, as I climbed out of the Stearman.

"I've got some aviation fuel for you. You can park the plane in front of my office while I tell Tim you're here," he said, talking over his shoulder to me as he turned back toward the building. "He wants to see the plane."

A few moments later, Tim Cameron, a mechanic for Wesaya Air, came out from the large hangar that formed the base of the control tower.

"What the hell is this coming all the way to Churchill?" The question was followed by a big guffaw.

I was checking the plane to make certain everything had survived the flight in good order as he approached.

"You the fella flew this thing up here?"

"Yepper, that's me."

"Huh," he said, comically inclined, "We don't get many darkies up here, especially crazy ones."

Ordinarily, I would have been offended, but the way he said it just made me laugh.

"I'm surprised you get *anybody* up here," I said with a smile. "What type of stupid s.o.b. would come up here to make a living?"

As we walked together into Cameron's office, Tim immediately started farting and smelling up the place. It was 12 degrees Fahrenheit outside but we all went back outside.

The north is full of interesting characters. Cameron was what you might expect of a young entrepreneur, while Tim was a northern wild man, with a heart of gold and the social graces of an alley cat. These two men could not be more dissimilar. Cameron was skinny and, most always, serious, and quiet. Tim, on the other hand, was built large, a boisterous man with few serious bones in his body.

Tim took me to the hotel that Mary had arranged for me to stay in. When he saw the room, he insisted that I stay somewhere else.

"We can do better than this," he promised. "Hell, you're a VIP. You should have the best room in Churchill."

As things turned out, Cameron Doll and Tim Cameron, those walking, talking, twisted versions of Laurel and Hardy, became two of my closest friends.

That night I called Mary to hear about the disasters and near disasters of her day. I tried to keep my problems to myself. I told her about Churchill and she said she could not wait to see it one day. I did not think Churchill was one of the places that would be on her "can't-wait-to-see" list, but as I was there and she was at home dealing with the day-to-day problems, it would have been a welcome change for her.

The next day, Tim managed to secure me a suite with a living room, dining room and kitchen, and a bedroom upstairs. It was a lucky find, although at the time I did not know how lucky. After Tim had taken care of my accommodations, we both went to the airport to take a look at the plane. I told him about the problems I had been having with the tachometer.

"It hasn't been working for a while. But overall I don't think it's a big problem, 'cause I can tell the rpms of that plane just by listening to the engine hum."

"That's not a good idea," Tim said, with unaccustomed seriousness.

"One rule of Arctic flying is don't go until everything's perfect, because up here, when one thing goes wrong you can count on other things goin' bad. I'll fix it for you. While I'm at it, we should stop-drill some of these cracks in the canopy."

Unfortunately, the Arctic's version of Murphy's Law proved to be just as true on the ground as in the air. While climbing into the Stearman to fix the tachometer, Tim busted the base of my headset. And after taking a good look at the tachometer, he decided it could not be fixed and that I would need to have another one sent to Churchill and installed before I could leave. I called Don Sanders to tell him I had solved the problem of the fuel consumption on take-off and then called Bruce to tell him about the problem with the tachometer.

"I'll find one right away," Bruce promised. "I'll ship it up as fast as I can."

One thing about Bruce—the man is a genius at finding things. If there is only one of something on the planet, Bruce will have it located by sundown and on its way. And by the time he finds the part he will know as much about it as the manufacturer. He is a virtuoso of scrounging.

Later Tim told me that if someone could get the part to Winnipeg, he could pick it up when he made the run from Winnipeg to Churchill. So that settled it. I could not leave Churchill until I had the new tachometer. I didn't mind this too much because I had a great place to stay, good company, and better food than in most of the northern villages. Pickle Lake had one restaurant, with bad food; in Nakina, the one restaurant had *worse* food. Churchill had two restaurants and the food was adequate in both.

Later that afternoon, Tim asked me if I could put on a small air show for the people at the airport: "Just fly around and do some stunts."

He did not have to twist my arm. I called the tower on the landline inside the airport.

"Hey," I said, excited by Tim's request. "Do you guys mind if I put on an impromptu air show?"

"What do you mean?" a voice in the tower asked.

"You know, a couple of loops and rolls and buzz the airport a few times to give everybody a show. You mind?"

The tower manager laughed. "Would we *mind*? Wait thirty minutes. I'm going to get the other controllers over here to watch!"

I removed the canopy and readied the plane till the tower radioed me.

"Airport's officially closed for the show. Do your thing."

A crowd of about thirty had formed outside the tower and many others were watching at the windows.

Now, I have often been called a showoff—and sometimes for good reason—but when someone asks me to show them what I can do in my airplane, I do not mind doing some wild stunts. I put on forty-five minutes of the best perform-ance I could summon up. I would not say the performance was award-winning, but at the conclusion the audience was grateful and the pilot was extremely happy. It was an easy room—entertainment in Churchill is rare, and everyone there loves airplanes.

After heating up the airport, I flew to Churchill village, five miles away, and gave the townspeople twenty minutes of the same show. Since I was used to fly-ing around cities where people are aircraft-adverse, I cut the village show short for fear they would not be as thrilled with the intrusion as they had been at the airport. When I arrived back at the airport, I looped the plane, did another couple of rolls, and landed. I pulled up to the ramp, my adrenaline still pumping, pleased that the stunts had gone so well. As I was shutting down the plane, Tim approached with a crowd of townspeople following him.

"Somebody from town called the airport," he said, looking a bit down.

Oh no, I thought. Damn. "Were there complaints?" I asked, already feeling ashamed.

Tim chuckled. "No, of course not. They were upset you didn't stay longer. You finished up just as they let the kids out of the classroom to see the airplane."

A weight lifted and a lightness came into my voice, "Oh, well, in that case, send my apologies. Tomorrow I'll do a show for the school."

What a difference from what I was used to at home. Unfortunately the encore show never happened because Churchill was socked in for the next six days, tethering me to the ground.

For most of the year, Churchill, Manitoba, is a village of eight hundred stalwart souls. That number swells to almost four thousand during tourist-favorite polar bear season, which lasts from mid-October to mid-November.

Most polar bear spend a solitary winter on frozen Hudson Bay. But in the warmer months, when the bay ice breaks up and there are no more seal, they migrate south of Churchill and mate. This migration lasts from July to November. Deprived of seal, their primary food source, the bear mostly fast during the mating season. But once the bay begins to refreeze and the seal reappear, the bear return to the ice. For the past fifty years or so, the bear, likely enticed by the smell of rotting food in the Churchill dump, have stopped in Churchill on their way back to the bay. And where the bear go, so go the tourists, who come from all over the world to see the migration.

Although the town's bustle is relative to other northern Canadian towns during the migration season, during the off-season, when the bear are either on the ice or south of Churchill, the tourists return home and there is not a great deal to do in Churchill.

In addition to the airport, Churchill houses the northern terminus for the rail line, and its station operates year-round for the transport of supplies to the more isolated northern villages. Churchill is also one of the largest grain ports in the world, although when I was there, nearly three months before the thaw, no one was manning the grain elevator. In the summer months, its harbor supports a port, where ships from as far away as Russia dock to load Canadian grain.

The U.S. Army used to have a base at Churchill. While the airport uses a few of the base's buildings, the base itself has been closed and most of its facilities plowed under, returning the land to tundra. When the base was active, Canada built a town center to service the increased population. The complex is still the envy of all the northern towns. It houses a school, a hospital, a theater that plays one film a month, a curling rink, an ice hockey rink, and shops, all under one roof.

As luck would have it, the six days that I was marooned coincided with the town's annual curling competition. The Canadians borrowed curling from the Scots, who take credit for inventing the sport. Curling is easy to describe but difficult to appreciate. One member of the team slides a forty-pound stone across a frozen surface toward a line opposite the start. It is like shuffleboard on ice, with a comical exception: as the stone slides, broom-carrying team members busily sweep the ice in front of the stone in an effort to control its path as it heads toward the goal. You have to see it to believe it. In the end the stone that gets closest to the finish line wins. I never thought curling was particularly interesting, much less a sport, but in Churchill everyone is crazy for it. Worldwide, the sport has grown in popularity, so much so that it was made a gold medal sport in the 2002 Olympics, where the Canadian men's team lost in a squeaker to the Norwegians.

Tim Cameron served as one of the coordinators of the Churchill event. The competition brought out the whole town. Everyone seemed to play and the last team standing had bragging rights for the year. Like everyone else in town I went to the town center every day for the competition. I was not drawn to the matches, which I found about as exciting to watch as a washing machine in the spin cycle, but I was drawn to the people, and the partying, and the fun. I told Tim what I thought of curling and even nicknamed it "hurling." A couple of times, I told people in town that I was on my way to the hurling competition. Some found it amusing; others found it insulting. In Churchill they take their curling seriously.

My third day in Churchill was rather warm, with a high of 29 degrees

Fahrenheit. Tim lent me his four-wheeler for the day, so I could check out Churchill and the bay. Before heading for the bay I visited the ruins of old Fort Churchill, circa 1858. Churchill, I discovered, had been a popular wintering spot for the British in the nineteenth century. Then I drove out to the shore, parked the four-wheeler on the beach, and took a hike out onto the frozen Hudson Bay.

On the way back to town, I noticed large animal tracks in the ice that appeared to lead back to town. On closer investigation, I determined they were polar bear tracks. I was curious to see a polar bear so I mounted the four-wheeler and followed the tracks to their terminus, where I discovered that "polar bear Wade," the person in Churchill responsible for bear safety, had darted the bear. The bear had already been taken to a holding area, fondly known as the "polar bear jail," where it would stay until it could be moved safely away from town.

Later I saw a group of three women and two men who looked like tourists. I stopped to ask if they were visitors and was told that they were part of the Born Free Society and were in Churchill to talk to people about the bears.

"Really," I said, with interest. "What's going on with the polar bears?"

I was told that the society was concerned for the safety of the bear population as it comes into contact with humans. They were in Churchill to do something about the situation. Their plans included planting noxious food in the Churchill dump that would sicken the bears, discouraging their attraction to human food.

They seemed like well-intentioned people and I liked the sound of their ideas, so I asked them if they needed a ride back to town. They accepted and we all crowded into the four-wheeler. On the way back I took them onto the ice to see the tracks I had found. I later asked Tim what the townsfolk thought about of the society. He told me that 80 percent of Churchill's revenue came from tourist dollars, and that while the society's mission may help to save the bears it would do little to save Churchill.

Every time I went to a curling match, I was asked what the society was up to. Everyone laughed when I said that they just wanted to help the bears. But the town never warmed up to the society members, and some even thought they should be run out of town. I invited them to various events, but they preferred to stay to themselves.

By far the most memorable party during my time in Churchill was the annual dance held in the Legion Hall at the end of the curling competition. I dressed for the event in my finest attire—a warm pair of pants and shirt, one of only two suits of clothing I had with me. The party was already in full swing when Tim, his wife, daughter, and I arrived. We got a drink and walked to one side of the hall, somewhat removed from the dance floor. Tim was not much of a dancer, and the beer and conversation were good enough for me. As the salute to the winning curling team was drawing to a close, a rather large Inuit woman approached me. She smiled, grabbed me by the genitals, and pulled me onto the dance floor. It was the most unusual way I have ever been invited to dance. Immediately, I whirled around to see Tim's reaction. For all I knew, this woman's behavior could have been normal, even a native custom. Tim was not looking my way and nobody around me seemed to have noticed, or cared about, what had happened. I decided to go along with her. Once we arrived on the dance floor, she let go of me and started to dance on her own. Again I looked around searching for a clue to what was going on, but everyone around me was still drinking and talking, as if nothing out of the ordinary was happening. The music continued to play and she continued to dance, while I stood at a polite but safe distance, just in case she tried to grab me again.

At that moment, a guy ran up, leaned over, put his head into my stomach, grabbed me around the waist, and pushed me off the dance floor. I was so surprised that it took me a while to react. I remember noticing the people from the Born Free Society staring at me with a "what the hell?" expression on their faces. But they were the only ones. Regaining control, I reached up in an effort to push the guy away. As I did, the man let me go and stood up.

"Hey, I was rescuing you!" he said, a big friendly smile on his face. "I thought you were Creet and the Inuit was messing with you. Whiskey Jack's my name. I'm Creet, up from the south to work on the railroad."

"So what was that all about back there?" I asked.

"She always does that on the first dance. From the side and the back, you look Creet," said Whiskey.

"Well," I said, "I appreciate your rescue. I'd be mighty grateful if you could stand between me and her tonight."

Whiskey chuckled. "It's all right. She only does it once. She's got an image of the package now."

At the end of the dance, we went to a house party, a short walk away, no more than 150 yards from the Legion Hall. When we got outside I noticed that everyone was getting into trucks or cars to drive to the house. Even those without vehicles waited outside the hall for someone to ferry them over to the house, which was in full sight of the hall. I asked one of the townspeople why they did not walk.

"Who wants to walk, when you can drive?" was the response. There were only twenty miles of road in the area and not many places to go, so people made an adventure out of driving down and across the street. Things that seem out of the ordinary to me are perfectly normal in Churchill.

The next day I called Mary. I did not quite know how to tell her about the Inuit woman grabbing me, so I told her that I had met a woman at a dance who had the strangest way of inviting a person to dance.

"Was it some sort of local thing?" she asked.

"I certainly hope not."

"She grabbed your privates, huh?"

I cannot keep anything from Mary. I am convinced the woman can read my mind.

After six days of bad weather the new tachometer finally arrived in the mail. Tim installed it and I was good to go, just as another three days of bad weather arrived. On the fourth day I left for the Hudson Bay.

4. The Quest and the Hawk

▼

The telephone rang in the hotel room where I was sleeping off a long night of partying. It was the airport controller calling with word that the weather had cleared. There was a three-hour window opening for VFR flights, after which Churchill would be socked in for another three days. In a sixty-year-old biplane without instruments, flying in anything less than VFR conditions is not only a violation of FAA regulations, but of good sense as well.

The weather in the north was getting worse by the day. It was already May 3 and I had been warned to be out of the Arctic before June, when the air warms and the potential for wet snow and freezing rain is a certainty. Because the Stearman has more surface area than most modern aircraft and no way to deal with ice buildup, an encounter with freezing rain is almost always fatal. Had everything gone as originally planned I would have been home by now, not still going north. This was my last chance. All I needed was three hours. Pilot reports from the north showed all clear at Rankin Inlet and Baker Lake. Churchill was clear with 1,500 feet overcast and forecast to hold for at least a couple of hours. I needed one hour to prepare for the flight, allowing me two hours in the air before the storm—enough time, I thought, to steer clear of it.

It took me fifteen minutes to get to the airport and another seemingly endless thirty minutes to pump seventy-five gallons of fuel into the airplane. The storm was still more than two hours away. Pilots who had just come in from Rankin Inlet, 300 miles to the north, assured me that the sky there was clear with a ceiling of 20,000 feet.

"You'll be all right," one of them said. "The ceilings pick up as soon as you get about a hundred miles north of here."

Sure, I thought, that is easy for you to say. You guys are flying those big transports capable of handling rain and snow.

My nerves were on edge. The Stearman was designed for fair-weather use and pilot training. I could be in real trouble if I were to get stuck in a severe storm. On the other hand, if I stayed in Churchill for another three days I might never make it any farther north. It was now or not at all.

Tim struggled with my headset while I prepared to get underway.

"I can't get this thing working," he finally conceded. "But Cameron's got one just like it. I'll take his and swap it with yours and have yours fixed by the time you come back through Churchill."

While I was relieved to know that I would have a working headset, the exchange took another fifteen minutes. The clock on the storm was running and I was standing still.

During the preflight preparations, the engine ran a bit rougher than usual. I thought it was likely a fouled plug, so I worked with the mixture controls and it smoothed out nicely. The rhythm of the seven cylinders roaring in sync calmed me. As I climbed into the small, cramped cockpit, the controller came down with a couple of locals to take pictures. As he snapped the last photo, he gave me some good advice:

"You'd better get going." (Indeed, I thought.) "Still forecasting clear at Rankin Inlet," he added.

I cried, "Clear!" and cranked up the Stearman's radial engine, which started easily.

I was optimistic as I took off into a heading for Rankin Inlet. The cloud ceiling had dropped from 1,500 to 1,000 feet, but everything else was fine. I had been assured that it was clear to the north, and the old Stearman was now running beautifully. But ten miles out of Churchill my composure crumbled. A massive, thick, and churning gray-white wall of clouds fueled by an eighty-mile-an-hour wind was building from the west off my left wing tip. The sight of a monstrous Arctic blizzard heading straight for me took my breath away. It looked to be no more than fifteen miles away and coming in fast. The temperature had taken a dive from 30 to 20 degrees and the ceiling had slid precipitously to 800 feet, pushing me closer to the ground.

I thought about heading back to Churchill and turned to the right 90 degrees to check out the situation behind me. I was hoping to see a clear path back, but Churchill had vanished in the huge storm. Already well out over Hudson Bay, I decided to turn east and head out farther into the bay to evade the approaching storm. Hoping to outrun the storm, I took a heading of .035 degrees (the heading for Rankin Inlet would have been .014). Twenty miles off course, the storm was still chasing me. As the cloud ceiling closed to 500 feet, I could hear myself saying, "The sky is clear at Rankin Inlet. The sky is clear at Rankin Inlet."

At thirty miles off the course, I realized I would not be able to get around the storm. I had no hope of returning to Churchill, which, without radar, lacked the means to talk me in. I considered landing on the bay and waiting for the storm to pass, but one look at the roughness of the ice below, and I decided against it. The ice was breaking up, folding from the force of the wind, large chunks of it piling up like pieces of a giant jigsaw puzzle. The water was 28 degrees Fahrenheit. With the extra forty pounds I had put on for the trip, I could survive for ten, maybe fifteen, minutes if the plane broke through the ice on landing. Since I did not have enough fuel to continue east to the other side of the bay, my only option was to turn north, cut through the storm, and head for Rankin Inlet. The temperature was still dropping, which was good news. The plane can handle snow because it does not stick to the wings.

Two hundred miles from Rankin Inlet, the clouds increased — zero visibility in all directions. The plane shook and groaned in the turbulence. The clouds were so thick I could barely make out the tips of the wings. I had never flown through weather as violent. I descended slowly, hoping to get low enough to use the sight of the bay to keep the plane level. I located the ice at twenty feet, but the forward visibility still remained at zero. As I inched closer to the surface, I saw the pack ice—ice supported by ice, making it susceptible to breaks and tears from the force of wind and currents—churning and folding up from the vicious force of the storm's wind. I climbed a bit higher. If I went too high I would lose the ice; too low, and I would risk ramming into one of its pressure ridges. I went back up to fifty feet, and once again the bay vanished.

I both needed and feared the ice, but did not know how to weigh the need against the fear.

The more air the better, I thought, remembering the advice of an old pilot in Corinth. The ground is the enemy. The more air the better.

I climbed slowly, straining against the force of the storm to keep the plane steady and level at the same time. Did I really have the ability to pull this off? Would it take more than skill?

"It takes skill, luck, and pluck," the old pilots used to say.

I thought I had the skill, knew I had the balls, but the luck I was not so sure about. Alone and in the middle of the Hudson Bay, fear visited me in the cockpit. I began to sweat, even in the freezing wind. The only working instruments I had were an oil temperature gauge, a tachometer, an airspeed indicator, a GPS, a turn and bank indicator, a radio with a ten-mile range, and a clock. My compass had stopped working north of Pickle Lake, and I was not sure what would go next. The clock was the only instrument I had come to trust completely. It was an earned trust and it would never fail me. I used the airspeed indicator to keep the plane level. As long as I stayed at ninety-five miles an hour I would stay level. Any faster would mean I was diving, any slower and I would be climbing. The GPS kept me on a straight path. I kept glancing at the clock, thinking that as long as it worked everything would work.

Thirty long minutes after I had entered the clouds there was a sudden break in the storm and the sky cleared. Nothing but blue above and open water below, where the storm had ripped a hole in the ice thirty miles wide. As I looked behind me I saw the massive cloud mass sliding into the distance. Relief shot through me like a bolt of adrenaline. I had made it out. I was relieved to the point of exhaustion but felt a surge of joy and pride that I had tangled with and survived something that fierce. Now all I had to do was sit back and enjoy the ride to Rankin Inlet.

Minutes later, I heard the unmistakable sound of the engine sputtering. It coughed a few times and then quit completely. It is eerie when a plane's engine dies. The vibrations slow and the noise level drops significantly, but the propeller continues to windmill until the pilot either feathers the prop by turning the blades knife-edge into the wind, or slows the plane to nearly a stall. A plane stalls when it flies too slowly for the wings to produce enough lift to keep it airborne. I attempted to restart the engine, but it would not catch. Two, three, four, and five times I tried. I looked below for any signs of ice on which I could land, but the nearest solid surface looked to be about ten to fifteen miles away. I could not make it that far with a dead engine gliding from 2,000 feet. I thought about radioing for help, but knew no one was within range. Even if there had been, no one could have reached me in time. Only an oceangoing helicopter hovering above me when I ditched could have rescued me, and there were no long-range "helos" in Northern Canada.

I was down to two options: either land the plane in the water and swim until I passed out, or dive straight into the bay and get it over quickly. I decided on the quick route. The choice was not made as coolly as I now relate it. At the time I was convinced I was going to die, a certainty that so terrified me I almost passed out. But once I had determined how I would die, and had made the decision to take control of my final flight, I calmed down. I thought about all the fool stunts I had pulled and the unintended dangers I had survived. Now I was going to die on a mission undertaken specifically to prove to myself that I was a man of substance. The irony of it, I thought. I had really screwed the pooch this time.

My plan was to wait until I descended to fifty feet, then pull the nose up to a high angle so that the plane would stall, then plunge straight into the bay. I was keeping up airspeed by descending. I was calm and strangely happy. I would be dead in less than fifteen minutes and there was nothing I could do about it. The sky was the bluest I had ever seen and the air was perfectly clear. I was flying, doing what I liked doing best, living the life I had chosen. It was, I thought, not a bad way to go.

As the plane descended, my thoughts went to Mary and the kids. Lara, my youngest, would probably take it the hardest. I supposed Gustavus and my daughter Hera would be all right. They were old enough to have lives of their own and that should lessen their pain. I had wanted grandchildren and wondered how many I would have had. Would any of them become pilots? Or better yet, astronauts. Mary, I was sure, would be okay. She is strong, strong enough to have put up with me for all these years. I remember worrying about their imagining my last moments. I knew my body would never be found. I was at least forty miles outside my expected flight path. I wished I had a way to tell them that this death was not so difficult. I would have a few more minutes of perfect flying and then nothing.

I was at 600 feet and ready to give in to the inevitable when the engine caught. My blood pressure went up so fast that I almost fainted. I was jolted back into the real world. Now I had to think the hard thoughts of survival. With that, old Mr. Fear returned, singing with a vengeance, and this time he brought his brother, Panic, to play the piano.

What should I do? Think, think! More air. Climb, yes, climb!

The engine continued to sputter and cough but somehow it kept running. There was ice in the distance that looked solid enough on which to land. I might be forced to crash, but I could survive. I hoped I could at least make it that far. I was at 2,500 feet, still not close enough to glide to the ice if the engine shut down again.

Ninety miles from Rankin Inlet, I saw that I was within gliding distance of the ice. The engine continued to struggle as I began the descent. At first glance, the surface ice looked smooth, with outcroppings of rock here and there. I was certain I could land on it if I had to. I realized I was nearing shore because the ice was land-fast, held in place by the rocky outcropping that protected it from the ravages of the wind.

I descended to fifty feet and eased the airplane down, setting the wheels on the makeshift runway all the while maneuvering to keep the craft stable. Forty miles out, the engine was still having problems, but it *was* running. Once again I had two options. I could cut power, land here on the ice, and await rescue, which could take a couple of days. I had filed a flight plan before leaving Churchill. If I did not show in Rankin Inlet today, someone would eventually come looking for me. Or I could let the engine run as long as it could and try to reach Rankin Inlet. Although the terrain ahead might not be good for landing, I chose to continue, letting the Stearman take me as far as it could. I pushed the throttle to full power and rose back into the air. If the ground ahead looked to be too rough, I would turn back and land here.

Ten miles from my destination, as I was beginning my descent into the airport, the engine started acting up again. I radioed Rankin Inlet.

"Rankin Radio, this is November 29743. Do you read?"

"Roger 743, I read. What is your intention?"

"I'm ten miles out, in-bound VFR and would like the straight-in approach, please."

The answer from the tower crackled through my headset, "November 29743, we've been expecting you. No traffic. Any runway you choose will be fine. The winds are 210 at thirty gusting to forty. Our runways are thirteen and thirty-one."

I had no time to talk to the tower. As I lined up for final approach, I realized I was drifting too far left. What had they said about the winds: "thirty gusting to forty." Stearmans are designed to handle seventeen-mile-an-hour crosswinds. Twenty-knots was the strongest crosswind I had ever landed in. The tower called again.

"November 29743, do you read? Winds have picked up."

I did not answer. I could not reach the talk button on the instrument panel as both of my hands were working to keep the plane steady. Then the tower called again.

"Do you read? Winds have increased. State your intentions."

My intentions would be obvious in a few minutes. I would either make the best landing of my life or litter his runway with antique aircraft and human body parts. As I flew the airplane down onto the runway, the wind pushed it violently to the right. I tried to hold it steady, giving it all I had. Finally, the main wheels touched. I was on the ground, rolling fast. The wind was fiercely pushing the plane to the right. The Stearman was still traveling too fast for me to get the tail wheel down. I did not think I could hold her on the runway. I decided that adding power would only make things worse, so I stayed off the throttle. The nose of the airplane suddenly swung 90 degrees to the right. I was sure I was going off the strip. Then the tail wheel hit the strip and the plane stopped abruptly. I looked out to the side. The plane was sitting crossways on the runway, facing the tower. The main wheels were right on the edge of the pavement.

"November 29743, nice job. Do you require any assistance?"

My left hand was still on the throttle and my right hand on the control stick. I tried to release the throttle, but my fingers would not move. I was in shock. I tried to break my hold on the controls and the same thing happened.

"Relax now," I told myself. "You're on the ground. You're safe and the plane is safe. Let go of the damn controls."

I leaned my head on the back of the seat. It was over. My left hand slowly let go of the throttle. I was alive and on the ground at Rankin Inlet. I radioed in.

"Tower, this is 29743. Where can I park?"

In the Keewatin district of Nunavut, Canada, where the Arctic cold wraps its fingers around everything in sight, the small village of Rankin Inlet sits on the shores of Hudson Bay. Snow and ice cover the region ten months of the year, and there are no trees or vegetation of any kind. Without exaggeration it could easily be described as a wasteland. But to its Inuit inhabitants it is home, and it is beautiful.

Rankin Inlet, the largest village in the Keewatin district, is the spiritual hub of Inuit activity. The Inuit call the area Quivaleg, the meaning of which depends upon whom you ask. Each Inuit I asked gave me a different answer. Some said "home," others said, "land of the people," "meeting place," others, something else. "Keewatin," the Canadian government's official name for the area, is a Creet word from the language of the Creek Indians. Keewatin lies in the eastern part of what was once known as the Northwest Territory, and is now called Nunavut, an Inuit word meaning "our land." In recent years, the names of some of the villages have been changed from English back to their original, precolonial names. Spence Bay, for example, is now named Taloyoak, and Eskimo Point is Arviat.

Rankin Inlet has a population of 2,300, greater than that of Churchill, which is more than twice as large in area. The whole village of Rankin Inlet could easily fit into one block of a compactly designed American town. The main road, a Nunavut version of the Capital Beltway in Washington, D.C., is a mile and a half and loops around the entire town, which sits along the perimeter of the circular road. There is one hotel on the road, and in the center of the loop there is a lake. The airport lies about a quarter of a mile south of the village. There is an emergency barracks along the south side of the airport designed to house five hundred U.S. troops. The complex, now mothballed for a war with some future foe, has of six hangars, each of which could house one fighter aircraft. The base stands apart, almost hidden, from the rest of the airport, and I daresay most of the residents of the village have not seen the inside of it, or even been close to it.

I parked the plane and was still sitting in the cockpit when an Inuit man and woman came up and leaned into the plane.

"I've never seen anything like this," the man said. "What kind of airplane—"

Before he had a chance to finish the question, I grabbed him by the shoulders, lifted him up, and kissed him square on the mouth. I had never kissed a man and was a little surprised at myself for letting my emotions get away from me, but I was so happy to be alive I could not contain myself. The woman (who turned out to be the man's wife) was standing beside him, so I grabbed her and gave her a big kiss too.

News of my arrival spread quickly across the entire community. Steve Fredland, at Keewatin Air, a local airline operating out of Winnipeg that services many of the northern villages in Nunavut, offered to let me house the plane in Keewatin Air's heated hangar. Keewatin's base at Rankin consisted of a large heated hangar (a rarity in the north) and an aircraft used for emergency medical evacuation. While I was putting the Stearman in the hangar, villagers with questions—each question was preceded and followed by giggles—started streaming in. The questions were flying right and left.

"Did you fly this?"

"Where you from?"

"You part Inuit?"

Among those stopping by were Johnny Onosolouk and Thomas Norkitique. During my stay in Rankin Inlet, Johnny and Thomas (Studly, as I came to call him) designated themselves as my personal Inuit ambassadors.

Thomas always seemed to be burdened with women problems. Every day I was there he showed up with new stories of his romantic woes. I assured him that the reason he was experiencing all that strife was because he was such a *studly* man that the ladies could not stay away from him. The nickname stuck, and to this day, whenever I call a friend in Rankin Inlet, they tell me what Studly is up to.

Johnny and Studly went everywhere with me, proudly describing my flight in the Stearman to anyone they happened upon. The Inuit appear to share a natural affinity for anyone who takes on the full force of the Arctic.

I met one man in Rankin Inlet who had made the 200-mile trip from Arviot to Rankin by snowmobile in two-and-one-half hours. He had covered the same distance on the ground almost as fast as I had in the air. The man looked me up and down, paying close attention to my cheeks. I later found out that he was looking for frostbite, little of which I had. He was curious to know what I had worn on my face. I told him that all I had worn were my helmet and goggles. He smiled and nodded in approval. We both had known the same bitter bite of the northern wind. I felt like a heroic pilot-explorer, imbued with the spirit of the hawk.

My arrival coincided with Rankin Inlet's village days, an annual gathering of Inuit who travel to Rankin Inlet from all over the Keewatin district to be with friends and relatives. Before joining in the evening's festivities, I called Mary and told her a watered-down version of the ordeal over Hudson Bay. After assuring her that I would not leave Rankin Inlet until the Stearman's problems had been resolved, I called Bruce and told him the full story, holding nothing back.

I learned later that Bruce told a reporter the unedited version, which appeared a day later in the *Gaithersburg Gazette* and frightened little Lara.

After checking in with Mary and Bruce, I went to the evening's gathering. I was standing by the side of the dance floor watching the fun when Johnny motioned to me to join in.

"I don't have a partner," I shouted to him over the music.

"All you have to do is come stand in the middle of the floor, and the women will come to you," he shouted back, a laugh in his voice.

With the memory still fresh of the genital-grabbing woman in Churchill, I was cautious. As the music ended, Johnny came over and led me out to the center of the dance floor. I stood there alone and awkward, waiting for the next dance to begin. As the musicians tuned up, a group of men and women surrounded me—the women in front and the men behind. Silently and without ceremony we were partnered as the music began. The music continued on for more than a half-hour. When I could take it no longer, I asked my partner if we could sit out the rest of the song. She gave no indication of wanting to and I wondered if she had understood me. I asked again. Her only response was to look at me and giggle. Getting nowhere I shrugged my shoulders and went to sit down, as she continued to dance.

A few moments later, an Inuit man with a big smile approached me and asked, "Are you the walrus?"

Earlier, I had heard a few of the men talking about "the walrus" but had not realized they were referring to me.

"Just like a walrus," the man continued. "When it finishes playing with a polar bear, it just turns around and sits."

Everything I did seemed to reinforce my walrus image. At different times I was "tough walrus," "dancing walrus," "flying walrus," and so on. I did not appreciate the joke, although I could understand it since I had put on so much weight for the trip and was chubby by almost anyone's definition.

The hotel in Rankin Inlet often doubled as a courthouse. A rape case was being tried there during my stay. The trial was a lesson in northern law. Because it is difficult to live on one's own in the north, the most meaningful punishment is some form of ostracism. While their sense of justice seemed to me to be right on track, they had a hard time enforcing the punishment because relatives of the criminals would simply bring food and supplies to the ostracized. The rape trial resulted in a hung jury, because one half of the jury was related to the victim and the other half to the accused.

After my Hudson Bay mishap, I knew I would be grounded until I corrected the engine problem. I needed a good mechanic. I called Tim Cameron in Churchill and asked him to give me the names of any he knew in the area. I had hoped Steve Fredland would help me find a reputable mechanic, but shortly after I arrived in Rankin Inlet, Steve and his family left town on vacation, traveling thirty miles into the tundra to hunt seal. Steve's father had been a missionary in the area, and Steve had married an Inuit woman. He even spoke the native language, Inuktitute.

To most people, the prospect of a vacation conjures up thoughts of Hawaii or some other tropical region, but a typical vacation for the Inuit is to go eighty miles or more into the tundra for fish, seal, and caribou hunting. God has got to love the Inuit. Any people who could find the Arctic both tolerable and enjoyable have got to be chosen.

My days in Rankin Inlet soon developed a pattern. Each morning I went to the hangar and called Don Sanders to discuss the engine problems. I would tweak the engine and then take the plane out for a loop and roll over Rankin Inlet, only to have it sputter and cough again. Then I would call Don again to talk through another plan and go back over the whole process again. At the end of the day, I would go back to town to eat some torturous food.

The food throughout the north was bad, but the food in Rankin Inlet set a new standard. The hotel dining room had a minimal selection of poor-imitation North American dishes. They had fish and chips, eggs and ham, beef in various states of abuse, pie, and sugar-flavored drinks. I liked the orange-flavored sugar water and tolerated the egg sandwich, minus the ham. To break the monotony of the hotel food, the local store had a sit-down pizza section, where you could get an imitation of a cheese pizza. I complained so about the food that my Inuit friends felt sorry for me and invited me to their homes for dinner. The government subsidizes most of Rankin Inlet's housing; the structures are prefabricated in the south and shipped north. Inuit homes are plain by American standards, without the bric-a-brac and over-furnishing that Americans are attracted to. The homes, like the people, are simple and reliable. While I was touched by my new friends' generosity and accepted their invitations gratefully, I could not develop a taste for whale blubber, caribou, or seal, so more often I settled for the hotel's eggs and sardines and bought some bread, cheese, and cookies to keep in my room.

I was enthusiastically included in parties, dogsled races, and snowmobiling, all of which served as opportunities for my friends to teach me how to survive in the northern wilderness. Under their guidance, I learned not only to identify land-fast ice, pack ice, freshwater ice, and to find north by the direction of the snowdrifts, but to enjoy the Arctic's hard beauty and to open myself to the secrets it reveals to the humble and the patient. In the Arctic, life is a test you know you are taking. To survive requires the kind of self-understanding I was pushing to acquire. The Choctaw say that if you sit in the woods and listen, they will speak to you: they will tell you where the deer are, the predators, the clearings, and the river. It is the same for the Inuit. They listen to the wind, read the land and sky, and survive in a land more forbidding and dangerous than any on the planet.

The welcome pressures of life lessons and entertainment not withstanding, I found the necessary time and energy to solve the Stearman's engine problems. Concluding that the air was too cold for the engine to operate properly, Studly, Johnny, and I weatherproofed the Stearman's engine with insulation and rebuilt the carburetor. To test our work, I flew circles around the town for three hours. The engine stayed lit. Its temperature was constant at 104 degrees Fahrenheit, more than 10 degrees above its seizing temperature, but nowhere near normal.

With the successful test fight under my belt, I planned to leave the next morning. But in the night an ice storm hit the village, coating it with four inches of ice. The town looked like an ice sculpture. I had never seen anything like it. It was then that I understood why the Arctic is no place to fly in the spring. As weather begins to warm, freezing rain and snow fall constantly. On the next trip, I decided to be out of Rankin Inlet before the start of spring.

When the weather finally cleared, I said goodbye to my friends and took off for Baker Lake, where I had prepaid for three barrels of fuel. One hundred and forty miles from Rankin Inlet, my tachometer failed again. I had waited for weeks in Churchill for a new tachometer and now the new one was dead. I decided to go on without it. I knew how to tell the speed of the engine by the sound it made and the airspeed I was traveling. Come what may, I was not going to wait on another tachometer. I did not want to spend much time in Baker Lake for fear that I would get boxed in by another ice storm. As I quickly refueled the plane, someone from the tower came outside and took pictures of my airplane. Not many people that far north had ever seen anything like a Stearman.

I got out of Baker Lake as planned and started for Taloyoak, 318 miles away. As I headed deeper into the wilderness, I began to lose myself. The hours to Taloyoak were the most difficult and lonely of my life.

I never thought I needed anyone, thought I was at my best on my own. I had always sought to be alone, to get away from people and their complications. But out there, where the cold, empty tundra stretches for thousands of miles, there is no one to escape from, nothing to duck out on, no voices to block out, no complications. There is just cold, impassive, and unforgiving space. As I searched the emotionless ice beneath me, a terrible loneliness set in upon me, like a fog bank blanketing my entire being. All I could see was snow and ice. There was no difference between the ground and the sky, no definition but a soft gray extending to what seemed like the ends of the earth. Was this purgatory, somewhere between heaven and hell? Alone with myself, my demons taunted me. What I would not have given then to hear a voice other than my own.

A forty-mile headwind (nearly half the speed of the Stearman, which travels at ninety-five miles per hour) slammed into the plane. The headwind reduced my ground speed to fifty miles an hour, considerably lengthening the trip to Taloyoak.

About 100 miles out of Baker Lake, I thought I saw a black spot on a ridge in front of me. It was the first variation in color that I had seen for the past two hours. As I got nearer to the spot, it seemed to be moving. When I passed over it, I realized that it was a herd of Arctic bison or musk ox. They had heard the plane and were circling, as they do, for defense. The adult bison had formed a protective circle around the calves. There were about thirty in the herd. I felt an immediate connection to them—a connection to all life on our small planet. Together they looked like a flower of life with the calves as the center and the adults as the petals.

About ten miles later I encountered an enormous herd of caribou. As the plane approached them, they started to run. At fifty miles an hour, I was not catching up on them quickly, but gaining nonetheless. As a caribou exhausted, I noticed it break off from the herd and make a stand, looking skyward toward the plane. The herd kept running, until four caribou remained. Soon three dropped out. The last caribou continued on until he could run no longer. Then it too stood and with dignity prepared to face what it feared was death. Will forces us on, but it is courage that gives us the strength to suffer the inevitable with honor. I was like that caribou.

After I landed in Taloyoak and settled into the hotel, I called Bruce and Don to tell them I wanted to turn back for home. I had gathered enough data on Arctic flying and had put the Stearman through its paces.

"You're close to the magnetic pole, aren't you?" Bruce asked. "Why not go for it?"

"I don't know," I said. "If the temperature drops the plane won't fly."

"It's only a hundred miles away from you now," he countered.

"The Stearman needs major work before it can go farther north," I parried. And for good measure added ominously that I thought the Stearman had had it.

But Bruce stayed on the offensive, and I soon heard myself saying, "Well, I might be able to make it there and back without a problem."

I called Mary that night to wish her happy anniversary and to tell her that the Stearman and I were going to give her the magnetic pole for an anniversary present.

"If you are doing this as a present for me then you may as well leave the airplane where it is and come home now." She was upset and in no mood to humor me. "This is your thing; it means nothing to me."

With a whimper in my voice I told her that I was dedicating the flight to her and that it would be a record breaker.

"I would have done it today, but I didn't get here in time," I said. "But no matter when it happens this record is ours." I was lying and she knew it.

"I thought this was only going to be a test flight," she said coolly. "Weren't you planning to turn around as soon as you'd learned enough to make the geographic pole attempt?"

I was caught. She had me. I came clean and told her that I was too close not to go for the magnetic pole and that I had everything under control. Still a lie but not as blatant as the first one.

Since Taloyoak carried only jet fuel, I had to cart the auto gas to the airport from town. It took seventy-five gallons—three and a half loads—to fill the Stearman. The Stearman's engine did as well with auto gas as it did with aviation fuel. Aviation fuel is 100 octane, while cheap auto gas is 87 octane. The Stearman only requires 73. It needs the lead that aviation fuel has, but running unleaded auto fuel for a few tanks will not harm it.

For the flight, I decided to remove the canopy, which by that point had nearly cracked in half. I gave it to Dennis Lyales, the mayor of Taloyoak and an Inuit who owns most of everything in town, including the hotel, in witness of my attempt to cross the magnetic pole in an open aircraft. He took it with all the pomp and ceremony of a politician.

I knew that the attempt on the magnetic pole was unnecessary. Mary was right, I should have been heading home. The Stearman was having problems and would not benefit from the added ordeal. I had learned all I needed to know on the trip, and I would have been better served to go home as fast as I could. This last flight, I thought, was just dangerous grandstanding. I could say that Bruce had goaded me into it, but that would be passing the buck. I was going to do it, although I did not fully understand why.

The directions to the pole were uncomplicated, direct, and reliable.

"Follow Boothia Peninsula until you run into the bay. The magnetic North Pole is right on the other side," the Inuit said.

But as I prepared to take off, a thick fog rolled in, so thick I could not see more than 100 yards in front of me. Frustrated, I taxied back, got out of the plane, and walked to the tiny one-room terminal. By the time I reached the terminal, the fog had blown off the runway and cleared to the 3,500-foot-high mountains that surround the town. I got back in the plane and taxied to the runway, gunned the engine, and took off.

Thirty miles out, another fog bank formed beneath me. The unpredictability of the fog concerned me. Would I be able to locate Taloyoak on the return from the pole?

The Stearman's oil temperature hovered at 80 degrees Fahrenheit. An oil temperature less than 77 would cause the engine to quit lubricating itself and seize. The air temperature remained at 3 degrees Fahrenheit, which was far too cold for the plane. Just as I had decided to turn back toward Taloyoak, the last fog bank lifted and the temperature suddenly rose to 14. The engine shot back up to around 93 degrees Fahrenheit.

Continuing on, I reached the point where I could see the edge of the island, the very spot that the Inuit had described as the magnetic North Pole. (Current maps show the magnetic North Pole at 78°27′N, 104°24′W, which is much farther north than I traveled that day. I found out later that I had made it to where the magnetic pole was in 1945.) I had made it, but I had no time to celebrate. I quickly turned the plane and beat it back to Taloyoak.

5. Going Home

By the time I reached the magnetic North Pole I had traveled 2,800 miles, burned 560 gallons of fuel, and flown forty-two hours. It was May 10, 1999, 1:30 P.M., eastern daylight saving time. It was one day after my twenty-third wedding anniversary. I had been gone almost one month. Now, all I wanted was to go home. The flight to the magnetic North Pole meant little to me. The goal was set simply to have something to shoot for. The only reason I had come to the Arctic was to familiarize myself with the route, scout out fuel stops, learn Arctic flying, and test the Stearman in the extreme conditions. I had done all that. I had made that old engine operate at 40 degrees colder than it was designed for. With a little more work, I could make it operate in even colder weather. Although the trip had deepened my conviction to reach the top of world, I felt no sense of satisfaction on reaching the magnetic North Pole. The geographic North Pole was still 1,400 miles north, half the distance I had already come. The top of the world was a world away, in conditions far worse than I had already seen, over mountains higher than I had ever flown, and through temperatures colder than I had ever felt. But I *had* gotten a taste of the Arctic and was thirsty for more. I wanted to see more of its wonders, smell more of its cold air, master the air as my Inuit friends mastered the tundra. Of course no one ever masters the Arctic. One may learn to survive it, but the Arctic will always be the master, killing those who do not heed its laws or listen to its wisdom. The Inuit say that you can never work against nature, you can only work with it. It was time for me to return home, time to prepare my airplane, and myself, for the spirit of the challenge. Was I made of the same stuff as my childhood heroes? Was my soul truly that of the hawk?

The wind traveled in my direction the entire way back to Taloyoak. I gathered a ground speed of 130 miles an hour. When I arrived in Taloyoak, I circled the town, performing a victory roll and loop. When I landed, Dennis Lyales was there to congratulate me and tell me that he had talked with someone from Guinness World Records.

"Really? What did they say?" I asked, with skepticism.

"They had heard about your attempt on the pole and asked if you'd made the village yet. I said you'd already left going north."

I never followed up to see if Guinness made anything of the trip.

Bruce had called Dennis Lyales, who told him that I had gone on to the magnetic pole. And Bruce told my Mary about it. I had not bothered to tell anyone and simply wanted to return home to start work on the real trip.

There was a storm coming down from the north, and I wanted to ride it as far south as I could. I made a trip into town for more gas, reattached the canopy, and took off, riding the front 500 miles back to Rankin. Thanks to the forty-knot tailwind, I made the trip in only four hours.

I looked for the wildlife I had seen on the way up to Taloyoak but saw none, no life of any kind. This time the emptiness did not frighten me. I was going home. The only thing I saw was a radar station set up by the United States as part of the defense early warning line (DEW) against nuclear missiles approaching, presumably, over the north from Russia.

When I arrived over Rankin Inlet, I circled, doing rolls and victory loops. My friends were waiting.

"We heard you went to the North Pole," Johnny told me. "You made it, didn't you?"

I had made it only to the magnetic North Pole I told him.

"But now that I know what I need to do, I'll be back, and then I'll make it all the way to the geographic pole," I said with renewed faith and determination.

That night I returned late and had not eaten, so the manager of the hotel gave me the keys to the pantry and told me to eat whatever I wanted. In Rankin Inlet, none of the townspeople are allowed to drink, although in the hotel, nonresidents can drink in the evening from ten to eleven o'clock. My nightly drinking buddy was a scientist from Winnipeg. He was in Rankin Inlet to count seals. Evidently, knowing the seal count is a good way to calculate the bear population. He was at the hotel anxious to welcome me back. While we talked and drank my Inuit friends waited outside.

I had a terrific meal that night. It consisted of a can of salmon, fried with mashed potatoes, ketchup, applesauce, cheese, a can of spinach, and some rolls. After I had eaten my fill, I called Mary to tell her that I had made the magnetic pole and was safely back in Rankin Inlet. She told me that Bruce had already told her and anyone else who would listen. I told her that everyone in Rankin Inlet and, probably, everyone as far south as Pickle Lake had heard about it too. News travels fast in the Arctic. I joked with her about my Inuit nickname. I wanted them to think of me as a polar bear or some scarce Arctic bird. But no, I was a walrus, and that was that. Mary laughed and said I looked like one with all the weight I had gained. I told her I was planning to put on another twenty pounds for my next trip. "Maybe then they won't call you Walrus; they'll call you Whale," she said. At three in the morning I finally turned in.

The next morning, I said goodbye to my friends. They invited me to come back during the summer for a whale hunt. I knew, but did not say, that I would not have the heart to take them up on the offer because I found it hard to kill any animal that could survive in the Arctic. Later in the year when they called to ask if I was coming, I told them I could not kill something smarter than many of the people I know.

The tailwind that had carried me to Rankin Inlet held out to Churchill, where Tim Cameron once again found a place in his hangar for the Stearman. We pulled the tachometer to try to fix it, giving me a looked-for excuse to stay in

Churchill overnight. Tim got my old room. The Born Free Society had stayed in it after I had left town, but they were gone.

I received word that Bernie Cox was planning for me to come back through Pickle Lake. He sent news to Churchill that he planned a large party for me that would begin as soon as I reached the town.

A headwind prevented me from flying directly to Pickle Lake. Instead, I flew to Gillam, 150 miles south of Churchill. In Gillam, I was invited to tour the town. I wanted to pass on the tour because I did not want to delay my arrival at the party in Pickle Lake, but ended up taking the tour, which included Gillam's hydroelectric plant. By the time I got airborne the winds had changed again. I ended up running smack into another headwind and had a hard time making it to Bearskin Lake, the next stop on the route to Pickle Lake.

Life in Bearskin Lake had changed. On the way north everything had been covered in snow. By the time I returned not a patch of snow could be seen anywhere. With the change of season, Bearskin Lake was actually a handsome community surrounding a lovely lake. All the airport's aviation fuel had been used up, so I was forced to scare up auto gas from the village. I went into town to look for a gas drum. I found one and filled it at a local co-op, returned to the Stearman, and fueled up for 150 miles to Pickle Lake.

I left Bearskin Lake in the late evening, hoping to make Pickle Lake before nightfall. The sun slipped below the horizon one-half hour out of Bearskin Lake. Up until then I had been using my wind dodging technique, dropping down under the tree line to just above the lakes. But this maneuver was too dangerous in the dark, so as the night fell I was forced to wrestle with the headwinds higher in the sky. It was the first time I had ever flown the Stearman at night. I enjoyed it. There was no light anywhere, which was fine because I had no need to see. I could hear the engine and feel the stick and rudders. All was well. Outside the temperature rose to a balmy 40 degrees Fahrenheit. I did not have on a flight suit, just my good clothes. The lack of bulk gave me some room, and I could even move around in my seat. What a luxury! I had forgotten how good it felt to move my body around on long flights and shift my weight to relieve the seat pressure.

It was exceptional flying the entire way to Pickle Lake. In the warm outside temperature, the engine came within normal temperature boundaries, reaching 130 degrees Fahrenheit for the first time in weeks. The only light came from the faint glow of the GPS. In the darkness, I could peer out from the cockpit and see the flames of the exhaust. In the extreme darkness, the flames bring an eerie glow to the cockpit and the tips of the wings. In the glow, the prop appears to be standing still, a perception that is created by the strobe effect of the firelight hitting the moving propeller.

I made Pickle Lake around 11:00 P.M. My pilot buddies were waiting for my arrival to begin the party. They were expecting to see the plane coming in with running lights. The Stearman, of course, had none. They heard the sounds of the craft nearing, but all they could see was a tiny glow of exhaust steadily lining the runway.

Pilots I have talked to say it is difficult to land a Stearman at night. That night, I realized just how true that is. I could not see out to the front of the craft, so I had to rely on peripheral vision to land. Depth perception is good in the main line of sight, but not peripherally. The runway at Pickle Lake was a mile long, giving me plenty of room to float for as long as I needed. I put the plane into a gentle descent, looking out from side to side as I went. Because I could not see the ground, I waited until the wheels touched down before I pushed forward on the stick to hold the plane to the ground. It was one of my smoothest landings ever.

The party went on until the wee hours of the morning. I was having a good time, but I was tired from my long flight and wanted to get some sleep before getting an early start for home. I said good night and told the group I would see them in the morning before takeoff.

"What are you talking about?" one of them asked.

"I may not get much, but I need to get a *little* bit of sleep," I pleaded.

"I don't think you're going to get any if you're planning to leave in the morning," one of the pilots said with a chuckle. "It's already seven o'clock."

I passed on sleep, packed up the gear I had left at Pickle Lake, climbed into the Stearman, and headed to Geraldton.

By 11:00 that morning, I arrived in Geraldton in one of the hairiest landings

I have ever made. I was in a rush to leave Pickle Lake and had shoved all the extra gear into the compartment behind my seat because it was easier to get to than the compartment we had made in the front seat. But what I had not anticipated was that the shift in the load would knock the craft's center of gravity way out of kilter.

As I landed in Geraldton, the main gears were still in the air when the tail wheel touched down. I could not get the mains to touch down so the tail began to slide out. It was all I could do to keep the plane from rolling over on the runway. After the difficult landing, I took the time to reload the plane correctly. It seems that we never have time to do it right, but we always have time to do it over.

Huge float planes were stationed at Geraldton for use as water bombers against area forest fires. I was invited to look at the water bomber and go for a flight. I wanted to decline because time had become a factor, but I was intrigued with the craft and ended up taking the tour, but not the flight, and left Geraldton later than planned.

The next fuel stop was Wawa. Nobody was manning the airport when I arrived, so I had to call someone to make the trip to the airport so I could buy some fuel. The guy wanted to charge me an extra fifty dollars U.S. for the call. I told him I thought that was akin to the Yankee speed traps the police set on interstate highways in the American south. A lively discussion followed. I did not like Wawa. But I did get the fuel and continued south, with hopes of reaching home by the next day.

The sun dropped below the earth on its daily cycle as I crossed over Manitoulin Island, the largest freshwater island in the world. With the satisfactory night landing under my belt, I was well prepared to make another. I followed the GPS. I had the airport's radio frequency memorized, keyed it in, and pressed the microphone button as I circled the airport.

Most small airports are not manned at night. A pilot activates the runway lights by keying the radio to the appropriate frequency, which is connected to a device that brings up the lights. It is simple and effective way to save time and the airport's money. I keyed the code, but nothing happened. I knew I had remembered the correct frequency. I had checked it twice before dark. I continued to circle the airport, keying in the frequency and pressing the button on the mike, but still nothing happened. I was getting concerned about fuel. I shone a flashlight on the fuel gauge, a small tube hanging down from the gas tank on the wings. It read empty. I pulled out a flight registry. The next nearest airport was fifty miles away. I had no desire to go down in Lake Superior trying to reach that airport. I had to land at *this* airport. I put the flashlight between my teeth and the flight stick between my legs, located the Manitoulin Airport on the registry, rechecked the radio frequency, and started clicking the mike again. Nothing. I was beginning to get afraid, so I called on an approach frequency to find anyone in the air.

"I'm getting ready to land. What's the frequency for the airport up here?" I asked, worry in my voice.

A voice responded, "122.8."

"Damn! That's what I'm using! Runway lights refuse to come up. Maybe something's wrong."

"Well, you can come over here to Elliot Lake."

"No can do. I'm out of gas," I said, trying to remain calm.

"I don't know what to tell you, then. Try Ottawa radio," the man replied.

I tried to reach Ottawa, but my radio signal did not make it that far. I kept clicking the mike in hopes the lights of the airport beneath me would spring to life. The moon was high and the sky was cloudless, so I descended as close as I could get to the runway. I noticed a windsock, as well as a bunch of airplanes on the ground. I circled again, buzzed the windsock, and saw what appeared to be a runway. I was still clicking the mike. I was sure that the engine would begin to sputter and shut down any minute.

There were few choices. I could ditch the plane in the lake, come down in the woods, or try to land on the runway. I decided to take my chances with the runway. It may have been closed for construction, but I figured it would be better to crash on a runway than into trees or a lake. With the light of the moon, I could roughly make out the runway. Lining up the plane with the dark silhouette, I cut the power and brought the Stearman down slowly. The blood was pumping furiously through my body as the plane settled toward the strip. At any moment, I thought, I would hit a ditch, truck, car, or fence. When I dropped below the trees, my pulse accelerated. Suddenly, the tires squeaked as they hit the runway. I worried about running into the planes that I had noticed collected on the field on my previous pass. I thrust the stick forward to keep the tail up as I looked down the runway. I did not see any obstacles. Then, I lowered the tail until the tail wheel touched. I slammed on the brakes as hard as possible without flipping the plane and came to a stop.

I turned three or four 360s on the runway to check the surrounding area before deciding I could safely taxi in. I located an empty spot to park the Stearman, got out of the plane, and quickly tied it down. I wondered whether I would be in trouble for landing at a closed airport. Or perhaps I had the wrong airport—I could not understand why the runway lights had not come on.

I found a pay phone at the airport and with a little help from the operator located a grungy cheap motel on the island. The next morning, when I returned to the plane to check the tanks, I felt a cold chill of fear. The front seat tank was dry. I climbed up to the wing—nothing in the main tank either. I had been minutes away from running out of fuel. I remembered the scolding that I had given Doug in Pennsylvania for allowing the very same thing to happen. After checking the plane, I found the airport manager and told him what had happened.

"Did you dial in the right frequency?" he asked, perplexed.

"The one every resource gave me."

He slowly read off the frequency.

"That's what I used! I circled for twenty minutes trying that damn frequency!"

"That's impossible," he returned.

"It sure as hell wasn't impossible!" I retorted.

We went back to his office, where in a few minutes we had unraveled the mystery of the missing frequency. He had forgotten to activate the light system before leaving for home for the night.

I called Mary from Buffalo, New York, where I stopped to clear customs, to tell her I would be home in four hours. She told me that my friends wanted me to hold off for another day so they could arrange a homecoming party at Montgomery Airpark on Saturday. I told her that I did not want to wait another minute to get home, so we arranged for me to fly to Frederick, where she would meet me and take me home.

During the last leg of the flight, I went over all that I had experienced in the six weeks that I had been away. I was concerned about the upcoming trip to the geographic pole. Some of the technical problems seemed insurmountable. How could I keep the engine warm in temperatures much colder than I had already faced? How could I land and take off on the Arctic ice pack? How could I get more range out of the Stearman? How would I survive the colder temperatures? While I had never been dangerously cold during the test flight I had not always been comfortable. I had learned to shiver when I felt cold. That always seemed to help. But I would have to face temperatures at least 30 degrees colder than I had experienced. I would have to figure out how to carry a minimum of thirty additional gallons of fuel. How would it perform? One thing I have learned from years of engineering experience is that you must take problems one at a time, instead of trying to solve them in a clump. I made a mental list of what needed to be done and how to do it. By the time I landed in Frederick, I believed I had worked out most of them.

I had not realized the toll the trip had taken on my family until I saw Lara. She had read about my ordeal over Hudson Bay. But no one had taken the time to talk to her about it, so she was under the impression that I had been going through that kind of ordeal every day of the trip and that it was just a matter of time before I would be killed. She spent the whole time I was away thinking she would never see me again. When she saw me in Frederick she broke from her mother and ran to me as though I had returned from the dead. I had never seen her respond that way before. She ran for me, rushed into my arms, and started crying.

"Daddy, I thought you weren't coming back. They said you would get hurt, they said you would die. Please don't go again."

I have always prided myself on never having public displays of emotions. Mary calls me a cold fish when I am in public. But, Lara's speech broke my heart in two, and I looked away to hide my tears. She had paid far too much for the trip. After reassuring her that I was fine and that the stories she heard were overstated, I gave her the same speech I had given Mary twenty-five years earlier.

"Flying is my thing, an airplane is never going to kill me."

Mary reached me a few seconds after Lara. She too was crying. My trip had taken its toll on her as well. I assured her that everything was fine, and hugged her, giving in to a rare display of affection. I put on my best smile, choking back my own emotions.

"I've got this thing licked, next time will be a piece of cake."

The conversation with Lara and the overall effect of the trip on Mary and the children confirmed for me the necessity of keeping the dangers of future trips to myself.

Bruce and Valerie drove up a few minutes later. We all decided to go over to the airport restaurant to talk about the big homecoming party planned for the next day.

As soon as we sat down, Bruce declared that neither he nor Valerie wanted anything to do with a geographic North Pole trip. The problems I had over Hudson Bay had convinced them that the venture was too dangerous.

"You could be killed," he said. "Besides, you have a record now. Isn't that good enough?"

When he said that, I knew he had no understanding of what I was trying to do or why—not that I should have expected him to understand. I had not shared with him that I was driven to reach the pole by a more complicated and vastly more important reason than a notation in a record book. It was not the pole, but myself, that I needed to reach.

And then Bruce added, "And, furthermore, I don't think your family would like you to try that again."

When he said that I took a deep breath. He had gone too far. I knew that if it had been Mary's choice I would not be returning to the Arctic. But I also knew that Mary would never side with someone else against me. Keep going, Bruce, I thought, you are doing a great job of convincing Mary that I should go for the pole.

Mary spoke before I had a chance to.

"Bruce, I never told you I didn't want him to try again. If my husband says he can make it, he can make it. And I support whatever he wants to do."

I cut in before Mary really got her Irish up.

"The most dangerous part of the trip is over. I have all the information I need to make it to the pole. I can understand if you don't want to be a part of it. It is dangerous, and anyone who follows me in the chase plane will have to take care of himself. It won't be easy. But I'm going back, with or without you."

Bruce and Valerie continued to try to talk me out of the return trip. The more they tried the more they helped me. I could not help but smile. By attempting to set my wife against me, they had driven her into my corner. They said they would no longer give financial help and that we would have to sell the chase plane. This did not bother me too much. They had already paid for half of the test flight; I could fund the rest on my own. And, thus far, the chase plane was a dead issue since I had not found anyone who would fly it to the Arctic. Anyway, after what I had been through I did not want to be responsible for two antique aircraft in the Arctic at once.

"You've made the magnetic North Pole in an open-cockpit plane," Bruce said. "Nobody's ever done that before. You don't have to go back for the geographic North Pole."

But I did have to go back. The quest and the test had to be completed. If I didn't go, I wouldn't have been able to live with myself.

6. Finding My Way Back

▼

It proved to be no easy task finding the ways and means for the return trip to the pole. Bruce and I had shared expenses for the first trip, which cost us about $10,000 each, not including the modifications I had made to the Stearman. Now that Bruce was out of the picture I would have to handle all the expenses—far exceeding those of the magnetic pole trip—on my own. To bolster the bottom line, I had sold my Beech Baron, but that money was soon spent. High-end credit cards and second mortgages would to be pressed to carry most of the burden, including the hefty cost for a chase plane to carry extra fuel for the Stearman on the last leg to the ice cap.

I also had some family fence-mending to do. The episode over Hudson Bay had really frightened my children. While the vehemence of Bruce's withdrawal from the expedition had rallied Mary to my cause, I still had some explaining to do.

"Do you really think you can make the North Pole in that thing?" she asked.

"Piece of cake," I responded, adding that I now knew what I needed to know to keep the old bird together.

I admitted to her that in hindsight the first trip would have been easier in the Beech 18, but explained how that same hindsight convinced me that I was lucky to have taken the trip in the Stearman.

"Now," I told her, "I know what to expect. I've got the key to making this work."

"I'll stand by you no matter what," she said. "But remember, if you don't come back, we are the ones who will have to live without you. We are the ones who sacrifice for you."

There was no masking the seriousness in her voice. I was deeply struck by their loyalty. I was about to launch into a defense of my flying skills and survival instincts, and the importance of the trip to me, but instead I put my arms around her and said, "Honey, airplanes are my thing, an airplane is never going to kill me."

We smiled knowingly and remembered when we were young, naive, and ready to take on the world. With that Mary was on board. She would keep the family together—she would calm their fears, deal with the sleepless nights, and handle the problems of the business while I was away. All I had to do was come back alive. My part seemed easier than hers did.

Hera, my oldest daughter, had grown cold toward me since my return. I did not understand why and asked Mary to find out. This is my typical way of handling our children's emotional problems—"Talk to your mother about it." Mary explained that Hera thought the trip was too risky and that I was being selfish.

"She doesn't think you take us into consideration when you do things like this," Mary reported.

Mocking me, Hera asked me how I would feel if she went camping in an alligator swamp and used raw meat for a pillow. Then answered her own question by saying that the probability of a gator attack was low, but if she were attacked she could take care of herself because, "Gators are her thing, no alligator is ever going to eat her." I had to laugh at that one. Hera was not going to give me an inch. Like her mother, she always spoke her mind, and like me she was stubborn. I told Mary that I would talk to her, but Mary and Hera knew I did not like to deal with emotional issues. We would talk, eventually. But it would be Hera who would see to it.

My son was not going to talk about it at all. Although I knew Gustavus did not approve of the expedition, I also knew he would not talk to me about his feelings. His ploy was to act as though the trip was just another one of my adventures. From time to time he would casually ask me how things were going, but I could tell from his voice that he was concerned. Mary would have to allay their fears. I was going to the pole.

I lost no time in making a list of technical difficulties that needed to be addressed.

1. How to keep engine warm: The outside temperature would be colder than I had experienced. The engine was designed to operate at no colder than 20 degrees Fahrenheit and had barely functioned at 12. I had to plan for −48 degrees Fahrenheit at the pole.

2. How to navigate: I was near the magnetic pole when my GPS had stopped working, forcing me to rely on directions and landmarks to visually follow the landmass to the magnetic pole. How would I navigate visually on the Arctic Ocean where there is nothing but ice for as far as the eye can see? A compass would prove useless: the nearer the magnetic pole, the greater the error for all compasses and, particularly, the Stearman's compass, which is generally unreliable most of the time anyway (it was unreliable even before I got to Churchill). I would have to find a GPS that could take the cold.

3. How to make the propeller perform more efficiently: It took the old wood propeller 3,500 feet to get the plane into the air. I would not have that much space on the ice. Since the Stearman could not make the final leg of the trip without a fuel stop, I would have to land on the ice to refuel. Arctic pilots had told me that 800 feet was the best I could expect for an ice landing. The Stearman would have to perform far better than it had on the test flight, and it would have do it carrying more weight. A bigger engine was not the solution because it would burn more fuel and would not give me any more speed. The answer was in the propeller. I had to get a more efficient propeller.

4. How to get another forty gallons of gas into the plane: I had carried fifty gallons of extra fuel in the front seat area. For the longest leg of the flight, I would need to carry twice that amount. If a scheduled stop were iced- or fogged-in when I arrived, I would have to return to the last stop. There are few alternative stops in the Arctic. Because ice cap landings would be the

most hazardous of the mission, I would want to keep them to a minimum. If I could carry an additional forty gallons of fuel it might be possible to fly to Russian Siberia and skip the ice pack landing altogether, if necessary. In any event I would need to carry more gas.

5. How to afford a chase plane: I had no way of ferrying fuel out to the ice by myself. After experiencing Arctic conditions, I knew the Beech 18 was not the support plane I needed. I needed a ski-equipped, modern aircraft with a pilot who had lots of time landing on the ice. I would also need a good chase plane if I needed to be rescued. First Air, a Canadian airline charter, flew to the North Pole every year carrying tourists. They would be perfect for the job, but their fee was $40,000. It might as well have been $40 million. The chase plane loomed as my biggest hurdle, but I knew I would go without one if I had to. I also knew I would have to keep that fact to myself.

6. How to document the trip: Robert E. Peary and Richard E. Byrd documented their attempts with sketches. There is still controversy over whether Peary or Byrd actually made it. Roald Amundsen solved the documentation problem by flying from one side of the Arctic Ocean to the other, passing over the pole as the shortest route. Without a chase plane I would be forced to fly to Siberia via the pole, as Amundsen had. But I would need witnesses; the chase plane was the solution.

7. How to keep myself warm: On the previous trip I had relied for warmth on the canopy Bruce and I had installed. I had removed it only for the air show in Churchill, the test flights in Rankin Inlet, and the last leg to the magnetic pole. The geographic pole trip would be made in an open cockpit, no canopy from start to finish. In 0 degrees Fahrenheit without the canopy, I had felt the cold down to my bones. I would need a more cold-resistant flight suit and would have to gain more weight. I went on the test flight at 280 pounds; I would go to the Pole at 320 pounds—no longer Dancing Walrus but Flying Whale. What would an additional forty pounds do to my health? Mary said I had started to snore at night with the extra weight I had already put on. Health concerns and vanity aside, I enjoyed gaining the

weight. To keep the weight on I did little exercise, ate like a pig, read a lot, and worked on the Stearman.

8. How to check the plane for mechanical problems: This, I thought, would be the easiest of my tasks. I enjoyed being at the hangar working on the plane. Now I would have an excuse to do it every day. Life was good.

9. How to pay the bills: Two things were certain. First, more money meant a safer and easier expedition; and second, I would never have enough for everything on my wish list. I resolved to put in as much as I could afford and what I could not afford I would trust to luck, pluck, and skill—another detail I felt it wiser to keep to myself. So I started thinking about how to make do with what I could afford. Like everything I do, I figured that if I just got started solutions would present themselves as I went along.

Rick Galvin, a pilot at Montgomery Airpark, asked me to go with him to an aviation vendors' convention at which he had a booth. I jumped at it because I thought it would be an excellent opportunity for me to talk with people in the field and round up some needed gear for the trip. I was right. Bendix-King offered me a GPS that was guaranteed to work at temperatures to −70 degrees Fahrenheit. A company named ICOM agreed to give me a high frequency radio, along with a handheld radio. Iczos Instruments, an Iridium satellite phone dealer, offered a satellite phone for the trip. Telford Aviation in Bangor, Maine, promised to put in FAA-certified ferry tanks, adding one hundred extra gallons to the fuel-carrying capacity of the Stearman.

Robbie Vajdos, an aircraft restorer I know in Texas, asked his crop-dusting friends what modifications could be made to increase the amount of weight the Stearman could carry. It would need enough power to lift me at full weight and one hundred gallons of extra fuel. They all advised using a metal prop and suggested a McCauley "ground adjustable." Props come with various pitch angles to the blades. A prop with a shallow pitch offers greater acceleration but a slower cruise speed. A greater angle on the blade slows acceleration but quickens the cruise speed. The best configuration is a variable pitch prop that can be adjusted from the cockpit for a shallow angle on takeoff and readjusted in the air for a greater angle in cruise. I could not afford a variable pitch prop, so I set out to find a ground adjustable prop—the pitch is adjusted by loosening the bolts that hold the blade in place and setting the desired angle before takeoff. All agreed that the McCauley was the best prop ever made for a Stearman with a 220 horsepower engine. The only downside to the McCauley was that it had to be removed, X-rayed, and completely rebuilt after every one hundred hours of use.

No problem, I thought. One hundred hours of flight-time would be more than I would need to reach the pole and return home.

I had been back for only two months, and already the new trip was coming together.

It took another three months for me to locate a prop I could afford. I contacted everyone I knew who flew or had an interest in Stearmans. Finally I found a guy, Doug Work, in Tulsa, Oklahoma, who had a McCauley prop in his garage. When I told him what I planned to do with it he let me have it for $2,200, about half its value. I had the prop shipped off to be X-rayed and rebuilt, which added another $500.

Don Sanders and I discussed the problem of the engine temperature and decided to protect the engine with a cowling. The engine is uncovered in the original Boeing design, and as a result not many cowlings were made for the Stearman. I insisted that the cowling was essential to the trip, giving us both an added incentive to find one.

Northern Outfitters, the company that had made my cold-weather suit for the first trip, said they would make improvements based on my feedback. I found the company through a research project the Canadian government conducted on cold-weather gear. The Canadians had tested every piece of gear in the world and found the gear made by this small American company to be the best. When worn properly, the suit was guaranteed to −65 degrees Fahrenheit. I told Northern Outfitters that the boots and suit I used on the test trip were much too bulky and the suit's buckles needed to be improved. The company agreed and offered to provide a new suit and boots free of charge.

Problems were being solved one at a time. But as irony would have it, the one

problem—checking the Stearman for mechanical problems—that I had anticipated would be the simplest (and most pleasurable) to solve, turned out to be
the most troublesome. And in the end, was solved in a painful and unusual way.

I decided to visit Baughers Orchard, the tiny grass field airport I flew into with
Bruce soon after our initial conversation about the Arctic trip. A return flight to
Baughers Orchard would be good practice, I thought, for landing on 800 feet
of ice. As I had on the earlier flight, I brought down the plane and got it on the
strip. This time though, in an eagerness to show off, I taxied in too fast and hit
the brakes too hard, flipping the Stearman bottom side up.

The fall from the backseat of an overturned Stearman is a fifteen-foot drop.
The year before, at the Sun and Fun Air Show in Florida, a pilot flipped a Second World War fighter on landing and smothered to death before he could be
retrieved from the plane. So this is what it is like to break your neck, I thought,
as the plane went over. With my head resting two inches above the ground and
my entire body in pain, I could see Dwight Baughers, who was standing about
forty feet from the plane, and heard him shouting, "Are you okay?"

"Yeah, but I need some help with the seat belt," I moaned.

"Is it going to catch on fire?" Dwight said, spotting the gas that was leaking
slowly from the tank.

"That's probably a good reason to get me out!" I cried.

I noticed Dwight's arm about to hit the latch for the seat belt. "No!" I yelled,
right before he released the latch and I fell, head first, onto the ground. Two
inches does not seem like much of a fall, but it hurt like hell. I was wearing a
helmet—only the second time I had ever worn one—given to me by Greg
Thalamus. Greg owns a motorcycle paint shop. He had given me the helmet as
a gift to take to the North Pole.

I must have been a sorry sight. I did not know it at the time, but I had a gash
on my nose that was bleeding, making me look far worse than I was. I lay there,
relieved to be resting on my back. I told Dwight I was in pain.

"Can we move you away from the plane?" Dwight's father asked.

"That's probably a good idea. Grab my arms and pull me out."

"I don't know," Dwight said. "I don't think we should move you until the ambulance gets here."

"No, no, don't call an ambulance," I shouted. "Just get me from under the plane."

They pulled me clear of the plane, and, as I lay there, I heard an ambulance approaching. I pulled myself up and grabbed my helmet, enduring the pain— I did not want a doctor to mess with me—as two paramedics carrying a stretcher rushed toward me.

"We have to take you to the hospital," one of them said.

"That's okay. I'm fine," I answered them, not wanting to be bothered.

"But we have to," the other asserted. The tone of his voice bothered me.

"You and what army are going to take me?"

One of the attendants went to the ambulance, returned with a form, and handed it to me. "You have to sign this release form, then."

"Look, I didn't ask you all to come out here," I said angrily. "I'm not going to sign it."

They did not back down, and I did not want to make things worse for the Baugherses. I had already put them out enough, so I signed the form and handed it over.

A few minutes later, a police car pulled up. The policeman asked to see my driver's license. I laughed as I told him that I did not need a driver's license to fly an airplane.

Unfazed, the cop said, "Some form of identification, then."

"Look," I snapped back, "I'm not asking for your help. This is private property and the airplane is mine. Leave me the hell alone!"

Since I did not have any identification, the police asked to see the paperwork for the plane, which I did not have. The Stearman does not have a floor, just panels for the pilot's feet, so I always fly with empty pockets. Pilots have a saying that when something drops into the depths of the plane, it falls into the wishing well, because anything that falls becomes something you *wish* you could retrieve.

"If you don't show me some form of ID, I will put you under arrest," the officer threatened.

"If you want it, you go under that plane and get it."

Once he noticed that the Stearman was leaking fuel, he changed the subject.

While I was talking to the policeman, the Baugherses brought in a crane to right the plane. The cop stopped them, asserting that I would have to get permission before I could move the plane because it was now government property. Any airplane that crashes, I learned later, belongs to the National Transportation Safety Board (NTSB) until released. The NTSB, which investigates all types of transportation mishaps, takes possession of all crashed aircraft so that an accident investigation can be done without interference from the owner. I immediately called the NTSB, told them what had happened, and they gave me permission to right the plane and tie it down until they could investigate.

As we finished repositioning the plane, I remembered that I was supposed to pick up Lara from her gymnastics class. Mary had gone hiking with her sisters. I called my office and asked one of my employees to pick up Lara and stay with her until Mary came to get her. The employee asked me what was wrong, and I told her I had had an incident with the airplane and could not get back for an hour or more. When she picked up Lara, she told her that I had crashed the airplane and that she would have to wait here for Mary.

Dwight gave me a ride back to my hangar at Montgomery Airpark. I sat there for an hour, depressed. I wanted this catastrophe to be over with. I was angry that the NTSB had impounded my aircraft. I felt put upon by the government, and more than anything else, I was afraid they were not going to return the airplane and that plans for the pole trip would have to be abandoned. As I look back on it now, especially through the shock of September 11, I know that the NTSB's response was reasonable and prudent.

Mary finally showed up with Lara in tow. No one had told Lara that I was safe. When she saw me, she started crying and hugged me, which hurt my ribs. But I put up with the pain, proper punishment for the distress I had caused her. It turned out that I had two broken ribs, and for weeks after, whenever I sneezed or tried to sit in an upright position, my ribs hurt like hell.

Overnight I fretted that the accident would ruin the trip. But the next day, when the NTSB released the aircraft, I realized the ordeal had been fortuitous. Since the plane was in no shape to fly, it had to be completely disassembled. Dwight put the fuselage on a trailer and hauled it back to Montgomery Airpark, where I planned to strip and repaint it. While Dwight handled the fuselage, I put the wings and the engine in a U-Haul and drove nonstop to Oklahoma City, where I handed over the engine to Don Sanders, and then drove to Texas to drop off the wings with Robbie Vajdos, who restores classic airplanes for a living. I met Robbie through a mutual crop-dusting friend about eight years ago, and not long after he helped me with a problem aircraft I had purchased. We have been friends ever since. Once the wings reached their destination, I turned in the U-Haul and caught a flight back home.

That trip solved two problems: professionals would rebuild the plane and in the process assess the toll the Arctic test trip had taken. Don soon discovered that the front of the pistons were more worn than the back, which he attributed to the cold and the front-engine exposure. A cover for the front of the engine would be essential.

I spent September 1999 through January 2000 repairing the fuselage. I had a lot of fun redoing the old girl. When you own a Stearman people often show up angling for a ride. But when you are rebuilding one, hardly anyone shows up. During that fall and early winter, there was no hangar flying, no one stopping to ask questions. There was just me and the airplane and lots of time to think about the next trip north.

The fuselage of the Stearman is nothing more than metal grids covered by polyester fabric. The more I stripped down the fabric, the worse the wear from the Arctic trip showed. I ended up redoing all the fabric on the plane. I did a decent job on the top and sides of the aircraft, but by the time I got to the bottom I was running out of both patience and seam tape. Seam tape is made of the same material as the fabric. It is about two inches wide and lies on top of the fabric along the ribs of the aircraft. After the fabric is taped, the entire surface is covered with a dope compound and painted. When I reached the bottom of the aircraft I ran out of seam tape. I was on a roll and did not want to take the time to order some more, so I improvised by cutting some seam tape from the fabric I had left. It looked like hell—crooked instead of straight—but I figured that no one would ever look under the aircraft to see this workmanship, so I used the crooked tape. All it has to be is functional, I reasoned. That is true. But I wish that I had done a better job on that tape, because the Stearman now hangs in the College Park Aviation Museum and the bottom is the part that everyone sees.

To repaint the fuselage, I decided I needed a space away from the other planes in the hangar. Devon Berkeley, the owner of Rockville Harley Davidson in Rockville, Maryland, let me use one of his warehouses for the job. To transport the plane to the warehouse, I put the back end of the fuselage (tail-wheel first) in the trunk of the car and pulled the plane on its front wheels. I made the move at midnight to avoid the police. A friend of mine drove behind me with his car blinkers on so that no one would run into the fuselage. Once the fuselage was safe in the warehouse, Jerry Lewis, an aircraft upholsterer, and I spent the entire Christmas holidays painting it.

When it was time to put the Stearman back together, I called everyone who had been working on the different parts of the plane and arranged to meet them at the end of February 2000 at Robbie's place in Texas. I chose to reassemble the aircraft at Robbie's because he is the best Stearman restorer I know. He can rig a Stearman to fly hands-off and dead level. If a Stearman is not rigged properly, it is a fight with the controls to keep it flying straight. But if it is rigged perfectly, it can be flown in cruise no-handed, and the plane will stay straight and level. The rigging of a Stearman is a dying art, and Robbie is one of the few who has mastered it.

That January, Jay Rosenburg, a good friend, put me in touch with Lori Butterfield, a producer for National Geographic Television. Lori expressed some interest in filming the flight for the National Geographic series "Explorer." Later that month, after clearing it through their approval cycle, she called to tell me that she and her crew would accompany me to the pole. I was very excited—for years I had watched National Geographic documentaries, now I would be one. It felt kind of weird always being introduced around National Geographic as the crazy guy who is going to try to get to the pole in an open-cockpit airplane. But I got used to it. They were not the only ones calling me crazy. As part of the documentary Lori wanted to film me reassembling the Stearman, which I told her would take place in Texas late in February.

I ran into trouble trying to come up with a way to get the fuselage to Texas. The Stearman's landing gear is seven and one half feet wide. I could not find a rental truck with a door wide enough to handle it. Paul and Robert Thommesen, my auto mechanics, helped me with the solution. Paul is an automotive genius. The guy can hear a car engine at thirty feet and tell you what is wrong with it. Whatever strange mechanical solution I come up with, I always pass by Paul to see if he thinks it might work. In this case we took a U-Haul car carrier, pulled out the ramp meant for getting a car on to the trailer, and bolted it into place. Next we made a cradle of six two-by-fours to hold the plane's tires and put the tail of the aircraft on the tongue of the car carrier. Then we threw the rest of the parts inside a U-Haul truck and hitched the car carrier to the truck. It worked like a dream.

The trip to Texas seemed a good time to test my stamina for the pole trip, so I drove nonstop from Gaithersburg to Louise, Texas, pulling the Stearman all the way. I was on route when I received word from Northern Outfitters that the improvements they envisioned for the cold-weather suit would keep me warm to −65 degrees Fahrenheit. They also came up with a way to restyle the boots so that they would better fit the craft's foot pedals. Once I reached Texas, Robbie and I took two days to assemble the plane. Don arrived with the engine and the good news that his friend, Randy Smith, had just bought a Stearman and was willing to lend me the cowling for the trip. It was a break to have found a cowling designed for a Stearman, because it meant that I would not have to worry about it fitting the engine. The day we finished the assembly, Lori Butterfield and Dwayne Impie, a National Geographic cameraman, showed up at Robbie's to get some footage of my test flight and of some of Robbie's other Stearman projects. Things were going well. I still needed a chase plane, a pilot to fly it, and money for the trip, but little by little my problems were being solved.

National Geographic had agreed to film the expedition from the chase plane, but they could not be persuaded to pay for the chase plane. I still did not have enough money to rent First Air's ski-equipped aircraft, so I told Lori that I would arrange to fly her and her crew as far as Resolute, just over 900 miles from the pole. I was fairly sure I could get someone to ferry her and the crew that far as a favor to me. From Resolute, they would have to catch a commercial flight to Spitsbergen, Norway, where I would meet them as I came off the Arctic Ocean. I showed Lori on a map that the only way to fly from Eureka in Northern Canada to Spitsbergen, was over the pole—proof enough that I had accomplished what I set out to do. She was not keen on the idea. Then I told her that if First Air flew the chase plane I would not have to fly to Spitsbergen, but could return via the route I had taken to the pole. Whereupon she said that she would try to arrange for some funding from the National Geographic Society to help with the cost of booking First Air for the chase plane.

The reassembled Stearman looked terrific and flew like a dream. Don had rebuilt the engine to perfection. Instead of reinstalling the front seat, Robbie made a metal cover to fit over the seat well. His work was so seamless that it was difficult to tell if the plane ever had a front seat. The cover had the added benefit of holding back the wind—always a factor in a Stearman. The new prop also performed well. When I took it out for a test it flew well enough—twenty miles an hour faster than with the wooden prop—but not as well as I had hoped. I then realized the prop had been set for maximum cruise performance. The man who worked on the prop thought that flight-speed on an 8,500-mile round trip was more important than increased takeoff performance. Normally I would have agreed. But for this trip, I was more concerned about takeoff performance since the ice cap would give me so few feet to get airborne. Robbie readjusted the prop and I soon was getting off the ground in less than 1,000 feet and cruising ten miles an hour faster than with the wooden prop. For a final touch, I had the registration numbers changed from N29743 to N8NP. NP was for North Pole. Eight was the lowest number the FAA had with NP at the end.

The only instrument that was installed at the time was the airspeed indicator, so for practice I decided to fly the plane back home using nothing but a map. Thirty minutes after I left Robbie's place following a road to Galveston, Texas, I plunged into a hell of a storm. For ten miles the shiny, newly painted Stearman was racked up, down, and around. The windshield in a Stearman is not, strictly speaking, a windshield—the shield gives little protection from the wind—but it is a great rain shield. While I was completely dry by the time I landed in Galveston, the rain had blasted some of the paint off the prop and the engine. What a sight! At least it looked good for an hour.

My next stop was Jennings, Louisiana. Jennings is a base for a bunch of crop dusters. I spent a fair amount of time swapping stories with them and won the hangar flying contest when they heard about what I planned to do. From Jennings, I flew to Jackson, Mississippi. The flight to Jackson was tough going, traversing the bayou without a compass or roads to follow. It is no small task to look at a chart while flying the Stearman. With the wind coming in from every direction, I would have to hold the chart with both hands and fly with the stick between my legs. Rather than deal with the charts, my tactic was to line up the course right after takeoff and hold the heading without turning. This turned out to be a good strategy, because it gave me practice at holding the Stearman directly on a course for long periods. On the pole trip, I would have to memorize the charts in advance of a day's trip since I would be wearing heavy mittens in flight, making it impossible to hold the charts.

It was around noon when I landed in Jackson. I borrowed the airport courtesy car and drove to a nearby cemetery where my parents and grandparents are buried. With the pole trip and all its dangers ahead of me it was a fitting time to visit their graves. My Choctaw grandmother, Annie Easterling Gray, had died in 1974 and my grandfather, Areather McLeod, in 1988. My father, John McLeod, died in 1993, the year I bought the Stearman, and my mother, Jonell Gray McLeod, died four years later. I am the next generation of this family to face eternity. Those four people had such a great impact on my life that it seemed strange none of them would share in the fruits of this labor or even know what I was setting out to do. The truth is, I sometimes questioned why I was so determined to take on this challenge. Deep within me, I knew the assault on the pole was not an end in itself, but the means by which I would gain something far more important than a notch in the record books or a half an hour on TV. I was in search of self-knowledge—a harrowing but necessary journey. I wondered why it had taken me so long to take this journey and regretted that I had not done it sooner, for the sake of my grandparents and parents. I wanted their approval. But as I looked down at their graves, I understood that when they were living I did not feel the need for self-discovery because I saw myself so clearly in them. When I lost them I lost myself.

My grandfather McLeod always told me I had the bloodline of the McLeod's, eight hundred years of Scottish heritage. To him that meant that I was something special and I believed him when he told me that. I am also part African. But it has long appeared to me that most Americans are unable (and unwilling) to see through the color of my skin to my Scottish heritage. Part of me must not have been able to see through it either because I did not travel to Scotland until after my grandfather's death. When I went in 1989, I was surprised by how well the McLeods treated me.

My Native American grandmother is the source from which I trace the mysterious streams to my interior self. My secretiveness, my guardedness, my spirituality, my outward suppression of emotions, they are all aspects of my personality that flow from her. My parents were in college when I was born. My grandmother took care of me until I was six. She had left the Mississippi Choctaw reservation when she was eighteen. Her family had nearly starved to death, and her father and half of her siblings had died in a flu epidemic. She did not marry a Choctaw or raise her children in the Choctaw ways, because there was a law in Mississippi that all Indians caught off the reservation would be shipped back to reservations in Mississippi or Oklahoma. She learned to keep her heritage and beliefs to herself. I was her last chance to pass them on.

My father represented that confusion and duality of ethnicity that marks the Black American experience for many. At home he was just like his father, proud to be a Scot. Outside of home, he was the soul of the black preacher or whatever the popular culture dictated he should be. He flew with me for the first time five years before his death. On one of his visits to Washington, we went pheasant hunting on Maryland's Eastern Shore. He loved hunting, bird hunting in particular. But he hated flying. I told him I was going to fly over just for the day, but he could take my car over and stay the night.

To my surprise, he said, "That's okay, I'll ride over with you."

It was the worst possible day for flying. It was bumpy, rainy, and cold. We landed in a grass field next to the farm where we were hunting. He expected us to land at an airport. When I started the approach for a landing in the field he asked if we were going to crash. I had forgotten to tell him that we were landing at the farm. He was quiet during the fairly smooth landing, but once we were safely on the ground his eyes lit up with excitement.

"I've never seen anything like that," he said, with a thrill in his voice. "You put this thing down in a pasture without a hitch. Boy, that's something! You really do know how to fly."

I think that was the closest moment we ever had.

I blushed red with the kind of pride that only your parent can make you feel and said, "Flying is my thing."

After that he flew with me whenever he could.

A week before he died—we all knew he was dying—he told me that he understood the differences we had on religion.

"No matter how much I pushed and prodded, you stood your ground," he said.

To my surprise, I detected admiration in his voice. Then he started crying. I was unprepared and responded in the most miserable possible way—I turned away from him and left the room. I regret having done that. I returned when he composed himself, and we made our peace. I never embraced his religion, but I have his passion and aggressiveness. And his face—I look like him. I hope he found what he preached. Despite our differences, I looked up to him.

My mother flew with me from the start.

She would always say, "I would rather fly with him than anybody else."

She loved to take the controls, and now and again I would oblige her. I am certain that if we got lost when we were flying she would say, "You're not lost, the world just got screwed up."

That is a mother talking about her son.

My mother was away at boarding schools most of her childhood. Her parents had not wanted their children scarred by the Mississippi school system. As a result she had always striven to get along with others, no matter what it took. I often told her she played to the cheap seats.

She would say, "You can't change people, you have to deal with them the way they are." In this, she was 180 degrees from my father, who believed everyone could change and he was the one who could change them. I am midway between them on that issue.

My mother loved tinkering with stuff. She always hid her toolbox from my father, because he believed it was not ladylike to be mechanical. My father's mechanical ability stopped at sharpening a pencil. If anything was broken in our house, either my mother or I fixed it. My younger sister, Jovonsia, loved to hunt and was a much better shot than my father. But because she was a girl, he would not hunt with her. When my father was around, my mother was the preacher's wife. When he was not, she was a fix-it person who loved telling stories. Mary once asked me why I talk about my mother only in relation to my father.

Mary was right, I always do. And it is because my mother's personality was so tied to my father's that one would have to know him to understand her. She was point to his counterpoint. I did not like that about her, but if I was going to deal with my mother I had to understand that. She never talked about religion. When anyone else did she would smile and say nothing. I did not know where she stood on the issue until she made a deathbed confession, but that is too personal and painful to talk about. I am a lot like my mother too.

The trip from Jackson to Birmingham, Alabama, gave me another difficulty. All the roads looked alike, making it extremely difficult to find the roads listed on the map. I called aircraft control to ask which way Route 20 pointed, relative to my direction. I heard laughter through the radio.

"It's about 40 degrees to your right."

I thanked him and headed for the highway.

I like the solitude of flying without the radio. I only talk on it when necessary. When you fly VFR you are not required to talk to anyone unless you enter controlled airspace, that is, the airspace around major airports and cities. If a pilot has to go through controlled airspace, all the needed frequencies are on the charts. Prior to September 11, 2001, a pilot entering controlled airspace without approval would be given a warning, a fine, or a suspension. After September 11, they might be shot down. I called Birmingham approach.

"Birmingham, this is Stearman N8NP. I'm coming in on Route 20."

"Stearman N8NP, follow Route 20 to abeam the airport and come on in."

Ah, how sweet it is to fly in a free country with great people to help you out. Flying does not get much better than this.

After I landed I called Mary to tell her I was down for the night. In one of those rare moments when I let down my emotional guard, I told her about the visit to the graves in Jackson. I told her how lucky I was to have her beside me while I was off in search of my holy grail.

She laughed. "Now you're a crusader. Your father always said you would get religion."

The route from Birmingham to Richmond, Virginia, was the toughest of the trip. I had to cross through Atlanta airspace and that of other major airport areas. All major airports control the airspace around them. Without the proper equipment a plane cannot enter that space—Birmingham had given me a waiver, but Atlanta was unlikely to do so because of the higher volume of traffic—so I spent the entire trip dodging big-city airspace. The plan was to follow Interstate 85 all the way to Richmond. After traveling a few miles over what I thought was the Interstate, I looked down and saw a traffic light on the highway. I turned the plane around, backtracked for five or six miles, found I-85, and carried on. I managed to reach Richmond before dark, rented a car, and drove home for the night. The next day I drove back down to Richmond to pick up the plane.

I was pleased with myself. With nothing more than a roadmap, I had flown the Stearman from Texas to Maryland and all stops in between, the same way pilots from the 1920s and '30s would have.

Most of the plans for the pole trip were falling into place. But I still was short of money and did not have a chase plane. I was able to solve part of the money problem when a banker friend of mine told me to put the expenses on a credit card. The bank would cancel it when I returned from the trip, after which I could pay it off like a loan.

The problem of a chase plane was solved in a most serendipitous manner. On a trip down to Durham, North Carolina, to pick up the engine cowling from Randy Smith, I was introduced to Joe Hunt. Joe asked me if I would speak about the pole trip at the Lakeridge, North Carolina, chapter of the Experimental Aircraft Association (EAA) at the Lakeridge Airport in Durham. The meeting was scheduled for a Saturday morning at 9:30. I showed up a half-hour early. I was waiting outside the building when Steve Pearce, a member of the EAA chapter, walked up and started a conversation. I explained to Steve that I was planning an adventure some might consider silly, even foolhardy. I could tell Steve was interested in my plans.

After the talk, several people gathered around with questions. I mentioned that the National Geographic team wanted a supply plane to make the trip, which meant that I needed another chase plane and pilot. Steve, who owned a Cessna 182, approached me after the talk and asked if I thought a 182 would do the trick.

"Heck, yeah," I answered.

"Then I'd like to go, as far as I can," he told me.

"You only need to go as far as Resolute, because I have chartered an Otter from First Air to accompany me from Resolute to the pole."

"I guess I'm in then," Steve said. And there it was, settled.

It was a bit foolhardy on both our parts to accept such an offer. I did not know anything about Steve as a pilot or as a person. But I liked his spirit and I was desperate. I needed a chase plane to get National Geographic to Resolute. I had thought I would be turning volunteers away for the job, but Steve was the only taker and he was willing to pay for his own way north. That was an offer I could not refuse. I hoped he was pilot enough to handle it.

When I returned home, Lori called me with the news that the National Geographic's expedition council would grant me $30,000 for the trip. Now I only needed to come up with $25,000 more—$15,000 to cover the remaining cost of the First Air chase plane and $10,000 to insure the Stearman for the polar attempt. The money problems were causing many sleepless nights. I was tapped out.

Then Mary came up with the answer. She knew without asking that I would go with or without a chase plane. But she did not want me flying over the Arctic Ocean on my own, and she did not want just anyone in any plane up there with me. She wanted First Air—they were the professionals; they knew the Arctic. Mary had saved $16,000 in hopes of getting enough to pay for the chase plane. She thought that if she gave me the money too early in the process I would spend it on something other than the chase plane. She was right. Even though I knew I needed a chase plane, it was at the bottom of my priority list. Had she given me the money earlier I would have sprung for a bigger engine, one with a variable-pitch prop. The woman is a wonder. I do not know what else to say. She handled the business, took care of the children, and still managed to put aside money for my trip. I almost cried when she told me what she had done. I often kid about how unlucky I am, but with Mary as my wife I am the luckiest guy I know.

With Mary's infusion of cash, only $9,000 stood in my way. When I found out that I could take another loan on the Stearman, the money problem was solved and I was on my way to the Arctic with National Geographic in tow.

Telford Aviation in Maine agreed to install the fuel tanks in the Stearman for no charge—a stroke of good luck, considering I had nothing left to pay them.

Bangor, Maine, about 500 miles from Gaithersburg, seemed to be within a range that would not adversely affect my budget by too much. For this trip I used a handheld GPS and had a compass installed. I did not want to take the chance of busting airspace in the Northeast, where it would have been too easy to wander accidentally into someone's airspace.

On a brisk early March morning, I took off to Maine to have the tanks installed. The temperature at 6:00 A.M. was 38 degrees Fahrenheit, which felt a bit cold to me. I must be losing my edge, I thought. I had been at 0 at the magnetic pole. That March morning I was only wearing a light jacket, but the added room in the cockpit more than made up for the chill.

With a favorable tailwind I cut a path for Bangor. This was the last step in preparation for the polar journey. The usual cool moist air near the Pennsylvania border filled most of the Allegheny Mountain valleys with fog. When the fog lifted, I dropped down to see the people coming out of their houses on their way to school or work. Those who shot up glances to see the source of the loud noise were surprised to see an old yellow and blue biplane overhead.

With the tailwind pushing me onward, the ground speed in the Stearman reached 125 miles per hour, which is really cooking when you consider that the normal speed is ninety-five. With that wind I felt I could have made it all the way to the North Pole. But all I had to do was reach Bangor.

The first stop was Poughkeepsie, New York. When I landed, people were waiting to see the Stearman up close. One of the guys manning the gas pumps called up some of his friends, local volunteer firefighters, to tell them to come get a look at the strange plane that would (I hoped) fly over the North Pole. When they showed up they gave me their business cards and asked me to place them at the North Pole. Their vote of confidence was exhilarating. While most of the pilots I talked to thought I was not only nuts but would never reach the pole, those firemen took it as a foregone conclusion that I would bring the old biplane to the northern ice cap and back. It was the first time anyone talked to me as though I would actually reach my goal.

I called Lori before leaving Poughkeepsie to see how their plans were progressing. The trip to the pole was still more than a month away, but I called her at every stop on the way to Bangor. When the winds picked up—again in my favor—I took leave of the kind firemen and headed north. Not long into the flight, I experienced my first bout of nausea as I passed over the mountains. The harsh wind from the mountaintops tossed the plane about, shaking me around like a sock in a dryer. With the wild jostling, fumes released from the engine began to flood the cockpit. I was not expecting the nausea because I had never been sick in either a plane or a boat. Nonetheless, somewhere around the New Hampshire border I became so intensely ill that I seriously thought I would keel over and die behind the controls. Let me tell you, going 100 miles an hour in an open-cockpit plane is not the place you want to be when sick. When I did vomit, the air stream sent the stuff back into my face, all over my goggles and mask. At that moment, I could almost hear the great Roscoe Turner laughing at me as he had laughed at me on that fateful day at the airport near Corinth.

Everything was spinning and I could not keep my head level. It became difficult to keep the plane straight and on course. But I also thought I might be too sick to land, afraid I would crash on the runway. I had to decide what to do. The closest airport was in Concord, New Hampshire. I could land there and sleep off the illness, or I could keep on trucking and hope that the nausea would lift before I lost control of the plane. I was about to take the latter course when stomach cramps hit without mercy. I headed for Concord.

Somehow, I managed to place the wheels on the pavement with a hard crosswind trying to toss me off the left side. My head was spinning as I taxied in and pulled to a ramp. A signalman gestured me to stop and park the plane where it stood. I shut down the engine and in a dizzy haze stepped slowly from the plane, dropped to my hands and knees on the black tarmac, and puked again. But nothing came out of my mouth. I had emptied my stomach in the airplane. The signalman approached the plane and asked me if I was okay.

I could not answer him because the stomach cramps flared again. I stood up and with his help made my way into the terminal and onto one of the couches where I slept off the nausea as the lineman refueled the Stearman. When I woke up, I noticed two pilots sitting near me, looking at a map. I put my hands to my head slowly. The sickness had faded, if not entirely lifted.

One of the men smiled as I lifted my head.

"That was a great landing you made back there. Hell of a crosswind in here today, too."

The other man joined in, "Yeah, damn good."

I thought they were patronizing me, because it had not been a good landing.

"Do you guys know if there are any mountains between here and Bangor, Maine?" I asked.

"I don't know if I'd call 'em mountains. More like hills," one of the men answered.

"Can I avoid the hills?"

"Sure," the other man chimed in. "All you have to do is fly a little farther east to go around them."

For the first time in my life, I could hear myself making plans to avoid hills and mountains because the ride would be too rough. It almost did not seem like a decision made by me. I would fly up the coast, avoiding the "hills."

Once I was out of the airport and back in the air, I was ashamed of myself for planning to avoid some little hills. My stomach felt much better. So I decided to return to the old flight plan and travel directly to Bangor through the hills.

Ross Merry, the manager of Telford Aviation's Bangor facility and the man who would rig the Stearman with its new and improved fuel tank, was waiting for me at the airport in Bangor.

"How much extra fuel did you want to fit inside?" Ross asked, trying to make an estimate of what was possible.

"I was hoping you could get at least eighty gallons into it," I said.

Ross scratched his chin, staring at the Stearman. "I should be able to do that. It'll take about a week, though. Willing to stay up here that long while I work on it?"

"I don't know," I said. "I've got some things to handle back home before the polar trip. Is there a way for me to get back home and then come back in a week?"

"You can leave this afternoon on one of our FedEx runs to Manchester, and catch a plane from there."

"Done deal," I quickly replied. "Then in a week, I'll come back up."

We talked about what needed to be done to the plane. When it was time for me to leave, I asked Ross how much he was going to charge me for the flight to Manchester.

"Don't worry about it," he answered. "Just consider this my contribution to the cause." We both shared a laugh at that.

The ride to Manchester was in a Cessna Caravan. The pilot asked me if I wanted to fly it. But I was still tired from the flight up and was just as happy to sit back and enjoy the scenery.

Before I went back to Bangor to pick up the Stearman, National Geographic reconfirmed that they were definitely coming along for the trip and that the $30,000 they had promised was in the mail. I was relieved that they were still on board for the trip but was a little bothered that even with the grant for the chase plane, which they would get more use out of than me, the trip would still cost another $15,000. But Mary convinced me that the money would be well spent if I went down on the polar ice.

With the money issue settled, I bought the airplane insurance, and sent money off to Resolute for the chase plane. Steve Pearce, my chase pilot for the trip, agreed to take the National Geographic team to Resolute. Ali Telapore, another pilot at Montgomery Airpark, volunteered to fly with me only as far as Churchill.

"Gus it's just too cold for me up north. I can't take it. You have antifreeze for blood. I would love to go with you all the way, babes, but I can't take the cold."

"Oh, come on Ali," I coaxed, "it's not that bad. I'm the one out in the wind. Not you, you have heat in your plane."

I had known Ali for a long time. I was glad he was coming with me. Even an extra plane going only as far as Churchill would help. I understood Ali's reasons for not going farther. He wore a heavy down vest on days that were mildly cool. If the temperature got anywhere near freezing, he would show up at the airport dressed like an Inuit.

Everything was set. All that I had left to do was pick up the plane. Early one morning at the end of the week, I caught a plane to Manchester, New Hampshire, and from there I hitched a ride to Bangor.

Ross greeted me excitedly. "Well, I got your eighty gallons in there, and then some."

Pleasantly surprised, I inquired. "Really? How much did you get?"

"We put 110 gallons in the front."

"Hot damn!" I shouted.

"Counting your weight and gear you should be only 30 percent over grossed with full tanks. We counted your weight at 200 pounds with fifty pounds of gear."

I was not about to tell them that my true weight was 320 pounds. I had gained an extra forty pounds since my test flight to the Arctic. The extra weight was for added body insulation. If they knew about my hundred pounds of body fat they might want to take out the same amount of gas before certifying the aircraft. I needed the 110 gallons they had installed.

Bangor had a nice long runway. Perfect for a full-weight takeoff. I had on my ten-pound Arctic flying suit, twenty-five pounds of baggage, and my 320-pound girth. We had loaded thirty-five pounds of oil and 960 pounds of fuel. A total of 1,350 pounds in a plane designed to carry 700 pounds. I figured if the plane did not come off the ground in 5,000 feet, I would cut power, come back to the hangar, and offload some fuel.

I had more gear than I had planned to take to the pole. Four power bars, a small metal cup, a flare, matches, and a tiny hatchet—total gear, five pounds—and me, fully suited, was all that was traveling to the pole. The power bars were for food. The hatchet was to chop up the Stearman wings for firewood, and the flare would scare off polar bears. The cup was to melt ice for water and the matches were for lighting the fire. I would take the bare minimum for life until rescue. The twenty-five pounds of gear I carried out of Bangor were twenty pounds more than I would carry to the pole. I was going for a full-load test out of Bangor.

Before leaving Bangor, I was interviewed by the local CBS affiliate. It was my first television interview. The reporter actually thought I could make it to the pole. We conversed about the new gas tank, which was mounted a little too close to the rudder pedals.

Loaded with fuel and cameras running, I taxied down the Bangor runway. I wondered if the plane would get off the ground with all the weight. I had had problems on the test flight with even less weight on the plane. But in Bangor, the wheels lifted after only 800 feet. Amazingly, I had taken off easily while fully loaded. I was now convinced that I had a good chance of making it to the pole. In that moment of triumph, I felt that with gas at an ice fuel cache I could make it from the pole all the way to Europe if I had to.

The temperature was 20 degrees Fahrenheit when I left Bangor. I wore the new Arctic boots, a test to make sure that I could fly while wearing them. They worked well—not great, but good enough. I could control the rudder pedals with my toes. Luckily, Northern Outfitters had made the new boots one-third smaller than the ones I had used on the test flight. I would not have been able to fly the plane if I had been forced to use the original boots.

By sundown that night I had made it to Hartford, Connecticut. I spent the night there and called Lori at National Geographic to ask about their plans. Now that the First Air chase plane was in the bag, we killed the idea of flying over the pole to Spitsbergen, Norway. The safest and easiest way would be to return from the pole the way I had come. National Geographic would be there to witness the flight.

The next day's sky shone so clear that I did not need the GPS. I simply followed the coast back home. Although just after I took off, I got a bit lost and came close to busting a commercial airport's airspace. I radioed a controller and asked him to direct me around the situation, which he gladly did. He was even kind enough not to write me up for getting into controlled airspace without permission.

When I landed back home in Gaithersburg, the reporter from the Washington CBS news affiliate (WUSA) was there to meet me. He too seemed certain I could reach the North Pole. I liked that. The WUSA reporter was so impressed with the story and the airplane that he asked if he could tape a camera to one of my wings to get footage of the view from the air. I gladly complied and took the plane for a few loops and rolls to get some good shots.

The airplane was now cruising at 115 mph, the fastest I had ever flown in a Stearman, and almost twenty miles faster than the average on the previous Arctic trip. We installed a winter front on the Stearman, to close off outside air to the engine. A winter front is different from the cowling. On a radial engine, the winter front covers the center of the engine. A cowling is a ring that covers around the outside of the engine. The winter front, which is designed to let in more air if the engine overheats, can be adjusted only on the ground. With few places to land in the Arctic, I wanted to be able to control it from the air. Paul Thommesen, my brilliant auto mechanic friend, came up with the answer. Paul ordered a choke cable designed for a Mack truck, hooked it up to the winter front, and ran it to the cockpit, where I could control it during flight. The Stearman has a flimsy cable to open up a manifold heat exchanger to let warm air into the carburetor. It is the only way to prevent carburetor icing, a common problem when flying through any precipitation. We also replaced the heat cable with the Mack truck cables.

The finished product of the winter front and carb-heat cables surprised me. The three-inch knob handle on the end of the Mack cables made them easy to grab, even with mitts on. The carb-heat cable had always been hard to reach while wearing gloves. With the larger handles, I could open the winter front and let in some air if the engine became too hot.

Ali Telapore flew a Cessna 337, fondly known as a "Push me–Pull me." It is a twin-engine aircraft with one engine in the front and one in the rear. The plane was ready for the trip, and he wanted to know what he could carry for me. I told him that National Geographic would give him some of their gear and maybe ride with him.

The scheduled departure was Sunday, April 2, 2000. As the day neared I was like a racehorse at the gate. I had hoped to leave on April 1, but National Geographic convinced me it was a bad idea, too much like an April Fools' joke.

7. Good to Go

On Saturday, April 1, 2000, the day before we left for the North Pole, Steve Pearce and his plane, a Cessna 182, showed up at my hangar. The 182 is a four-place, single-engine, tricycle-gear aircraft that runs about forty miles an hour faster than the Stearman. I hardly knew Steve. Although we had talked often by phone, we had met only once at the meeting of the Lakeridge EAA chapter. But there he stood in my hangar, ready to follow me all the way to Resolute in a 182. That said a lot about him, and I worried about what I was getting him into.

Steve is middle aged and spectacled, an enzyme chemist with a Ph.D. at the end of his name. I had told him that a beard is good protection against the Arctic cold. He showed up with a full, short-cropped gray beard that made him look like Santa on vacation. He had ordered an Arctic suit similar to mine, but in purple, the only color they had in stock in his size. I liked Steve right off. Anyone with the guts to take what I was offering was my kind of guy. On one of our many phone conversations I asked him what his wife, Ginny, thought about the trip.

"She worries but she's with me when it comes to something I really want to do."

I immediately liked Ginny too.

The time had come to buy a new battery for the Stearman. I liked to wait until the day before a big trip to buy a battery. It was part superstition, part good planning. The year before, on the eve of the test flight, I bought a new battery at the Clearview Airport. For the sake of tradition and the good luck that traveled with it, I decided to return to Clearview to buy the battery for the return trip to the pole. I asked Steve to go with me and suggested that we go in his plane. I had never seen the guy fly and did not feel comfortable taking him into the unforgiving Arctic without knowing if he had the ability to land on ice and tundra. The Clearview field, 25 feet wide and 1,800 feet long with a deep ditch at one end and a twist in the middle of the field, is a challenge to the most experienced pilot. At the very least I should see if Steve was competent enough to bring down a plane on Clearview's tiny strip. If he could then he could probably land on anything we would face. I considered telling him that he was being tested but did not.

We both jumped into his 182 and headed for Clearview. As we flew toward our destination, I began to question whether I could judge Steve's flight skills objectively. I had a great deal hanging on Steve and his plane. I needed him to get the film crew and equipment to Resolute to meet First Air. What if he turned out to be an incompetent, too poor a pilot to rely on? Could I compromise on safety? No. Would I? I hoped not, but given the circumstances, could I be trusted to know where to draw the line between good and not good enough? Yes. Maybe. I did not know. Without Steve and his plane, I was reasonably sure that National Geographic would back out of the expedition. I would still go—of that I was determined—but would I be expected to repay the grant money— money that I had already used—if they backed out? I looked over at Steve and knew there was a lot more than a new battery riding on the flight.

I watched Steve like a hawk during the approach at Clearview. On the takeoff from Gaithersburg, he had rotated the nose of the aircraft well and climbed out nice and steady. On the flight, I kept trying to goad him into different maneuvers. If he was easily distracted or his flying was sloppy, I would have to decide against his coming with us.

"This plane's pretty responsive," I said. "How fast is it?"

"Faster than that Stearman," Steve replied, as he pushed full-throttle and showed me the top speed.

When I asked him how slow it could fly, he slowed the plane, keeping it level. I looked for bad habits that might kill him in the Arctic and chided myself for not having tested him earlier in the planning.

The windsock at Clearview is broken most of the time, forcing a pilot to calculate the direction of the ground wind by the way the airplane is flying. It is best to land straight into the wind because the force of the oncoming wind helps to slow the plane's ground speed. A pilot must also be on the alert for a crosswind that could hit the plane from the side, making it difficult to land. A heavy crosswind is hell for a tail-dragger, like the Stearman, because their center of gravity is behind the main gear. Caught in a crosswind, it could rotate front to back, in what is called a ground loop. It is not as difficult to land a tricycle gear, like Steve's 182, which can correct itself if it does not land perfectly straight.

I checked the wind—no crosswind—and told Steve which way it was blowing, directing him on the sly to land on the downwind side but uphill, with the wind pushing at his back. I reasoned that if he could land the plane at Clearview in a downwind he could land anywhere we were going. If he botched the landing I knew I could take the controls and get us in safely. He came in a bit high and fast on the approach. Not perfect, but better than coming in too low and slow. We were at a moment of truth—his and mine. If he did not make it in I would have to steel myself to tell him that he was off the team and live with the consequences of the loss. I watched nervously as he began his descent. I did not think he would make it.

"Wow, this strip is shorter than it looks," he said with a rush of concern in his voice.

He put the flaps down full and cut the power. His technique seemed a bit awkward. I could not decide whether to take over or give him a little more time. I knew he had not logged a lot of airtime and that most of his flying had been in and out of little strips. It was not until much later that I learned he volunteers for "Angel Flight," an organization for which pilots using their own aircraft fly people who cannot afford to fly to needed medical treatment around the country. A little more time, I thought. I need him to do this on his own and do it right. A second later, he pushed the nose toward the ground and brought down the plane, planting it within the first third of the runway. And man, did he plant it!

"I don't usually land them that hard," Steve apologized, "but it looked like I was running out of runway."

Had I been at the controls I would have used a "side-slip," a technique that calls for the use of cross controls to make the plane fly slightly sideways, increasing the drag. As a tactic, it allows the pilot to make a steeper descent without picking up a lot of speed. Slow down to land short is a rule worth obeying.

"Don't you ever slip?" I asked

"I'm used to landing on small fields," he answered, "and this always works."

I could not complain. Steve's technique worked just fine.

"Okay, I guess, go with what works. Oh, one more thing," I added. "When we take off you might want to use the other runway. The wind's coming from the other way, and you probably don't want to do a downwind takeoff."

"I landed downwind?" Steve asked with surprise.

We were still laughing as we ran into the airport store to buy a lucky battery. And when we left, Steve performed a short field takeoff without a hitch.

"Good to go," I said. "I think you can do this trip."

Lori told me I would need to bring along a mechanic. I did not have the money to pay for a mechanic, but even if I had I did not see the need since I always do my own mechanical work in the field. But she insisted. Steve and Ali were willing to pay their own way because they saw the trip as a once-in-a-lifetime opportunity. Just when I was about to give up finding a mechanic willing pay his own way, Robert Thommesen, the brilliant auto mechanic's brother, offered to come along and play the role of the airplane mechanic. Robert is in his late forties and stands about six-feet-five with hands as big as pie plates and the smile of a kid who just played a joke on his sister.

"Just don't tell anybody you are an auto mechanic," I pleaded.

But when he met Lori, the first words out of his mouth were, "I've never worked on an airplane before."

After Steve's successful, albeit clandestine, checkout, I called Lori to let her know that we now had two chase planes—Steve's 182 and Ali's Cessna 337. Ali had agreed to fly Lori and Dwayne Impie, the cameraman, as far as Churchill, where they would catch a commercial carrier to Resolute. First Air would meet them in Resolute for the last leg to the polar cap.

"What about filming between Churchill and Resolute?" Lori asked.

"Maybe Robert can take some pictures and get some shots."

"We may actually charter a plane," she said. "We don't want to miss anything between Churchill and Resolute."

If I had known they were willing to pay for their own aircraft I would not have put any of Mary's money into the First Air charter. I was angry but kept it to myself, as is my way. Nothing would be gained by letting it get to me. The money had been spent. But when I told Mary she damn near blew a fuse.

After the conversation with Lori, Steve and I went back to my house and stayed up talking for half the night. Around eleven, Steve told me he usually was in bed by ten o'clock and was up at five-thirty. I told him I stayed up most nights until one or two in the morning and slept until ten. We compromised and went to bed at midnight. The next morning we rose at six o'clock ready to go.

My family and I had said our goodbyes during the week before the trip. Lara would sit on my knee every night and tell me she would miss me and to be careful. Hera avoided me. Mary and I did not talk about it much either. But when I saw that look in her eye, I would hug her and promise that I would come back alive. The night before Steve showed up Mary had given me a letter to open the day before my attempt on the pole. I packed it with my emergency gear so that it would always be with me in the aircraft. We said our final goodbye that morning at home in private. That was it. The rest of the day was spent like any other day in our house. The only difference was that the family came out to the airport to see me off.

I was apprehensive as I prepared to leave the house. I walked around the place, taking leave of it in a solemn and almost ritualistic manner, acknowledging at each turn that I might not return but at the same time unable to imagine that I would not be coming back.

Ali, Lori, Dwayne, and a mountain of baggage so high it blocked the view of the hangar were waiting when Steve and I arrived at the airport. Never in my life have I seen so much baggage for two people. Steve's jaw dropped in wonder. And after a moment of shocked silence, he shouted, "There's no way all that stuff is going in my plane."

"I sure can't carry any," I said, "maybe Ali can handle it."

Ali quickly piped in that he could only carry Lori and Dwayne, and maybe an extra camera, nothing else. Finally, Steve sighed and said that he would take whatever they could get in the plane.

While they were negotiating, Jay Rosenburg, owner of an advertising agency and the friend who had put me in touch with Lori, came by with a *Washington Post* reporter in tow to say that he would handle the press for me.

"Hey, Gus, come on and talk to this guy."

The *Post* reporter asked questions as I rolled the Stearman out of the hangar. At the same time flashbulbs—more than I had ever seen—started going off. Cameras were clicking all around me. Jay stood by my side, smiling nervously. The reporter was impressed.

"Wow! This plane looks great. It would be a pity to lose it in the Arctic."

He was right. That day the Stearman was a stunner. With the wheel covers attached, the big red cowling over the engine and the front cockpit closed up, it looked like an old racer from the 1920s. What a beautiful sight it was.

I got in the plane and taxied to the front of the terminal. The airport manager had asked me to relocate the plane in order to keep the crowds away from the hangar area and out of the way of other airplanes. I thought the move was unnecessary but complied. As I pulled around the bend from my hangar and headed toward the main terminal I was shocked to see more than three hundred people and reporters and a television film crew from channel 9, WMAL/WUSA, the local affiliate, were waiting at the terminal.

At first I was happy to see that channel 9 was covering the flight. Channel 9 had been a part of my life since I moved from Mississippi to Washington. The very first show I saw in D.C. was the evening news with Max Robinson and Gordon Peterson. To me, channel 9 *is* Washington. But then I began to worry that their presence was an omen that I would not return from the trip—there at the beginning, there at the end. I felt like asking the crew to tape somewhere else. It is strange how fear empties the mind. I later learned that Gordon Peterson, who is still a newsman for channel 9, reported on the Arctic trip and said of me, "There's a real man."

"Well, now it's official," I said jokingly to Mary.

People approached to wish me good luck and to ask if their children could touch the plane. I did not want anyone to touch the plane, particularly the kids, but I thought it would be rude to say no. It must have been the same for the barnstormers of the 1920s—crowds gathering, pushing to get a closer look at the plane and a nervous pilot trying to hold them back from the aircraft. I excused myself, found Robert Thommesen, and asked him to watch the plane like a hawk.

"Keep your eyes on anyone who approaches the plane," I told him. "And don't let anyone get inside it."

Amidst all the confusion, Doug Duff's mother, Henrietta, arrived holding a canister containing Doug's ashes. National Geographic filmed as she handed me the ashes. It was an unsettling moment and sadly bizarre. There I stood, preparing to take off on a flight that could end in my own death, as the bereaved mother of my best flying buddy handed me his ashes. Henrietta wanted me to take his ashes to the North Pole. She had placed the ashes inside a small container, then placed that container inside another, attached a note written by her, placed the two containers inside a three-inch white plastic pipe about a foot long, and closed off each end. It had the look of a pipe bomb. If Canadian customs were to open the container, they would very reasonably conclude they had found a bomb because the ashes were almost the color of gunpowder. My thoughts were jumbled. I was unprepared and a bit spooked by the moment. I knew she expected me to say something but with the cameras rolling, all I could think to say was, "Doug always wanted to go with me on this trip. Well, I guess now he's going to get the chance to."

I should have done better by Doug, but my mind was on other things. I let it go at that.

After the interlude with Doug's mother, I told Lori that I would not fly with the ashes in the Stearman.

"Why not?" she asked, slightly annoyed.

"The last time I flew with Doug, we were talking about death and heaven. I can't do it. I'd rather be by myself."

"What do you expect me to do with them?"

"I don't know, but he's not flying with me. He wanted to be the chase plane pilot. Let him fly in the chase plane."

With that, Lori agreed to take responsibility for them, but instead of taking the ashes with her on Ali's plane she loaded them onto Steve's plane.

Two days before takeoff, Dwayne had mounted three external cameras on the Stearman and had plans to mount one external on Ali's plane. But Lori balked because she was concerned about adding more weight to the plane in which she would be flying. She decided that the additional camera should be mounted on the Stearman, even though I was against taking on anymore nonessential weight because the drag would slow the plane. I asked her why she was so cavalier about overloading my plane and so adamant about keeping the weight down on Ali's plane. "You've only got to risk your life once," she said with cool logic. "I have to do it every day. I don't want to take any chances."

The news cameraman was taping me talking about the trip when Steve ran up shouting.

"What the hell is this? This thing isn't going in my plane until I figure out what it is!" Steve yelled, waving the PVC containing Doug's ashes. "It looks like a bomb!"

I turned to see what all the commotion about. I did not want to explain to Steve what it was while the cameras were running, so I grabbed the PVC and stuck it under my jacket.

"Not to worry," I said. "I'll talk to you about it later."

Steve was upset. It was obvious that the tension of the day was getting to him.

"I'm not taking anything more in my plane, especially something that looks like a bomb. Every time I come back to the plane, it's something different."

"Why don't you lock up the plane?" I suggested.

"I can't," he answered.

I knew why. Most recreational pilots lose the keys to their planes and never bother to replace them.

"We'll talk later. Just make sure everything's okay."

After the interview, I went to find Steve. I have never seen a plane so loaded down. A Cessna 182 is not supposed to look like a tail-dragger, but that one did.

"This thing won't even taxi, let alone get off the runway!" I said.

Steve looked at his low-riding plane and agreed that it was tail-heavy. But he figured that "it'll even out" when he and Robert got in the front. That sounded exactly like something I would say. Man, I thought, this guy sounds more like me by the minute.

While Steve and I were talking, Lori appeared with more baggage. The additional gear did not fit into Steve's 182, and unless Lori could talk Ali into taking on the extra weight it would have to stay behind. When I informed her of the situation, she ranted and raved screaming, "This is a deal breaker." It was a phrase Lori often used, even when the slightest thing went wrong. But this time it was to no avail: the Cessna was full. In the end, Lori was forced to hire a Beechcraft Baron from Congressional Aviation to transport the added baggage to Churchill, after which it would be loaded on to the commercial flight and travel with her to Resolute.

Just before takeoff, the weather changed for the worse, making it difficult for me to make it to Canada that day. I did not want to throw a wrench into the day's sendoff ceremony, but I also did not want to risk forging ahead in inclement weather. After conferring with Steve, I decided to leave as scheduled, then fly twenty miles north to Frederick, spend the night at home, and take off from Frederick the next morning.

Richard Blair has played the pipes for every president since Harry Truman. When he offered to perform the duties of official piper for the takeoff I was thrilled and honored. He also suggested that for the takeoff I wear my kilts, a gift from my Scottish relatives. But that was not the impression I wanted to make that day. It would surely have been a showstopper for the crowd to see my big butt in all its glory as I climbed into the Stearman.

Blair thought the bagpipes were a fitting tribute to my Scottish heritage, something I often ignored. When I went to Scotland to meet my relatives, I told them the reason I had taken so long to visit was that I was afraid of how I would be received. When they treated me like their long lost son I was as pleased as I was surprised. An old guy, who reminded me of my granddad, put his hand on my shoulder and looked me straight in the eye.

"Son," he said, "you can pick your friends, but you cannot pick your kin."

By the time I left Scotland for home, I was both kin and friend.

As I started the engine, Dr. Blair fired up the pipes. I had not expected to be affected by the mournful heroic sound, but I was, deeply. The McLeods came to the Hebrides a thousand years ago. Over eight hundred years ago, Olofe, the Black, gave the Isle of Skye to his son, Leote. The Celts called Leote's son, son of Leod or McLeod. We have carried the name ever since. At the sound of those pipes, I knew that to understand who I am and how I would eventually come to see myself, I would have to fish all the waters that converged in me. I was on a quest of discovery, and I was being urged on by all my Native American, African, and Scottish ancestors.

I taxied the old bird to the runway. Just before takeoff, a reporter from channel 9 news approached to ask me to hold the aircraft on the runway until I reached his camera position, then pull up into a spectacular climb.

"Done deal, I'm on it."

I lined the plane up with the center of the runway and pushed full throttle. As the plane sped down the gray strip, I felt a small thump, after which the plane did a jump, then rose off the ground, pulling sharply to the right. Almost as soon as I was airborne, several people radioed to tell me that something was hanging from the bottom of the plane. One pilot radioed an offer to fly under the plane to see what it was.

"No!" I shouted. "Don't do that. I don't have very good visibility directly beneath me. We could collide."

Soon after, I heard Steve's voice say with authority, "Only one person can talk to Gus at a time."

He then went on to break down the situation for me.

"There's something hanging from your tire. What do you want to do?"

I thought quickly—Stearmans love grass runways—and responded, "Maybe I should continue on to Frederick and check it out there. They have all sorts of runways, even a grass one."

The airport manager called in to say that he wanted to "keep the problem here." Was he afraid of the plane coming apart? Are the wings bent? What the hell is the problem? Oh damn, I wondered, am I going to wreck the Stearman and die right here before even leaving Gaithersburg?

"The wheel pant looks like it's hanging off," Steve said.

He then suggested that it might be a wheel chock (a wooden block wedged in front of the tire to keep the airplane from rolling on the ground).

When I heard that I knew it would be an ugly landing. If something was locking one of my wheels I was not sure I could even set the plane down.

"Okay, I'm going to come around," I said.

When the wheels touched down I felt a bump, similar to driving into a pothole. Then I heard an explosion.

The wheel covers had been mounted too close to the tires. When I accelerated at takeoff, the air inside the tire got hot and expanded, causing the tire to expand and make contact with and subsequently loosen the right wheel cover. With the force of the landing the wheel cover tore off, throwing wheel cover parts everywhere, including into the wing. Damage for the day: a four-inch puncture hole in one of the wings that ended the day's flying.

Later that day, I removed the other wheel cover. The covers were supposed to make the tires more aerodynamic, giving the plane an extra six miles an hour of speed. It was a good idea, but it didn't work. I did not put the covers back on for fear that the same thing might happen again.

The weather changed from bad to worse, guaranteeing that we would not get up for another couple of days. We spent the time fixing the hole in the bottom of the wing and pacing. By the second day, everyone was jumpy, like pent-up birds trying to escape their cages.

8. To Be a Part

By eight in the morning on Wednesday, April 5, a large crowd of onlookers and reporters from every local station had gathered at the airport to send us off. As luck would have it, the wheel cover incident a few days before had heightened interest in the expedition. The morning was cold and snow fell gently. A headwind was coming directly out of the north. It was a good day to fly, and the departure went off with ease and little ceremony. I took off first and the team followed—first out was Ali's Cessna 337 carrying Lori and Dwayne, followed by Steve and Robert in the 182 hauling almost all of my gear. The Baron, carrying Lori's additional baggage, left several hours later. The first objective was Hamilton, Ontario.

Not long into the flight we ran into a snowstorm and a vicious headwind over the Alleghenies. The conditions were similar to those I had encountered at the very same spot the year before. I lowered the Stearman between the valleys and fluttered around under the storm clouds, following roads and skirting mountains as I had done the year before. None of the others on the team knew the drill in those mountains, and I could hear them talking on the radio about the difficulty of the flight. Whenever possible I avoid using the radio in the Stearman because the radio does not have much range and the plane is so loud that I have to yell to be understood. It would have taken me ten minutes to explain to them how to handle that weather, and even if they had been able to hear me—which I doubt—they probably would not have been any better off and I would have gotten a terrible headache for the effort.

In an experiment to calculate the performance parameters of the Stearman's radio, I found that it picks up a plane traveling twenty-five miles in front and thirty miles to the rear. But the maximum range within which I can successfully transmit is ten miles to the rear and eight miles in front. The Stearman engine was designed in the late 1920s when radios were not an option in most aircraft, making it unnecessary to shield the engine for electromagnetic frequency (EMF) waves. Magnetos are little generators that make the electricity for firing spark plugs. Whenever electricity jumps a gap, EMF radio waves at all sorts of frequencies are produced. Although I had shielded the Stearman for EMF, as had others before me, the radio noise generated by the engine was so loud that it acted like a jamming station, limiting the radio's use.

The team made it through the mountain storm, as I knew they would, and decided to stop for fuel in Dunkirk, New York, before crossing the cold waters of Lake Erie. I did not join them, preferring to continue on across the lake without a break. With the headwind I was averaging only fifty-five miles an hour over the ground and had been sitting in the plane for five hours by then. I just wanted to get to Hamilton. Although I knew the other planes could outrun the Stearman, I was fairly certain I would be the first to arrive at Hamilton. After all, Steve had never even flown across open water.

When I landed in Hamilton, an unfamiliar man approached and told me that he had been waiting for me.

"Who are you?" I asked.

The man laughed and told me that he was the pilot of the plane carrying the Geographic team's gear and that his name was Bob McCormick. I asked how long he had been there and was depressed to hear that he had left three hours after me and had beat me there by almost an hour. He laughed and said that the headwinds were not so bad at 14,000 feet. I knew no Stearman would ever go that high or fast, still it was depressing to be reminded how slowly it traveled. After that I stopped trying to beat anyone else's time and just accepted my modest pace.

About forty minutes later the rest of the team arrived, all with complaints of how rough the ride had been. I told them that the farther north we got the worse the conditions would get. And I offered to let any one of them fly the Stearman for a leg if they wanted an idea of what a rough ride really means. I had no takers, and none of them complained again about flight conditions, at least not in front of me.

Soon after we were all in and accounted for, the suggestion was made that we get right back in the sky and press on to Elliot Lake, Ontario. I tried to veto that because I was tired and, besides, Elliot Lake gave me the willies. When I had landed there the year before I was told that it had been a uranium-mining town. When the mine played out, the Canadian government purchased the town and turned it into a retirement community. The last thing I wanted to think about at age forty-five was retirement. So I decided then and there to have as little as possible to do with Elliot Lake.

With a little coaxing, the team convinced me to continue on. It was a good call, because over Lake Erie we met the backside of the Allegheny storm and enjoyed its helpful tailwinds all the way to our destination. It took me less than two hours to make Elliot Lake. It took the others even less time.

Boy, was I wrong about Elliot Lake. It is a fine little town. By the time I landed, dignitaries of all kinds had assembled to greet me—even the mayor was there to give me a pin and make me an honorary citizen. Perhaps that was why Lori had been so adamant about getting on to Elliot Lake. They must have known beforehand about the reception.

That night everyone on the team wanted to get a shot at using the satellite phone to call home. The calls were free, but to get the phone to work properly we had stand on the roof of the small hotel where we were staying. Throughout the night one or another of the crew could be seen standing on the roof talking over the satellite phone.

The next day, freezing rain covered the area. We had no choice but to stay put. To make the time pass as quickly and painlessly as possible, the airport personnel put together a cookout and for the entire day we did little more than watch the rain, talk, and eat.

On the second morning in Elliot Lake I woke early. The weather had vastly improved. It promised to be a good day for flying. The rain had passed and the temperature was a relatively warm 33 degrees Fahrenheit, warm enough, I decided, to travel light. Whenever the weather allowed I jumped at the chance to shed layers of my cold-weather gear—the lighter my clothing the more comfortable the flight.

The next stop, Geraldton, Ontario, was 318 nautical miles away, which translates into three hours and thirty-five minutes of flight time. Everything felt good. I was comfortable and eager to get on the road again. But, twenty miles out from Elliot Lake the temperature dipped to 19. When the snow started the ceiling dropped, forcing the Stearman down to 200 feet. With the surface whizzing by underneath me, I threaded my way through the hills. None of this concerned me greatly. My first trip to the Arctic had taught me that it was not easy to predict the weather in the north.

About a half-hour out of Elliot Lake, I heard my team talking to one another over the radio. The three planes were traveling together—Bob on his own in the Baron, Ali with Lori and Dwayne, and Robert and Steve in the 182. I watched the snow as I listened to their voices over the radio. The weather in the north never fails to fascinate me. High up, the snow looks like a thin mist, almost like a light rainfall and, in the quiet, is both spellbinding and comforting. If you breathe in some of the mist, it is a crisp, fresh brush of wind that enters your throat, not the humid or dense air you might have expected.

As the snow fell, I listened to the voices of my team talking over the radio, their easy conversations leading me to thoughts about humans in general. Although we humans often yearn to be alone, we are more naturally social beings. The crew had nothing particularly urgent to say to one another. Yet their conversations overlapped seamlessly in the mist, like gentle tethers binding one to the other. And there I was, alone and not participating in the conversation, but listening to it. And in the listening my own needs for human contact were being addressed. Part of me was interested in the conversation and part of me wasn't. Part of me enjoyed the solitude, the thrill of being left to my own devices, and still another part felt a true warmth and connection to those voices emanating from the small speakers in my headphones.

As I maneuvered through the hills, I too began to feel the need to join the conversation.

"This is 8 November Papa," I said. "It's pretty rough down here, but I'm coming through."

There was no response. The rest of the team kept talking as though I had not said anything. It was one of those rare moments when I caught a glimpse of my inner self, maybe even my soul. I was overjoyed to know that part of me needed to make contact with the others. But I also saw that part of me did not really care to. I felt both the need to connect and the need to remain detached. As one need grew the other subsided. I do not understand what causes such dissonant needs, although I do understand them to be human.

Steve's voice rang out over the radio. "It's pretty bad down here in the lower altitudes. You think Gus may have turned back?"

Bob McCormick, the pilot of the Baron, answered. "Well, it's clear up here at 10,000 feet and should stay that way to Geraldton. If he turns back, I'll get a call from Elliot Lake."

Ali, flying with the film crew, chimed in. "I think I'm going to climb up there over the top of this storm with you. It's very rough down here. If Gus turns back, at least we'll all be in the clear."

"I don't know if I can stay down here, either," said Steve. "It's too tough. I'm going to see if I can punch out of this."

I could tell they were behind me from the position reports they were giving each other. I was still barreling through snow and ice. Since it was impossible for me to slip through the top of the storm, I wondered where the bottom was. If I went down, would I break out or would I be socked in all the way to the ground?

I have always been surprised by how quick pilots are to reach for the radio when they run into trouble. The first thing most pilots do is to ask an air controller for help. I had never understood that. To my mind there is absolutely nothing the air controller can do from an office on the ground. To the controller the plane is just a number on a screen. It is the pilot, the one behind the controls, who is looking at the problem.

But as I listened to my crew, I began to understand why the radio is so important. It is not that the controller can take over the aircraft and bring it in safely, but that the voice coming back at you makes the situation, no matter how dire, feel more manageable. That day, even as I was fighting the weather, I felt better about what was ahead than I had felt at any time during the previous year's trip. The reason being that this time other people were traveling with me. There had been times on the last trip when I was so afraid and lonely I almost wept. But on that day, as I listened to the team talking to each other and overcoming their problems each in different ways, I was not afraid to sit back and press on in the best way I knew how.

Another thirty minutes passed before I heard Steve's voice again.

"Eight November Papa, do you read? Repeat, 8 November Papa, do you read?"

"This is 8 November Papa, I read you loud and clear. Do you read me?"

"I read you. Repeat, I read you. What are you doing down there? We haven't heard from you."

"Well I've heard from you," I said with a laugh.

Steve asked me my altitude, and I told him I was at 2,000 feet and flying between ridges. With a trace of relief in his voice that confirmed he was glad he was not down in the mess with me, he relayed that he was at 4,000 feet and in the clear.

"Where are your buddies?" I asked.

He told me that they had gone on ahead and were probably in Geraldton by now.

"So you must have broken out of the clouds at about 3,000," I said, hoping that the tops were that low so I could get up there too.

"Yep. Up on top, beautiful skies. It's a little cold up here, though. It's 14 degrees."

"Well," I said, "it's not much better down here. It's only 16."

"Why don't you come on up?" he said.

"You know what, I will. I think I see a hole in the clouds in front of me. I'll go through and come out on top."

That was a good joke, one I often played. The Stearman is a plane without instruments, and technically is not supposed to be operating in instrument weather. It is supposed to stay 500 feet below clouds or 1,000 feet above them, and definitely should not be flying through them. Because of that, I often make up imaginary holes in the clouds, granting myself an excuse to climb through the soup—a tactic that kept it all legal in my mind at least.

In the Stearman, a climb through an opaque mist is always an event. That day I set up a gentle climb at eighty-five miles an hour and held it. After setting the control speed, I needed to get a heading and maintain it through the clouds to make sure the plane stayed straight. When flying in the soup with a non-IFR craft, like a Stearman, it is important not to do anything too quickly. Once control is lost it is almost impossible to regain it using only heading and airspeed. Why? Because there is a lag of two or three seconds between what is actually happening to the aircraft and what the airspeed and heading readings indicate is happening. The lag means that any big corrections or overcorrections are going to be made seconds too late to be effective—a situation that invariably leads to a total loss of control. To fly with only heading and airspeed, each correction has to be small and a pilot has to be patient, waiting several seconds after making a correction to see how the airplane has responded.

I climbed at a creep. It took twenty minutes to break through the cloud layer, ascending at 100 feet per minute. When I finally popped into the clear blue sunny sky, the cloud covered world below looked like a big cup of milk.

"You're right," I radioed Steve, "it is cold up here."

The temperature was 14 degrees Fahrenheit. Because it had been so warm at Elliot Lake I was dressed for only 32.

"I read you. Did you break out yet?"

"Yeah, I'm on top. I'm having a bit of a problem reading you, though."

We gave each other our GPS coordinates. Steve was about nine miles away.

I looked around and up and down, straining my neck as I searched for sight of Steve's plane. I felt like the Red Baron (Manfred von Richthofen) or Eddie Rickenbacher and other First World War fighter pilots out on a mission. The only difference between them and me was that I was looking for a friend, not an enemy. I noticed something off my shoulder, a shiny glimmer about 2,000 feet above me, going in the same direction at about seven o'clock.

"This is 8 November Papa. I think I see you. Look down, right above the clouds. I'm at your two o'clock position, skimming along."

"I've got you, 8 November Papa, I see you down there. I'm gaining on you quick."

"Can you slow down and stay with me?" I asked. "I may need some help."

"Sure. How fast?"

"I'm doing 105 mph."

"Okay," Steve said. "I was doing 130. I'll slow down and match you."

I could make out the small speck of Steve's plane. Every time his wings moved the sun gleamed on them. I knew that Steve and Robert sat inside that small speck, two people who are my friends. I found great solace in that.

As soon as I pushed through the cloud layer I wanted Mary to know I was all right. I radioed Steve to ask Robert to call her and tell her I was okay. Robert had the satellite phone, and Steve's plane ran quiet enough to use it. Even though I had a phone for emergencies, I could not get it out of my pocket. If I had somehow managed that outstanding feat, the intensity of the wind would have blown the thing right out of my hand. Within a few minutes, Steve called to say that Robert had reached Mary and told her everything was fine. I almost cheered out loud.

Two hours out the cold started to get to me. I was wearing only a light jacket, light boots, long johns, gloves, and a flying helmet. I was beginning to get really cold.

"Steve, it's getting a bit chilly in here," I said over the radio. "How much longer do you think it'll be?"

"Looks like we're an hour out of Geraldton."

"I don't know if I can take another hour of this."

"We're right outside of Wawa," Steve said, "why don't we aim for that?"

I did not want to go to Wawa because of the experience I had when I stopped there to refuel on the previous trip. The gas attendant had tried to overcharge me, and the weather I ran into on leaving was so taxing that I vowed I would not return for any reason. I can remember, long ago, arguing with my parents about the logic of making a decision based on a rush of feeling rather than reason. At forty-six I had become like my parents. I did not like Wawa and that was that.

Wawa had the last laugh though, and I paid dearly for skipping it. When I arrived at Geraldton, I was so cold I had to be carried out of the Stearman. When they got me to the ground, I was disoriented and did not know which way to go. Robert took my arm and guided me into the terminal. Inside there was a working woodstove, which stood in front of a cocktail table and sofa. Robert, in his infinite wisdom, set me next to the woodstove. The heat felt good for about two seconds and then it started to burn. I bolted from the stove and planted myself facedown on the cocktail table, where I stayed until it was time to leave.

My joints were still trying to soak in the warmth when it was time to leave. I was stiff but could move. I was still tired but no longer delusional. Pickle Lake, the goal for the day, was 150 miles away—an hour and a half flight or, with a good tailwind, an hour and change. I could handle that standing on my head.

"Let's go," I shouted to the team.

Steve spoke up. "Are you sure you're good to go?"

"Aw, it's only an hour. I'll see you in Pickle Lake. They have something planned for us."

"Do you want us to stay with you?" Steve asked.

"No, just get there as fast as you can. That's what I'm going to do."

"Well, we'll leave after you then."

After Geraldton I was mostly on my own. I wanted it that way. The test must always be taken alone—on one's own or not at all. Steve had flown beside me for an hour of the three-hour flight to Geraldton. It was the last time during the trip that anyone slowed down to stay with me. From then on, the crew would leave after me, check in by radio when they caught up with me, and then continue on.

"You'll probably catch up to me about thirty minutes out," I said. "I'll see you at Pickle Lake. We'll have a few in the bar."

"Are you warm enough?" Steve asked, as I prepared to climb into the Stearman.

At Geraldton, Steve established himself as my mother hen. From there on, he gave me his "Are you okay" and "Do you have enough clothes" speeches before every departure.

"Actually," I admitted, "I can probably use another jacket."

I returned to the terminal, put on more long johns, another shirt, another pair of pants, and two more pairs of socks. Then, I put on my leather jacket and another jacket over that. I felt pretty good.

I hopped in the plane, checked it out, and headed to Pickle Lake. The flight was the most comfortable hour and a half of the entire trip. My only goal was to make the next stop, where I would meet my friends for a beer. It was a sensible attitude, one that I would adopt for the remainder of the trip.

Before the flight to Pickle Lake, whenever I thought about the pole I would find myself dwelling on all the hardships that I would have to endure just to get there. It would depress me. But, I found if I trained myself to think less about the ultimate goal and take each leg of the trip as a goal in itself I did not feel so overwhelmed by the enormousness of the ordeal.

I counted down the miles to Pickle Lake. When the distance came down to fifty miles, I shouted out, "One tupelo to go!" Since my childhood in Mississippi I have counted distances as units of tupelos—fifty miles equaled one tupelo, the distance from my home in Corinth to Tupelo, Elvis Presley's birthplace. Thus 100 miles equaled two tupelos, 300 miles, six tupelos, and so on. I often rode to Tupelo in the backseat of my parents' car and on a couple of occasions even walked part of the way. One tupelo in a Stearman takes about thirty minutes.

Pickle Lake is a challenge for pilots because there are no landmarks to follow into the airport. The runway is almost hidden within a patch of trees, and there is nothing else in sight but forest. But that day the GPS worked excellently, and the airport was easy to find.

Even before I landed I knew there would be a party waiting. Pickle Lake is at the end of the last road in Ontario, and most of those who live there work in transportation. Trucks bring in goods that are then flown out to all the villages that can be reached only by air. As a result the town is loaded with pilots on route to and from somewhere else. The comings and goings are the best excuse for a party. Our arrival would be no exception. That night they prepared a special fish fry on the ice for us. The temperature was 15 degrees Fahrenheit on the lake. They fired up a big grill and skillet and cooked walleye, char, and native rice. It was the first time I had tasted the local rice. It is wild rice, and I cannot imagine how, when, or where it grows, but the locals swear it grows in Pickle Lake. There we sat eating fish on a lake in the light of a northern evening.

Ali decided not to take his plane any farther north because of the cold. So Bob McCormick agreed to take a load of gear to Churchill that night and then return to Pickle Lake to pick up passengers. Ali rode with him. When they returned to Pickle Lake, Ali could talk of nothing but the harsh weather (-20 degrees Fahrenheit in Churchill) and the failure of the Baron's heater.

Than night, we spent a lively evening of drinking and singing karaoke. Dwayne filmed my rendition of "Bad Leroy Brown," which must not have been a pretty sight because it did not make its way into the television special. I had a good night of sleep, and I rose early the next morning. Ali said his goodbyes and headed for home as we prepared for the day's flight. Lori replaced the batteries for the external cameras mounted on the Stearman and activated the camera she wanted to use for the next leg of the trip. While there were four cameras on the plane, only one could function at a time—a limitation that required Lori to plan ahead. In the cold, the cameras worked for fifteen minutes. Once the batteries froze, the cameras shut down. I was of no help to her, because once I was seated in the cockpit I was unable to move around.

The trip from Pickle Lake to Churchill, a straight run, is one of the longest of the trip. While there are many native villages on the path to Churchill, none are equipped for refueling. On the test trip, when the Stearman was burning fuel at a dangerously accelerated rate, Bernie Cox had arranged for me to make an emergency fuel stop at Bearskin Lake. Since then we had solved the fuel problems and a stop was no longer necessary.

The weather was still cold and miserable. I called Canada Weather and was told to expect scattered snowstorms between Pickle Lake and Churchill. That would be easy enough. I had flown through similar weather last year. I was reasonably certain I could thread my way through the big storms and stay out of trouble. But as I wedged myself into the plane that morning, I felt a strong desire to be heading back to Gaithersburg with Ali. It was not the first time on the trip, nor would it be the last, that a part of me dreaded going forward. I was often overwhelmed by an emotional chaos caused by the mix of pain, fear, loneliness, boredom, excitement, awe, and fun that I experienced in the north. Sometimes when I found myself looking ahead to the pain, my rational side would argue forcefully to end the madness and turn back for home. But in a swell of "give me more, I love it" my sense of daring silenced reason. Each time the battle raged I calmed myself and step by step moved on, farther and farther north.

The others had planned to take off after me, but Bob and the National Geographic crew left with me, while Steve and Robert took off an hour later. A lot had gone wrong that morning: a screw had fallen into the gas tank. It was a safety concern, so Robert patiently fished around for and retrieved it. Then, Steve discovered that one of the Cessna's break-lines was cracked, and just as I was about to take off, I could not find my airport directory that contained all the information on the airports in Canada. I had carried it with me on the last Arctic trip, and it had become a good luck charm. It comforted me to know that if I happened upon an airport during flight I could look it up in my handy book and find out all I needed to know about the airport. I taxied over to the rest of my team and asked if any of them had seen it. They had not. Since I was already strapped in and ready to go, there seemed to be no point in continuing the search. I could make the flight to Churchill without it and look for it later.

Forty miles out of Pickle Lake, I ran into a solid wall of snow—not the scattered snowstorms I had been told to expect, but a full-fledged blizzard. The milky cream soup I knew to be the real deal was approaching. It was about then that I felt a pain in my seat. On my first Arctic flight, I used a gel cushion Mary had given me. She figured that since I would be sitting for long periods of time a cushion would help. It worked fine until the temperature reached fifteen below zero, and the cushion began to freeze into one position. For the pole trip, I made sure to bring an air cushion. The air certainly would not freeze, allowing me to adjust the shape of the cushion by shifting in the seat. I could not make out what was wrong. Had the cushion deflated? I lifted myself up a bit and repositioned my butt, which gave me a moment of respite. But the pain returned quickly.

Before I knew it I was heading directly into the blizzard. At 800 feet above ground I lost all visibility. I talked to myself in the calm and authoritative way a controller would talk a worried pilot through a storm.

"Keep level, straight, maintain airspeed. Good. Now calmly lower down until you see the ground. All tundra, no mountains. Just keep the wings level and look for something. Anything."

The Stearman was flying level at 105 miles an hour. If I could maintain that speed without changing the power setting the plane would stay level. North of Pickle Lake there is nothing to run into—no towers or mountains. I put the plane into a slight descent until I could make out the ground. It was much easier holding on to the Stearman with the ground in sight. I kept the speed at 115 miles an hour, allowing for a nice gentle descent. At about fifty feet, I caught sight of the ground. In less than a mile the temperature dropped from 18 to −10 degrees Fahrenheit. I could feel the plane rearranging itself—the struts, the fuselage, and every other part—in the cold. When I entered the temperature gradient, it felt like a bucket of ice water had been poured over my head. Quickly I forced myself to shiver, as I always do in extreme cold. It made me feel warmer. I could practically hear the Stearman creak in the cold. I leaned down into the plane and whispered, "It's okay for me to shiver, but you're not supposed to."

Unknown to me, the oil gaskets were blowing out in the engine—a quick 28-degree drop would be tough on any plane. I closed the winter front to protect the engine away from the cold air, and the temperature climbed back up to acceptable levels. This is not too bad, I thought. It was far worse over the Hudson Bay last year.

Soon the clouds lowered almost all the way to the ground. I could fly no lower. About ten feet above the ground, just as the storm began to lighten up, I heard a faint signal on the radio. Excitement grabbed hold of me. I had never heard the radio out there before—I had almost forgotten that I brought a support team along with me. I could hear Steve talking to Bob in the Baron on its way back from dropping off the National Geographic team in Churchill.

"I'm in bad weather, trying to climb on top. Going through 12,000 feet," said Steve.

"Top of the clouds are at 14,000. I'm looking down on them. I've cleared them pretty good," Bob radioed back.

"Roger," Steve said, "I'm coming out on top." At 12,500 feet, Steve emerged from the clouds.

I was stuck down near the ground with an aching butt and only two ways to go—forward or backward. After sitting for three hours, I was certainly not turning back. I wondered how much longer the storm would continue and decided to call the chase plane.

"This is 8 November Papa, do you read?"

There was no response.

"This is 8 November Papa, do you read?"

I tried for another twenty minutes and still no response. Then, I heard Steve's voice.

"Eight November Papa, we read you. What's your location?"

"I'm down on the deck, riding a storm."

"Yeah, I see it down there. Looks pretty bad. Are you going to turn back?"

"Yeah, it's bad, but I'm going on. I think I've gone through the worst of it."

Concern in his voice, Steve informed me that from what he could see it did not look any better ahead.

"Maybe you should turn back to Pickle Lake."

"I'll consider it," I answered brusquely, still determined to get through the storm.

A few minutes later, I called Bob in the Baron.

"I hear you down there," he said. "You're under the overcast?"

"Yeah."

"Not to worry. It's clear about 280 miles south of Churchill."

Only sixty-five miles away. I could deal with that.

"I'm returning home," he said. "Good luck. Hope you make the pole!" With that, Bob and the Baron were gone.

The Stearman's rudders respond in unison but in opposite ways—when one is held down the other rises. My feet were getting numb from the pressure of working the rudders. I felt quick dull stabs, the proverbial pins and needles, attacking my muscles and nerves. I lifted my feet and moved them about as best as I could to get the blood flowing. But once my feet were off the rudders, the plane started falling off to the left. When I placed them back on the rudders, the plane straightened. But then the pain returned even worse than before.

To keep the Stearman flying straight, a little right rudder is used all the time to counteract the torque of the engine. As a result my right leg was more likely to cramp than my left. To ease the pain in my right leg, I wedged my left foot beneath the left rudder, which had the effect of keeping the left rudder in the up position and the right rudder in the down. The movement allowed me to release the pressure on my right foot and gave me the opportunity to move it around a bit. I could only move my foot about seven or eight inches in either direction, but that was better than no movement. But soon my left foot, bearing all the pressure, began to hurt even more. I could feel my legs swelling and could not think of any way to stop the pain. My rear end was also killing me so I moved around on the air cushion. Nothing seemed to help. It felt as if I was sitting on a railroad track. I had to think of something.

I came up with another plan, something I call "poor man's autopilot." I reached down to the bungee cord I used to secure the Stearman's controls when it is parked, wrapped a bit around the left rudder, then connected it to the seat. Most Stearmans are made with a control lock to keep the controls in place on the ground. The lock keeps the wind from beating the control surfaces up and down and possibly damaging them. My Stearman had lost its control locks long ago.

The makeshift autopilot did not work the way I had expected, so I put the control stick between my legs to hold the plane steady and then tied two knots in the bungee, hooked the cord under the left rudder, and tied it to the side of the cockpit. It was not tight enough so I tied one more knot and rehooked the bungee. It worked. I freed my legs and pushed myself up out of my seat as far as I could, hoping to discover what was causing the intense pain in my lower body. I assumed it was from the cold, although I did not feel cold and the rest of my body felt fine as far as the temperature was concerned. But my legs felt like they were being sawed in half by ants chewing them apart. The pain persisted, but I could find nothing wrong, so I sat back down, unhooked the bungee, and continued to fly.

Back up to 200 feet, the sky seemed to be clearing. I thought I could make out blue skies ahead. The pain had gotten so severe that even the blue skies did not raise my spirits. I was having serious second thoughts about the trip. If I could not sit on a flight from Pickle Lake to Churchill how would I make the 1,200-mile trip from Eureka to the pole and back? I started to yell and scream about the pain, in hopes that the antics would distract, if not relieve, the pain. Then I remembered back to younger days, when Mary and I prepared for the birth of our first child. We had attended Lamaze sessions for natural childbirth. The instructor had told Mary to pant and breathe heavily when she felt a contraction. Unable to think of anything else to do I braced myself against the dash and began to pant and breathe rhythmically. It did not help much. With all the breathing and panting, I must have leaned against the radio send-button, broadcasting what I was going through over the airways. I do not know for sure if anyone heard me but at the time it seemed to me that I heard someone say, "What the hell is that?"

I was beginning to be concerned that even if I did make it to Churchill, I might not be able to even walk, let alone fly, again. My boots were getting tighter and tighter from the swelling. The pain was so intense I was not sure I could take it for much longer. I thought I might pass out. I got to the point that I was too exhausted to fight against the shoulder harness and seatbelt in order to change positions. Should I undo the straps, I wondered. No, I knew that was not a good idea. Without a strap and nothing else to hold me, the heavy turbulence could pitch me out of the plane. I remembered that Bessie Coleman, who in 1921 became the first Black American aviator to earn an international pilot's license, had died in a freak accident when she unbuckled her straps and fell out of a plane. Of course, the Arctic weather suit I was wearing was so massive that I probably would not fall from the cockpit, even if the plane was flying upside down. On the other hand, if I fell even halfway out, into the slipstream, I would not have the strength to make it back into the cockpit. With that I put the idea of unfastening the seatbelt to rest.

The pain was so intense that my vision had blurred. I knew Churchill lay dead ahead but doubted myself when I caught sight of it on the horizon. When I was sure that what I saw was the airport, the village, and the grain silos, the need to land quickened to the point of near panic. I called up Churchill radio, but no one answered. Twenty miles out, no answer. Fifteen miles out, still no answer. The pain cut through my legs and back. Ten miles out of Churchill, I radioed in, a rush in my voice.

"Churchill radio, this is 8 November Papa."

"Go ahead, 8 November Papa."

"What's your weather like down there?"

"Winds here are out of the west at twenty-eight knots gusting to thirty. You can use any runway you want."

I did not even blink about the strong crosswind. No matter what, I was going in on the runway right in front of me. I had to get on the ground, out of the plane, and away from the pain.

Churchill has a two-mile runway. In that wind, I used only 900 feet at the beginning of it, a long way to the terminal. Once I was on the ground, I considered taking off and landing farther down the long runway, but one look at the windsock with the heavy crosswind displayed, I decided that was not a good idea. I taxied to the terminal. Steve's 182 was parked on the tarmac. I shut off the Stearman's engine and looked down at the ground wearily. But I could not move. As my team approached the airplane, I could tell they were expecting me to get out. But I simply sat there, unable to move. I had unbuckled the seatbelts, but that was all. I could not move my legs. Robert saw my worried look and came to the side of the plane.

"What's the problem?"

"I can't feel my legs," I said, in a monotone. "I don't think I can get out."

"Here, I'll help you."

Robert climbed up onto the side of the plane, gave me a tug, and up I came out of the seat into a standing position. I felt the little stabs digging into my muscles. A good sign, I thought, at least I was feeling something. Robert stepped out of the way as I leaned against the aircraft, sat on the back of the plane, threw my legs over the side, and slid to the ground from the back wing. I looked back up at the plane and noticed that the side of it was covered with oil, as if it had been painted black.

"Is this normal?" Robert asked me.

"No, it should leak a little, but not that much. We might have bigger problems, though."

"What's that," he said.

"I can't feel my legs and haven't for the past two hours. I don't know if I can go on like this. That wasn't even the longest leg, and if it's going to be like this the rest of the way, I won't make it."

"What happened?"

"I don't know," I replied, "maybe the cushion got hard."

Robert reached into the cockpit and pressed the air cushion. "No," he said, "it's still inflated."

Then he reached down under the cushion and grabbed something, brought it out of the cockpit hole. He was holding my Canadian airport directory.

"This thing was rolled up under your seat," Robert said.

My face dropped. "You mean I've been sitting on that damn thing for eight hours?" We shared a laugh at this.

At about that time, Steve bolted out of the terminal, a look of shock on his face.

"There's no one here!" he cried. "We've been here for forty-five minutes and there's no one here! This is damn freaky!"

"They're probably just down in town at some event," I chuckled, although I could see that the trip was beginning to take its toll on Steve.

"But everything's open!" Steve continued. "Terminals, shops. There's money's sitting out! Registers are open! It's like the twilight zone! It's like we've flown off the edge of the planet, and nobody's here!"

A large Ford van carrying the National Geographic crew pulled up to the tarmac. They had arrived three hours earlier and had gone to town to rent the van. Steve, still in a state of agitation, went to tell them his first impressions of Churchill.

Several minutes later, my old buddy, Tim Cameron, came onto the scene while we were pushing the planes to the fuel pump. Tim has a way with a joke, and no sooner had we gotten through our handshakes and hugs then he started telling funny stories about me. After some good laughs, he offered to house the Stearman in his new hangar.

"What happened to the other one?" I asked.

"New job," he said, and went on to tell us that Wasaya had lost its contract to deliver to the villages and that he was now working for Keewatin Air. (Churchill is to the Nunavut territory what Pickle Lake is to Ontario. The railroad, which ends in the town, brings goods from the south into Churchill, where they are loaded onto planes and barges and shipped north.)

I asked him what had happened to the forklift that he used to unload cargo. He also used it to get to the lake in bad weather and often took it to his vacation cabin twenty miles south. Tim told me he bought the forklift from Wasaya because they did not want to ship it south. He now was moonlighting with the thing loading other companies' aircraft. The Arctic never changes. I had to laugh.

Same forklift, loading different planes because someone else got the contract to deliver to the villages.

Tim is the only person, aside from myself, who talks about the Stearman as if it is an individual.

"Let's get the old girl in the hangar," Tim said. "Pull her over here. Can we tow her?"

"I don't think so," I answered, "unless you have something to do it with."

"Can you taxi?"

"I doubt it. She's been sitting out here at -15 degrees Fahrenheit without heat. I doubt the engine will start. Only thing we used to heat the engine were some oil dipsticks heaters."

Steve, Robert, and I set out to push the plane across the ice. The Geographic team sat in their van and held the headlights on us as we pushed and fell and slipped around. Had I the choice, I would have stayed in the van too, but Lori and Dwayne's unwillingness to help upset Steve. Annoyed, he approached Lori and asked her why they were not helping us.

"I'm a girl—*I* can't do it," Lori answered using reverse chauvinism.

"What about Dwayne? Why not him?"

"I can't have my cameraman come out there on the ice. If he falls and gets hurt, I don't have a documentary."

"If your principal falls out there and breaks *his* neck, you don't have a documentary, either!"

It was the first time I noticed the discontent growing in the ranks. Their personalities were clashing, but I was not the leader to fix it. I was on my own personal test, and deep down I resented anyone being along with me. I had put the team together, I had planned the logistics of the operation, but I really had not wanted the company. My responsibility was to concentrate on the objective and survival, which meant dealing with the fear, the loneliness, the boredom, and the pain on my own. When I was on the ground I was almost constantly in a state of reflection on what I had just been through and what I had yet to do.

Other than Steve talking to me about how things were going and sharing some of his fears (in that environment his plane was not much safer than mine was), I found their bickering, practical jokes, and schoolyard antics annoying. For the most part I kept my opinions to myself. Lori took the brunt of my annoyance. She had to interface with me. A less-dedicated producer would have left on the next transport going south. I yelled at her, blew her off, and acted like a total ass to her at times. I think it was out of character for me and have since apologized to her for my behavior. I am not sure that she got over the way that I treated her on the trip. I certainly hope she did. But I was alone on my quest, and as the trip progressed the more self-absorbed I became. That was the way it had to be. I do not know if they understood then and hope they understand now.

Steve, Robert, and I pulled the plane on our own into the hangar. Then Steve decided that his plane should also go inside. With the temperature at −20 degrees Fahrenheit and the wind blowing forty miles an hour, toppling us in the gusts, we must have looked like Keystone Kops, slipping and sliding on the ice. We would pull the plane forward a bit, then get blown back farther than we had advanced. When we found good grips on the ice for our feet, we would make it our task to get the plane to those spots, and then we would rest. All together it took about a half-hour to get Steve's plane into the hangar.

Once the planes were under cover, Tim asked me if I wanted to look at "the old girl tonight."

"She's got lots of oil on her," he said.

"Tim, I don't care if the old girl dies tonight. I'm going to get some rest. Let's go down to the Northern Lights. I'm buying."

"Well then, if you're buying. . . ." and off he went to call his wife to tell her that he would not be home until late.

9. Auroras and Revelations

▼

The Northern Lights is the best place in town to eat. During the season, they have a wide selection of foods. Unfortunately, during the off season, which April is, almost nothing on the menu is in stock. "I'd like this meal," customers would say, and the answer would come back, "We have none of that." "How about this one," pointing to a different item. Again, "None." Finally, they would come to the point of asking simply, "What *do* you have?" At that point, the waiter would go over what was available, and the customer would order from that. I had the routine down by the return trip but found it amusing to see my crew go through the drill the way I had the year before. I am not sure why they use a menu during the off season, since they never have more than two items to serve. Perhaps they think a nice restaurant calls for a fancy menu. And the menu certainly is a dandy. The cover has a red cord around the fold, much like the menu of an upscale place down south.

It was good to be back in Churchill. We spent most of the evening at the Northern Lights, catching up on everyone I knew there, and settled into the hotel late. I had been asleep for a while when I heard a knock on my door. It was Lori.

"I want to go out and see the aurora borealis," she said, her voice full of excitement.

I opened the door and looked at her. She has much too much energy, I

149

thought, but did not say. But I could not refuse a request to see one of the great wonders of the world, so I went with her to rouse the rest of the crew. Churchill is the ideal latitude for watching the aurora. To describe the aurora borealis to someone who has not seen it is like trying to describe a rainbow to a person who is colorblind. The light shimmers, sparkles, as muted colors sway and dance before a brilliant star-lit sky. I think of it as an orchestra of electromagnetic forces conducted by a wonderful god. It is absolutely breathtaking.

We loaded into a truck and drove out of town toward the airport. The night sky above us was alight with magnificent green and blue tints. The aurora is hard to capture on film—"God doesn't like to be photographed," said Steve—so not even Dwayne could get any good shots of it. There is an Inuit legend that if you yell or make loud noises at the sky, the aurora will change colors before your eyes. I think it changes anyway, but regardless, when I told the crew the legend they started howling into the dark night like wolves baying at the moon, their faces upturned to the stars. I stood at a distance, watching them. They looked ridiculous, but it was heartwarming to watch as they joined together in the magical moment, howling like the animals we are. There they were, just humans, unshackled from cultural, religious, and social restraints, freed to howl with others like themselves simply for the pure joy of each other's company. They did not notice me as I moved in among them and with them howled at the night sky. That night was the only time on the entire trip that my crew came together and acted as friends do.

The temperature had dropped to −40 degrees Fahrenheit by the time we worked our way back to the hotel. I told the crew if they threw a cup of warm water into the air that it would freeze and with a hissing sound turn to ice before reaching the ground. For about an hour after we returned there was a run on the hotel's hot water as they each gave it at least one shot.

On the days when I did not fly I would sometimes avoid calling Mary. I was afraid she would tell me that she was having a problem she could not solve and that I would then feel guilty and the guilt would affect the trip. Mary knew that and while I was away she did not—not even once—mention any of her problems.

The 1939 Stearman that made the record flight to the North Pole, ready for its final flight to the College Park Aviation Museum in Maryland. The adjacent airfield was used by numerous aviation pioneers, including the Wright Brothers and Hap Arnold.

Bernie Cox, bush pilot, covering the Stearman in Pickle Lake, Ontario, during the test flight.

The Canadian tundra, taken from the Stearman.

My grandmother, Annie E.
Gray, at forty.

My mother, Jonell McLeod, holding me, less
than a year old. Behind us is the Gulf of
Mexico.

Preparing the Stearman for the test flight to the magnetic North Pole.

Inuit friends, Thomas "Studley" Norkitique (on my
left) and Johnny Onosolouk, at Rankin Inlet,
Keewatin district.

Approaching Churchill, Manitoba. Note the cover over the front seat.

Minutes before taking off for the magnetic North Pole.

Rankin Inlet, during one of many test flights. The runway is under the wing, and the hanger area is off the lower wing tip. The frozen Hudson Bay is off the tip of the top wing.

The Stearman's cockpit during reassembly in Louise, Texas, before the extra fuel tank is installed.

Flipped over at Dwight Baughers' orchard in Maryland. Dwight is standing next to me. (Courtesy Dwight Baughers)

Just before takeoff in Louise, Texas, after reassembly.

The McLeods just before I departed for the geographic North Pole (from left: myself, wife Mary, daughter Lara [front], daughter Hera, and son Gustavus).

Me and National Geographic producer Lori Butterfield, College Park, Maryland.

Doug Duff's mother, Henrietta, with the container of her son's ashes.

Doug Duff next to the plane he flew in the fatal crash, and in which we flew together to Olean, New York. (Courtesy Henrietta Duff)

The specially designed suit for the geographic pole attempt.

Robert Thommesen (left) and Steve Pearce, in Steve's Cessna 182 over Elliott Lake, Ontario. (Courtesy Robert Thommesen)

Tundra south of Churchill, Manitoba, taken out the window of Steve Pearce's Cessna (Courtesy Robert Thommesen)

Flying 500 feet over a glacier. (Courtesy Robert Thommesen)

Takeoff from Weather Station Eureka, Canada, for the North Pole. Note the trailing antenna. (Courtesy Robert Thommesen)

Support team waiting for me at a fuel cache on the way to the North Pole. (Courtesy Robert Thommesen)

Thirty-six miles from the North Pole. (Courtesy Robert Thommesen)

Iceberg near Weather Station Eureka, Canada.

The Stearman three weeks after being abandoned on the ice cap — it had moved about 80 miles.

Repairing the Stearman on the ice. Don Sanders looking down, Shane with his hand on a carburetor, and a First Air pilot advising.

Landing at Canadian Forces Station Alert, after rescuing the Stearman.

Thirty minutes before the Stearman was disassembled for shipment south.

Loading the disassembled Stearman into a U.S. Navy C-130 Hercules at McGuire Air Force Base, New Jersey, for transport to Washington, D.C. Cathy Allen, director of the College Park Aviation Museum, is standing to the left and Tom Allison, director of the Smithsonian Institution Paul E. Garber Preservation, Restoration, and Storage Facility, is in a white shirt.

The unveiling of the Stearman during dedication ceremonies at the College Park Aviation Museum in Maryland, April 17, 2001.

While the crew played, I called Mary to see how things were going. She asked me why I didn't call more often. I told her that there was not much to report on days that I do not fly. Even before the sentence was out of my mouth I felt ashamed. Mary did not respond. She did not need to.

"I'm sorry, I'll call more often."

"You don't have to if you don't want."

I did want to, and there was no question that I should, but would I? That question would be answered on the journey north because it was tied to a larger question I had to find answers for.

"The aurora is beautiful tonight," I said, trying to change the subject.

"Is it better than when we were in Pickle Lake last summer?"

The summer before Mary and I had taken a trip to Pickle Lake without the children. Bernie Cox dropped us off in the bush for six wonderful days of hiking and camping. Each night before we went to sleep, we would go out on the rocks and sit in silence watching the Northern Lights.

"No comparison at all, it's ten times better."

Mary kept a large map of Canada on the wall beside her desk. Every night she marked my travels. She had also kept the map during the flight the year before. When I returned from that flight I saw it for the first time. I could see the notes she had made and the notations recording the time I arrived and departed each place. I could see that the farther north I journeyed, the heavier her handwriting cut into the paper. She had worried; the trail was obvious. My heart sank when I saw it. It affected me so that I could not talk to her about it. I even avoided going into her office so I would not have to look at it. Two days before I left for the return to the pole, I went by her office at night when no one was there and stood for a long time looking at that map. I did it to remind myself that my life matters. That night in Churchill I remembered the map and vowed to call Mary every night from then on. It was a promise I kept.

That same night, Robert and I decided to try out the polar suits Northern Outfitters had made for us. The team's suits were the same as mine in all respects except one—mine had more layers. It was midnight when I walked out onto the frozen Hudson Bay in the many-layered gear. To test the integrity of the suits we found an iceberg and laid down on it. Every five minutes, without fail, I saw a shooting star streak across the sky, coming from the west and trailing off in the east. I was confused until I figured out that the objects were not shooting stars but communication satellites orbiting overhead. Robert and I talked for a while, about the trip and the dangers ahead of us. The conversation and the fresh air must have lulled us because we both fell asleep and did not wake up until 3:00 A.M. It certainly spoke well for the suits that we could fall asleep for two hours with the temperature at −40 degrees Fahrenheit. And even after a hike back to the hotel we still felt warm. I hoped I would feel as warm in the cockpit with the Arctic wind blowing.

The next day, Tim, Steve, Robert, and I took a jaunt to the airport to check out the Stearman. Something had definitely gone wrong on the flight from Pickle Lake. Oil, smeared by the wind, had stained the entire side of the plane. It was so bad that the Stearman looked as if it had originally been painted black instead of blue. Oil leaked from every seal in the plane and ran in streaks down the side of the fuselage. As soon as I saw it I remembered the quick temperature change in the middle of the blizzard on the way from Pickle Lake and realized the gaskets must have blown when the temperature dropped.

I had not brought any backups because the gaskets had not failed on the test flight. It was shortsighted because I knew I would run into colder temperatures and bigger temperature swings than I had encountered on the test flight. I had expected the pole flight to be tougher on the aircraft but was unable to anticipate which parts would fail. The perfect solution would have been to crate a complete Stearman and bring it north with me, but that was never an option because I could not afford it. I took along extras of only those parts I believed to be the most likely to fail—fuel primer lines, brake, fuel, and oil lines. To that I added duct tape, minimum tools, and a dry de-oiled tachometer. The total weight of spare parts and tools stuffed into Steve's 182 was ten pounds.

I checked around the region but could not locate any gaskets. So I got on the phone to Dusters and Sprayers Airplane Parts in Chickasha, Oklahoma, and placed an order to have the seals Federal Expressed to Winnipeg, where Kee-watin Air would pick them up and bring them to Churchill on one of their daily flights. Then I went back to continue checking out the airplane. Most of the oil caked on the side of the plane had come from the oil pump gasket. I had en-countered that problem before—Stearmans are notorious for blowing oil pump gaskets—and kicked myself again for not having planned for it. Since we could not do a thing about the leaks, Tim and I tightened the gaskets around the push rod tubes and valve covers. One particular gasket on the valve cover had leaked especially badly. With a wrench we cranked it to the point we thought the gasket might break and let it go at that. With the leaks slowed, I fired up the plane and it held.

The pressure on the oil pump was a little too high to use a paper seal and we decided to wait for the replacements before pressing on. I was not bothered by the delay because my legs had not recovered from the lashing they got from the cold on the flight in. We were two days ahead of schedule and the thought of spending a few more days in town appealed to me. I needed the rest and looked forward to spending some downtime with Tim, with whom I always found something fun to do.

But after two days of rest and relaxation, my legs were still numb and the gaskets had not arrived. I was growing restless, and concerned that if we spent much more time on the ground the weather would take a turn for the worse, throwing the trip dangerously off schedule. When, on the fourth day, the gas-kets had still not arrived, I decided to take my chances and leave the next day, which was April 13. On the twelfth, Tim and I retightened the gaskets as best we could. Our efforts paid off in spades. They still leaked a bit, but far less than they had.

Once I was satisfied that we had done all we possibly could to shore up the leaks, I prepared to take a few test flights out over the bay to make sure the gas-kets would hold. Lori took advantage of the tests to get some footage of the ice pack from different angles. She had four "lipstick cameras" rigged to the Stear-man: one mounted on the outer port strut and aimed at my side view; one on the starboard inboard strut aimed over my head toward the rear of the plane;

another on the port side under the tail looking forward; and another on the instrument panel aimed directly at me. I do not know why they are called "lipstick cameras," except that they are shaped like a tube of lipstick, only three times the size. The cameras remained on the plane in the same positions for the entire expedition. One video unit, consisting of a camera recorder and battery that could handle only one camera at a time, was positioned between my legs in a backpack attached to the straps that held the 100-gallon fuel tank in place — it never got in my way. Since I could not shut off one camera to activate another in flight, four flights were needed to get footage from each camera. The drill that day was the same as other days. Dwayne, under Lori's supervision, activated one camera by wiring it to the video unit, and I winged out over the bay. When I was ready, I returned to the airport where Lori detached the hook-up on the activated camera and attached it to another camera. Then I took off again for the bay. It was a routine I repeated as many times as necessary.

On one of the flights over the bay, I spotted several walruses sunning on the ice floes. Because my Inuit friends had nicknamed me Dancing Walrus, I felt a warm sense of happiness when I spotted them playing around on the ice. It was an omen of good luck, and on the spot I decided to leave Churchill the next morning.

On the final flight for shots of the bay, I noticed that the open water leads were beginning to freeze shut. Leads are breaks in the ice that result from opposing forces within the ice. They are the opposite of a pressure ridge, which is caused by ice floes colliding. When the leads freeze over they create a flat, smooth, thick, and hard area that makes a good runway. One by one the walruses were sliding from the ice and into the water, until only one large walrus remained on the pack.

"That's the one. That's my man — the dancing walrus!"

By the time we were ready to leave Churchill, each team member had settled into their particular roles. Dwayne was the practical joker of the group. Some of his pranks were funny, but most were a pain in the butt. He was like a sixth grader on a field trip. Except when the camera was running. Behind the camera he had the intensity of a chess master. The rest of the time he was either playing a joke, thinking of how to pull one off, or reveling in one he had just executed. Steve hated the jokes even more than I did. I mostly tried to ignore them. Robert, who always rode with Steve, had become Dwayne's sidekick and audience. No subject was too trivial or sacred for Dwayne's sense of humor. His particular specialty was playing a joke on someone without the victim ever knowing they were the butt of the joke. No one was safe, especially anyone who thought they knew something about cameras or who was in awe of the National Geographic film crew. But when it came to filming, the man transformed into the model of professionalism and courtesy. Dwayne played his Dr. Jekyll and Mr. Hyde role the whole trip, always with Robert in tow.

Lori was the prima donna of the group. She played the crowd like a southern politician two days before election. She shook every hand, kissed every baby, and let no potential story go uninvestigated. On the days that we did not travel, Lori's energy level outdistanced the rest of the group by a factor of three. By the third day in Churchill, she was on first name basis with most of the villagers. By the time we left Churchill she could have run for mayor and won. The woman is a phenomenon. Steve thought she was a flirt. The two were like oil and vinegar. They were in constant battle, with Dwayne and Robert egging them on.

Robert played the part of mechanic better than I thought he would. Whenever the Stearman needed something tightened or loosened, Robert was there. Every night when we checked the Stearman to make certain the oil dipstick heaters were plugged in correctly and working, Robert was on it. If the wings had frost on them in the morning, Robert had it off before I could put on the second layer of my six-layer suit. If something needed attention on the aircraft, Robert usually spotted it before I did. He helped me strap in before I took off and was there to help get me out when I landed. On more than one occasion, Robert pulled me from the Stearman either too frozen to move, too delirious to know were I was, or too stiff to stand up. He was the one who duct-taped my suit to keep out the cold air on every flight. He was the one who put duct tape between the cowling and the winter front to keep the right amount of airflow over the engine. At every stop he and I would scrounge around for oil for the Stearman. What he did not know about airplanes he more than made up for with his knowledge about mechanical systems. And he developed a tolerance for the cold second only to mine. While on the ground, both Robert and I went around with open jackets or no jacket at all. I told him this was because he usually stood on the wing next to the cockpit to help me get strapped in while the engine was warming up. With my full gear on I could not see the seat belt let alone fasten it. After experiencing the blast of Arctic air pushed by the Stearman's prop, nothing else seemed cold. When it came to me and to the Stearman, Robert was a man on a mission. In their professionalism, Robert and Dwayne were a lot alike. In the off time, they were much alike too.

From the start, Steve established himself as my personal manager. He checked on my condition before I flew and after I landed. He kept a notebook in his pocket with every bit of information he thought might be helpful. If reporters were trying to bother me, Steve ran interference. If I was supposed to get back to someone, Steve reminded me. Before we would leave on a flight Steve made a note of the path I would take, the time I should arrive, and the approximate time his plane would pass mine so we could communicate. Because I had to wear four sets of mitts I could not hold a chart, so every night before a flight Steve made sure I reviewed the chart and memorized it. He filed all the flight plans and gave me weather briefings. Although Steve's craft is instrument rated, he always filed visual flight plans. In the far north there is no radar for traffic avoidance and no controller to talk to. That far north, it is not who is in the tower but what equipment and who is in the plane that counts. Either way you file, you are on your own.

The flight plans included closure times, which means that if any of us did not arrive at the destination by the closure time the Canadians would look for us at our expense. Until Resolute, that is. After Resolute no one would come looking. We would be on our own. Steve posted all the close times and kept me informed. Steve and I formed a real bond. More than anyone else on the trip he understood what I was going through. He loved to say that if the others, especially Robert, knew the amount of danger we are in "they wouldn't be so damned happy all the time." Steve was under a great deal of stress. He was a relatively inexperienced pilot for the kind of flying we were doing, and his plane was not much better off in these conditions than mine. He liked to say that the only difference between his 182 and the Stearman was a little speed and heat. In truth, that was about it. He had taken on a lot for me and I was relieved that he was flying his plane only as far as Resolute and from there would ride to the pole with the rest of the crew in the First Air chase plane.

At the hotel the night before, we had looked over the charts for the next day's flight. I was concerned when I realized the route would take me across the same part of the bay that had nearly killed me the year before. The next morning, the oil still leaked a bit, but I thought the patch job would get me through to Resolute, 800 miles and two layovers from Churchill. Our first stop would be Rankin Inlet, 252 miles north, where we would spend the night. If the gasket blew on route it would not leak any more than two or three quarts an hour. The plane might be messy, but I was sure I could make it with a loss of a gallon or so.

Lori and Dwayne chartered a plane for the next day from Keewatin Air to take them to Churchill, followed by a brief stop to meet us in Taloyoak, and then to Resolute. That was a piece of good luck because before I departed I made a deal with Tim to send the gaskets with Lori. As usual, I took off ahead of Steve, who got into the air about forty-five minutes after and arrived in Rankin Inlet forty-five minutes before me.

Rankin Inlet was not a particularly great place to stay, but after the Pickle Lake to Churchill flight I had no intention of doing any longer than 400 miles a stretch. No more, that is, until the last day when I would attempt to reach the pole. I needed to give my body time to recover from the pounding it had taken and prepare for the one it would take.

Churchill sits on the southern coast of Hudson Bay; Rankin Inlet is on the northern coast. The shortest route from Churchill to Rankin Inlet goes out over the bay, about thirty miles offshore. The safer way hugs the shoreline but adds fifty to sixty miles to the trip. Though the Canadian government frowns on flying over the bay in a single engine plane, most pilots do it to save time. Steve told me even he would fly over the bay if it looked solid enough.

"After the flight from Pickle Lake to Churchill," he confided, "nothing can intimidate me. That was probably the single scariest flight of my life. I'm going to fly over the bay."

I agreed that the bay is solid this time of year and with bravado said, "Let's do it."

I flew about ten miles out over the bay before my nerves got the best of me and I turned and headed straight for the shore. I could not stay out there. The bay looked perfectly frozen, but the more I surveyed it, the more I thought about how much it looked like it had the year before. That was not a place I wanted to go back to.

My detour put Steve and me on different routes. The closest we would get to each other's path was thirty miles, too far for me even to hear, much less talk, to him.

Steve and I usually touched base as we passed each other. The anticipation of the contact kept boredom at bay. And it was pleasant to have someone to check in with. That day contact was not possible.

During the long flight, I thought about old pilot stories I had heard. One story in particular always gave me a laugh.

It happened on a ferrying flight to deliver a new airplane to a customer living in the north. Worn down by the long hours on the flight, an old ferry-pilot decided to stop for a rest along the way. He landed at an airport on the route and went into the terminal to take a much-needed nap. A raspberry pie was sitting on a counter near the entrance.

"Damn," the old man said. "I sure would like a piece of that pie." He reached into his pockets and came up with only a nickel.

"How much of that pie will you give me for a nickel?" he asked the person behind the counter.

"Tell you what," the attendant said, a devilish smile lighting up his face. "I'll give you the whole thing, if you do something for me."

"What's that?"

"Take this damn cat with you when you go," he said, pointing to a black and white spotted cat languishing, its eyes half-closed, on the counter beside the pie.

"It's been around here all damn day, and I can't seem to get rid of it."

"You got yourself a deal," the old pilot said with enthusiasm.

After a quick rest and stretch of his legs, the old ferry-pilot grabbed his newly earned pie, collected the sleepy cat, and hopped back into his airplane. He put the pie on the seat beside him and placed the cat into the backseat, where it curled up and promptly fell asleep. Everything seemed fine and dandy.

But almost as soon as the plane left the ground, the cat leaped up out of its seat, hit the ceiling of the plane, and landed on top of the pilot's head, its claws digging into the old man's face.

"Ouch! Damn it!" he cried as he grabbed at the panicked cat and at the same time struggled to keep the plane steady. Finally getting hold of the cat, he tossed it over to the seat beside him, where it landed directly on the pie, splashing raspberry all over the seat. The cat then jumped back into the air and returned to the pilot's head, digging in its claws.

"You little bastard!" the man yelped, struggling to grab the cat. He gained hold of it with one hand and with his free hand went for the window and opened it. With the window open, he brought the cat toward it and tried to throw it out. When it did not work, he tried again. Each time he tried, the cat would claw back up his arm and onto his head. Blood leaked from the claw wounds on the man's arm and on his face while the frantic cat tracked raspberry all over the new plane. The old-timer tried to keep the airplane steady and on course all the while fighting the cat.

When the pilot finally arrived at his destination and the wheels touched down, the cat calmly curled up in the backseat and fell asleep.

"Well, I'll be damned," the old pilot said. "The bastard was scared of flying."

As he taxied in he could see the plane's owner waiting in anticipation. When he stopped the plane and opened the door, the cat awoke, stretched, and blithely jumped to the ground and walked away. The plane's new owner looked merely puzzled at the sight of the cat. But his jaw dropped when the weary pilot, covered with blood and raspberry pie, climbed out. And when he saw the mess inside his new plane he looked almost apoplectic, at which point the old ferry-pilot spoke. "I suppose a tip would be too much to ask for?"

"You're damn right about that!" the owner shouted heatedly. "Why, I ought to make you pay for the damage to the plane!"

And later that day when the poor old ferry-pilot headed for home he had nothing to show for the trip but some claw scars on his face and a nickel less in his perfectly empty pocket. I like that story. It always makes me grin.

By the time I reached Rankin Inlet, Steve had settled in and had even made a few friends. Instead of my usual forty-five-minute-late arrival, the detour had taken an hour and a half. When I saw Steve, I could tell he was worried.

"What happened? Why did it take you so long? Where did you go?"

"I lost my nerve and went along the shore," I confessed.

"What if you'd gone down? How would we have known where to look for you?" He was right. I apologized for making everyone worry and promised it would not happen again.

Steve, Robert, and I spent the rest of that day in Rankin Inlet looking for my old Inuit buddies Johnny and Studly. Everyone still called Thomas "Studly"—it may stick with him for the rest of his life. When I caught up with him I was happy to hear that he had solved his women problems. I found Johnny later that evening, and, after visiting friends all over the small town, we stopped for dinner at what I know is the worst restaurant in the Arctic.

When I called Mary that night she was surprised I had left Churchill without the gaskets.

"It was time to move on. We fixed most of the leaks. The others we can get in Resolute."

We talked for a long time and about many things, and I could tell from her voice that the talk was doing some good. It helped me too, but I was still too self-absorbed.

Steve and Robert, who had been sharing rooms to save money, each complained that the other snored.

"It's not me," said Steve emphatically. "I've had my head fixed for that."

"Then the operation didn't work," countered Robert.

That night I offered to room with one of them to give the other a break. I drew Steve. I have always been a light sleeper and that night got only an hour of sleep. The next morning I told Robert that he was right about Steve's snoring. I also told him that he would have to take him back as a roommate because I needed my sleep more than he did.

When we arrived at the airport the next morning a group of Inuit friends had gathered to see me off. For some farewell fun I got on the satellite phone and called an "oldies" radio station back in Washington and had the Inuit group sing the "Oldies 100" jingle in Inuktitute. They could have been singing *Parsifal* for all we knew. It was a good way to say goodbye.

The ground along the entire 440-mile stretch from Rankin Inlet to Resolute is barren endless tundra, sweeping in all directions. On the same route the year before, I had seen a herd of caribou. I hoped to spot the herd again. But as the hours passed I knew that there would be nothing that day to look into but the emptiness—an eerie white rough-ridged expanse as desolate as the Martian landscape—all the way to Resolute.

The cold, snow, ice, and the constant vibration of the plane soon got to me. It was on the long flights that I suffered most and not always in silence. But that day was different than the others. The scenery occupied my mind for a while. The year before I had been fascinated by the landscape. From the safety of the heights, it had allowed me to observe its terrible isolation and impassiveness without dread. But on the return trip, its intransigence mocked me and soon ceased to distract—to comfort—me. I was edgy and could not get to the root of my discontent. I began to sing to myself. But with the cockpit open, the Stearman runs so loud that I could only feel the vibration of the singing in my head, not actually hear it. On the test flight, I had been able to hear myself sing into the radio mike because I usually flew with the canopy on. Without the canopy the mike froze from my breath eight or nine words into the song.

It was then that the demons began to surface. They climbed slowly, ungainly at first, out of that place named by the poet, William Butler Yeats, as "the foul rag-and-bone shop." Their questions begin innocently enough, almost teasingly—

What are you doing out there all alone? Are you suicidal or just living the dream, old boy? At first, I brushed them off with ease. They were questions I had heard before and had already answered sufficiently, if glibly, I thought. All I had ever wanted to be was an airplane pilot, and that was what this adventure was all about. End of discussion.

But like gnats in the hot sun I could not turn them from their purpose. Suddenly there was no order to the questions and no breaks between them. You are being tested, an inner voice warned. But this is not a test of skill, but of will. It is not a test of knowledge, but of insight. I was cold, lonely, and perhaps almost delirious. I could have cared less about being tested. No, that is not true. It was not that I did not care about the test, it was that I was angry that I felt the *need* to be tested. "Who am I?" I shouted into the emptiness. "Who the hell am I?" I am an American of mixed heritage. That sounded good, but it was not accurate. I was born colored. But what was I now? Black? No, they have changed that too. Oh yes, now I remember. I am an African American. "What does that make *me*?" I could hear the booming voice of my grandfather McLeod. "*I'm* not African either," my grandmother shouted from the backrooms of my mind. "Hang around them long enough they'll call you one," I heard myself say back, mimicking her warning from my childhood. That was laughable. If they had not labeled her as "colored" she would have been shipped back to the reservation to starve to death like a good little Indian. "Hey guys," I shouted, "it's not *you* they're calling African American, it's *me*."

When I was a younger man I told my granddad that I would not go to Scotland because I was afraid that the Scots would not like me. He looked at me sternly and said, "Whatever I am, you are. It's not for them to like you. It's for you to like yourself."

"Well, who *are* you?" pounded that inner voice. I was getting a headache, the kind I got as a kid when I tried to contemplate the meaning of the universe and existence itself only to hit the wall of eternity, a wall that could not be breached and against which all my ideas crashed in on themselves. I was enraged that I could not break out of the tightening circle of thought. But somehow I knew this time I had to think it through. I am not Choctaw, not Scottish, not African.

I am sick of being called some kind of American. I am an American, pure and simple. And I refuse to continue playing a game in which others define me, a game where everything that is won also gets lost in guilt. I want to move my arms and legs. I want to stand up. I am thirsty. "It does not matter what you want," I heard the demon say. "You are four hours from anywhere but death. It's your choice."

As I look back on it, I understand that in those terrible hours of truth I performed my test. My grandmother often talked to me about a warrior's hard journey to a spiritual place somewhere between now and eternity and of the battle the brave fought to earn the right to dance with the sun. All along I had thought that I would earn that right when I reached the pole. But as fate would have it, I experienced my revelation on the desolate plain between Churchill and Resolute. After that flight, the kind of peace that comes with clarity settled over me. And in the hard days ahead, as I continued ever onward toward the pole, that peace did not abandon me.

10. Sun Dogs and Resolutions

▼

It is unusual for a town with a population of 180 to have an airport with a small terminal manned by a weatherman. Taloyoak, our only scheduled stop between Rankin Inlet and Resolute, is such a town.

Steve, Robert, and I left Churchill for Rankin Inlet, where we spent the night. The next morning we got a good start for Taloyoak. Lori and Dwayne, not wanting a stopover, took a charter out of Churchill the following day with plans to meet up with us in Taloyoak, stopping there only long enough to film my landing before getting back on the charter and heading on to Resolute. The team, as expected, arrived in Taloyoak well before me.

It was 9:30 at night when I touched down, but the sun was still shining, like mid-afternoon in Maryland during the late spring. In short order, we secured a place to stay at the only resting spot in Taloyoak, a bed and breakfast owned by the mayor, Dennis Lyles. I had met Dennis the year before and was glad to see him at the airport to welcome me back. Almost nothing had changed in Taloyoak since my last visit.

Once out of the plane, I immediately set off to check the weather and was given the discouraging news that a bout of bad weather was expected within hours.

"What about Resolute?" I asked. "What are the skies like there?"

"Clear. If you leave now you might be able to make it. But if you stay here, you'll be stuck here for two days."

I had just flown four and one-half hours, and Resolute was still 318 miles into the next morning. But I could not stay in Taloyoak for two days and keep to the schedule. I had to be in Resolute by the fifteenth and that was all there was to that. I briefed Steve on the situation and told him to get ready to fly. If we were to leave soon, we could expect to arrive in Resolute by two in the morning. The sun would set there in about four hours, around 1:30 A.M.; it would be dusk when we arrived. We were above the Arctic Circle now. The days would get longer the farther north we traveled. By the time we reached Eureka the sun would not set at all.

The mayor and I got reacquainted while Noah Nashaooraitoot, owner of the only taxi in town, took Steve to search for gas cans to fill up at Mayor Lyles's station. The town was too small and the roads too few for a thriving taxi business, unless, like the folks in Churchill, the citizens of Taloyoak preferred to drive everywhere. Steve and Noah found ten five-gallon cans and made two trips to ferry back the auto gas. I took sixty-five gallons. With the fifty I still had, I would have enough to get from Taloyoak to Resolute and back if I had to. Steve took thirty gallons and donated the leftover five to Noah. If all went well I would end up flying 700 miles that day—not a deal breaker, as Lori would say, but a long, long day.

One hundred miles north of Taloyoak, I crossed thirty miles east of the spot where I had circled over the magnetic North Pole the year before. It was a big deal for me to see it again. The truth is I had not really expected to make it back—so much was against me—but there I was, an hour and a half out of Taloyoak, heading farther north than I had ever been. From that point on I would be plowing new ground.

Another fifty miles north the scenery began to change. The mountains were no longer smooth. Instead they were a jagged range that at its height pierced the sky and then plunged deep into great crevasses that opened to expose snow-covered valleys beneath—a scene made more dramatic by giant shadows that threw a dappled darkness onto the mysterious valleys below. On top of one of the crags, I could see a small herd of bison—the calves in the middle, the adults in a circle surrounding them. They appeared to be defending themselves from some perceived danger, and I soon realized they were anticipating an attack by the great Stearman bird.

The valleys north of Taloyoak are astonishingly beautiful and held my attention until the torture of the unrelenting wind got to me. I was so cold and so weary from the day's struggle. All I desired was to get to Resolute where I knew there would be a warm bed, a big glass of water, and food waiting. I was very thirsty. My mouth felt dry and thick, as though it was lined with cotton. On long trips, pilots usually do not drink enough water because they do not want to stop. Where I was, there was no question of stopping. I expected at least a two-day wait in Resolute before First Air would be ready for the final leg of the trip. I was looking forward to the hiatus. I needed the time to rest. The long days of flight were taking their toll on me. Earlier in the trip I felt the cold more than the pain. But as the days passed the pain got to me long before the cold. My body was stiff from the hours of immobility, and I was never free of a gnawing pain in my joints. My tongue was swollen from the dryness of the air. I did not carry water with me because I had no way to keep it from freezing. I also did not drink or eat anything before a flight because I had no way to relieve myself—if I wet my suit in those temperatures it could mean my death. I had tried a catheter on the test flight but it had frozen. I had to get to Resolute to rest. Warm, hydrated, and full, I would tell the team to leave me alone and let me sleep for two days. If I could just get to Resolute I would be fine.

As evening approached, I could see Resolute Bay in the distance. It resembles Hudson Bay, some 800 miles to the south. I neared the town of Resolute as the sun was setting and the twilight was gleaming in the sky. The GPS showed the airport to be situated on the end of an island. Technology is wonderful, I thought. It is −37 degrees Fahrenheit, and the GPS is still ticking. On last year's trip, the GPS had frozen at 14. That is progress. Ten miles out, I radioed in.

"Resolute radio, this is 8 November Papa. I'm coming in. Could you turn up your runway lights, please? I've never been here before, so I'm going to need help locating you."

In short order, I spotted a dirt runway to my left, 5,000 feet long, lit up, like a city skyline, with the best approach lights I had ever seen. When the Stearman's wheels touched down, the dirt was so compact that it felt like the plane was riding on glass. I taxied to the terminal where Steve, Robert, Lori, and a woman I did not know were waiting for me. It was April 15, one o'clock in the morning.

She introduced herself as Terry and told us she would take us to our hotel. She cast a look of disbelief first at the Stearman and then at me, and said, "The silly season is getting odder and odder." In the Arctic, April through May is known as the "silly season," because they are the months when polar attempts are made. Silly maybe, but on the drive to the hotel we so impressed Terry with our story that she gave us free use of one of her cars during our stay.

Terry drove eighty all the way from the airport to the hotel. It is unusual in the Arctic to drive over sixty miles an hour because the roads are never much more than a mile long, which may account for the absence of speed-patrols in the Arctic. But Resolute is ten miles from the airport, so it is easy to get up a good head of steam before reaching town. At one time the town and the airport were closer, but the town was moved because it was thought to be dangerously near to the bay.

Terry is an Arctic legend in her own right. She and her husband had owned the hotel where most pole explorers stay. She sold the hotel after her husband died but still runs it for the new owners and continues on as the person to see in Resolute when planning a trip to the pole.

The hotel was a cut above most of the places we had stayed. The rooms are regular hotel size—not small, like most hotel rooms in the Arctic villages—and the furnishings were relatively new. Even the food was good, and there was an unexpected variety. When we arrived at the hotel I was told that I would have to share a room. I knew I would not be able to handle Steve's snoring, so I chose to bunk with Robert. Within minutes of turning out the lights, I understood why Steve and Robert had found it so difficult to room together. Robert snored even louder and longer than Steve did. The next morning when I asked about the possibility of an additional room opening up, I was told that all the rooms were spoken for by other teams making attempts at the pole.

Resolute itself, with its year-round population of 160, in most ways is a typical Arctic town. But during the "silly season," Resolute is how I picture an Everest base camp to be. The hotel was loaded with adventurous types with enough testosterone to melt the island—spirited and rugged people of different nationalities decked out in their high-tech gear followed around by television cameras. It was exciting. A team of Japanese was there to ski to the magnetic pole. A Norwegian team planned to walk to the geographic pole; and another group was there to organize the rescue of a team whose dogsled had broken through the ice on the Arctic Ocean. The Japanese team looked like an army, dressed alike in the best North Face outfits money could by. They not only looked like a team they behaved like one. They did everything together, even came to meals as a team. I thought they were marvelous. And they made me realize just how laid back and disconnected my team was.

Whenever we arrived in a new town or village, Robert, Lori, and I would always check out the nightlife. Steve might join us if the local culture was promising, but Dwayne usually passed unless there was something to drink or Lori wanted him to film. Invariably, Lori would manage to find someone in the dry towns to sell or give her booze—she would not tell me who. I thought I was a seasoned traveler. But Lori is a pro. She can get her hands on anything worth finding no matter if it is in town, out of town, or somewhere in between. If I ever get booked in hell, I am taking her with me to negotiate with the devil.

In short order, Dwayne and Robert found kindred spirits at the hotel. They and the ladies they met played endless practical jokes, keeping the cooks and assistant manager in stitches. Dwayne's favorite prank (and evidently everyone's favorite judging from the laughter that followed) was to put two apples under his shirt, making him look like he had breasts. He would then put on his coat, further concealing the wayward apples, pick up his camera and go about his work. After some fancy camera work, he would feign fatigue, stretching his arms wide as he let out a big yawn. Whereupon the coat would open and the unexpected apples would tumble to the floor. The prank always elicited shocked silence followed by gales of laughter. After the performance he would close his coat as if nothing happened and walk off, with Robert at his heels. Once they were out of sight, Robert would genuflect in front of Dwayne saying, "You're the master, Obie Wan. I am unworthy."

The evening after we arrived in Resolute, I borrowed the car Terry had offered us and drove the team to the airport for a briefing with representatives of First Air. It was the first time I had driven a vehicle above the Arctic Circle. I gunned the engine and, like Terry, took off down the road at about eighty miles an hour.

First Air is a Canadian Airline company with regular flights throughout Canada and the north. They have a base in Resolute that runs ski-equipped Twin Otters to remote bases throughout the region. In the spring they run rich tourists and various expeditions to the pole. I had hired them to carry the team for the final push from Resolute to the pole.

The plan was for Steve to leave his 182 in Resolute and pick it up on the way back. Before we left for the First Air briefing Steve came to me and, with a sullen but resigned look on his face, offered to forgo going to the pole if the Otter could not handle the extra weight of an additional passenger.

"If you don't get on that plane, nobody gets on it," I told him. Throughout the trip Steve always kept his eye on the tiger and his ego in check. I am grateful to him for that.

As we walked into the First Air hangar, I noticed a large black chalkboard hanging from the wall. On it was an up-to-date list of the teams on route to or being rescued from the pole. From the list it looked like they could handle two plane-loads a day if the weather allowed. The weather was everything. I figured that we would be told either that the window over the Arctic had closed up and that we were too late for a push this season, or that we should go back to town and rest up for a flight out in a couple of days. I did not think we were too late so I anticipated a few more days of rest before the big push.

The First Air crew was waiting for us. The captain of the Twin Otter, Poul, had come to Canada twenty-five years before, gotten a job with First Air, and has been a bush pilot for them ever since. He had spent many hours in the air, most of them in the Arctic. I would come to rely on his word as law. Kevin, the copilot, was a laid-off First Air pilot who had come north on a transfer. He had been flying on the ice for only a few months. Steve told me later that Kevin was more apprehensive than Poul in the cockpit. Poul was as comfortable there as he would have been on his sofa at home.

The plan was simple. We would fly from Resolute to Eureka, spend one night at the Canadian weather station, then push on to the pole, and head back as quickly as possible.

After a quick introduction, Poul informed us that the weather over the pole was −20 degrees Fahrenheit, the wind calm and the sky clear—a perfect window.

"Get your team ready. We've scheduled you to leave tomorrow morning. The weather's not going to get any better than this—no clouds, no wind—just cold."

I was stunned, unable to reply. I was not ready to go, mentally or physically. Not only did I need time to prepare myself for the flight, but time was also needed to prepare the Stearman. I tried to come up with a viable reason for staying put for a few days, but all I could think to ask was if it would be warmer in a few days.

He shrugged. "It might, but the weather could also get worse."

That hit me with the force of a tank. I needed more time. Now, I would have only one day of rest.

"Okay, then, we leave for the pole tomorrow," I said. The words echoed through my mind long after I spoke them.

At the close of the meeting, Kevin advised us that we would have to be back to Eureka within sixteen hours of our departure, explaining that if they stayed out any longer the Canadian government would write them up for breaking their duty day.

"If we get written up we'll be fined, and if we are written up too often we can lose our job."

I informed him that I did not think I could make it to the pole and back in that time.

"If you go over sixteen hours, we'll have to go on back without you."

He said it with so little emotion that I was sure I was not the first person to hear his warning. And then, he dropped another bomb. Kevin Williamson, a Transport Canada inspector, would be coming along as an observer.

Poul did not show any concern about the inspector. Poul was never going to be a jet-jockey. He was just a bush pilot, and no one in their right mind would fire a good bush pilot for getting written up. Bush piloting is about skill not about paperwork.

How many more times would I have to hear that tomorrow was the departure date? My apprehension was already cracking the thermometer. Even though the hangar was chilly, I broke out in a cold sweat. My blood temperature must have dropped three degrees. I felt clammy. Real fear took hold of me. The type that silently burrows its way into your belly and makes you feel you will puke your insides out if you do not get some air soon. The trip from Rankin Inlet to Resolute was the longest day I had spent in the air. I was drained, almost beyond the will to continue. While the trip from Pickle Lake to Churchill, when I lost feeling in my legs, had been physically the hardest day, I could see a longer, harder trip ahead. The trip from Eureka to the pole and back would take twenty-five hours, with fourteen of those hours in the air. The temperature would be −40 degrees Fahrenheit if I was lucky. I did not know if or how I could do it, but I tried not to show my fear and anxiety to the crew.

"I guess we're ready to go," I said, not too convincingly.

At the end of the briefing, someone handed me a small package—the oil gasket. I had gotten used to the leaks and dirtiness of the plane and had forgotten all about it. The gasket put another wrinkle in the schedule—how would I have time to replace it and still get some sleep? That was when one of the First Air mechanics, Peter Karttunen, came to the rescue. Peter told me that he had learned on radial engines as a kid and "would love to work on one again." I was concentrating so hard on the task ahead that I hardly acknowledged the help he was offering. By putting that oil pump gasket on correctly he may have saved my life. I did not thank him then but, Peter Karttunen, wherever you are, I thank you now.

At that moment, Robert stepped up and offered to help Peter install the part. "All right," I said, "then you can bunk with Steve—I need rest."

When he returned to the hotel late that night Robert slept on a couch in the hall. I still feel badly about that, but I would not have been able to sleep with him in my room.

In an interview with Lori later that same day, I admitted that I was afraid. It was the first time I had said it out loud. She did not take me seriously when I claimed to be "scared sick," but I really felt that way. From the beginning of the trip, I had daily interviews with Lori. Most of them were pretty mundane, so dull that I do not remember any specifically. But I do remember that one in Resolute.

When I woke the next morning it was perfectly beautiful outside. Sunlight flooding through a light ice fog had caused a phenomenon that made the sun appear as though it was encircled by golden rings of pixie dust. The Inuit call the phenomenon "sun dogs." (I don't know why, though; no one ever told us.) It was mesmerizing, and all of us who watched were transfixed with joy. We even made jokes, like "Beam me up, Scotty." Although it could not completely relieve my fear, the sight of the "sun dogs" eased the swelling tension.

Robert put the GPS—the one guaranteed to work in temperatures down to −75 degrees Fahrenheit—into his pocket as we prepared to leave for the airport. I had been advised by the manufacturer to take the GPS out of the plane every night, because it could freeze if it sat in the off position in the cold for too long. When I arrived in Resolute, I asked Robert to remove the GPS for me because I was too tired to attend to it. It was −42 outside when he retrieved it, and the wires were so brittle from the cold that they broke. Without realizing what had happened, Robert put the GPS back in the plane just before I took off from Resolute.

Robert and Peter had worked late into the night on the oil pump leak. In the process, they drained so much oil that there was not enough left in the Stearman for the trip. When we arrived at the airport that morning one of the airport's mechanics saved the day by telling me that we were welcome to use some leftover oil used by DC-3s, which, like the Stearman, have radial engines.

"You think it'll still be good after ten years?" someone asked.

"It'll be fine. It's just been sitting there, nothing's been done to it," the mechanic said. "It won't run in turbine engines, and I don't think anybody else with a piston engine will ever come up here."

He brought out two pails of the oil. One of the pilots threw one of them into the support plane, and the other I opened and tried to pour. Nothing came out.

"Are you sure this is oil?" I asked.

"Sure it's oil. It's just been sitting here for five or ten years. Let's heat it up; it'll run."

Consistency is the only difference between radial engine oil and regular aircraft oil. Radial engines have loose tolerances (the engines are loosely constructed—the parts do not fit as tightly as they do on modern engines) and call for thicker-than-normal oil, fifty-weight or better. Jet engines have very tight tolerances calling for thinner oil. If the oil is too thin, a radial engine will use it up so quickly that the plane may run out of oil before the pilot is ready to land.

Since the beginning of the trip, Robert and I had fought a constant battle to keep the thick oil warm enough to get the Stearmen started each morning. But I had never seen oil at −42 degrees Fahrenheit. It is almost a solid, thicker by far than molasses. Robert ran to the plane to grab the oil dipstick heaters we used for the Stearman. He handed the heater to me, and, as I forced the heaters down into the muck as far as they would go, he took the plug end to the wall. It would not reach.

"Move the pail a little toward me," he said.

I reached down and lifted the pail. Robert's eyes went wide. Steve also looked shocked.

"What's wrong?" I said.

Steve's jaw dropped.

"If I hadn't just seen that, I never would have believed it. You just lifted that whole five gallon pail of oil by the dipstick."

I was holding the Stearman's oil dipstick heater with the pail attached to it. We all shared in the laugh as we sat around waiting for the oil to heat up. Thirty minutes later, little had happened. In another ten minutes, the oil near the dipstick had melted enough to allow me to free it from the muck, but that was all.

Then, Peter got an idea. "I know what, let's cook this thing!" he said as he retreated into the hangar and came back pulling a large Herman Nelson heater, the kind used to keep jets warm in cold hangars. It was a real torch and it proved to be the ticket. In no time, the oil liquefied and I poured it into the Stearman. To keep the oil warm enough to flow I would have to maintain the engine temperature during the flight.

I had brought along a high frequency (HF) radio that was purported to have a range of almost halfway around the world. To make it work, we had to uncoil a sixty-foot antenna and attach it to the tail so that in flight it would hang behind the plane. I had not installed the HF radio earlier in the trip for fear it would get tangled on something during a low flight or landing. But from Resolute on I did not think there would be anything on the ground to hit so I decided it was a good time to set up the HF radio. Robert was not as certain and convinced me to wait until Eureka.

"Why take the chance? We won't need to talk between here and Eureka."

To use the HF radio, I would have to remove the headset plug from my radio, put an adapter on it, and then plug it into the HF set. The adapter was stored in a box next to my seat in the cockpit. In preparation, we had cut the bottom off a two-liter bottle of soda and affixed it to the end of the wire. Steve's theory was that in the air the bottle would act like a parachute pulling against the wind, keeping the antenna straight and stretched out behind the aircraft. It sounded good in theory.

At 8:00 A.M. on April 16, we were ready to leave for Eureka. Terry asked some of the hotel staff out to the airport to take pictures. I got into the cockpit, turned on the GPS, taxied out, and said goodbye to Resolute. That was it, no fanfare, no bells or whistles.

For the first ten miles out of Resolute, I did not even bother to look at the GPS—I knew where to find Eureka—but at nineteen miles out I glanced at it. I took a double take. It was still reading the coordinates for Resolute.

What the hell, I thought. And in the same breath I figured that it must need to be farther out of Resolute to get a signal or something was blocking the transmission. It could be anything. But minutes later it was still reading Resolute, and I knew something was seriously wrong. I decided to turn back and find out what.

As I backtracked I tinkered with it, hoping to get it working. There is an old saw in aviation that if a piece of equipment isn't working you should hit it. So I gave the GPS a rap on the top, to which it responded by shutting down completely.

"Son of a bitch."

The team was already aboard the Otter, preparing to take off, when I landed.

As I pulled in Peter, the mechanic who had fixed the oil-pump gasket, came running to find out what had happened.

"The GPS won't acquire," I shouted. "And now I can't even get it to turn on."

We went inside and Pete hooked it up. It still would not engage.

"What happened?" he asked.

"I rapped it—I don't know," I said, shrugging my shoulders in exasperation.

Then Peter gave it a quick smash with his knuckles, and the thing popped to life. Still, the GPS would not read. We sat there for a minute, waiting for a signal, but none was forthcoming.

"Maybe," Peter hypothesized, "the roof of this hangar is blocking the signal. Let's try bringing it outside."

We took a battery and the GPS out onto the tarmac to test it. By this time my entire team had left the plane to find out what had happened. We stood there waiting and watching for ten minutes and still no acquisition.

"I give up," said Peter. "Let's try something else."

He walked back into the hangar—everyone followed—where he wiggled the wires around a little and suddenly the GPS blinked on and off.

"Ah," he said, in a relieved voice, "you've got a bad power cord." He fixed it, and everyone walked back outside to test it. Still no signal. Then, Peter discovered that the antenna wire was also busted, which he was unable to fix.

I had no navigation without a reliable GPS. And I had no time to order a new one. The window was open, and if I did not go through it now I knew it would close for good. Could I go without a GPS? Yes. But should I? Without it, how would I ever get off the ice pack?

Steve had two portable GPSs—his main GPS was mounted to his plane—the best of which he retrieved from his plane and gave to me. I shook my head, knowing it would quit at −14 degrees Fahrenheit.

"What options do you have? You can bring this one to Eureka, see if it works, and keep your spare on you for backup."

I undid my polar suit and burrowed beneath the many layers of clothing until I reached skin, against which I placed the backup GPS. We then duct taped Steve's GPS to the Stearman, and I took off again for Eureka.

Steve's GPS worked for about ten miles before the screen grew faint and finally blinked out. Because of the terrible cold, I dreaded retrieving the GPS I was carrying next to my skin. To get to it I would have to undo my polar suit and expose my flesh. It would take less than a minute, but the pain would be excruciating. I opened my suit and reached in and under the layers and brought it out, took one reading, and shoved it back into the suit. Not long after the first reading I needed a second and again I opened my suit to retrieve the GPS. Easing it out from its warm perch, I was stunned to see that it had frozen over, even though it lay next to my skin.

I could see a mountain range ahead of me that looked to top out at about 7,500 feet. Before leaving Resolute, a fellow pilot advised me to get to at least 8,000 feet in order to clear the mountains that lay about 170 miles out. While I preferred to take them at nothing less than 9,000 feet, the very lowest I could go and still clear them was 8,000 feet. I did not know if I could even make it and began looking for an alternate route around the mountains.

The shore was easy to follow, simplifying navigation. All the islands have a distinct shape and had been easy to memorize from the charts. But I knew that I would never remember every valley. As I looked down, I thought there might be a path through the mountains at sea level because I could see what appeared to be a river flowing. But as I got closer the river turned out to be a glacier, solid and rising 7,500 feet high.

The higher I went I realized that if I did not get to at least 8,500 feet the wind shear could slam me into the side of the mountain. Five thousand feet was the highest I had ever taken the Stearman fully loaded. Even with the lightest load, I had never taken a Stearman of any kind higher that 8,000 feet. As I soldiered higher I hoped that the density altitude in the Arctic air would be of help—the colder the air, the thicker it is.

The scenery was spectacular. I had never seen glacial country before and can honestly say that there is nothing else I can compare it to. I looked down on white ice rivers pressing imperceptibly toward a frozen sea littered with icebergs that had broken from the tips of the massive glaciers. I saw small golden specks below, which for a moment I thought were ships, but were icebergs in the middle of the fjord, their rough-capped peaks catching the sunlight.

I started my ascent at 150 feet per minute. At that pace I knew I would eventually reach 8,000 feet. What I did not know was whether the Stearman would be able to continue to climb at that rate. By the time I neared the first mountain peaks, the Stearman was at 6,500 feet. With 2,500 feet to go, the climb had only fallen to 100 feet per minute. I was concerned that the engine might quit over the peaks, which could be fatal. But as I reached 7,000 feet at a seventy-five-feet-per-minute climb, I allowed myself a sigh of relief—the wind was not blowing, there was no worry of turbulence.

At 8,000 feet, the ascent slowed to fifty feet per minute, which was a concern. I still needed 1,000 more feet. At a rate of fifty feet per minute, it would take all day. I pulled the nose up a bit more, and the plane began to shudder and stall out. Then it dropped about sixty feet. I knew I could circle around and try to gain back some of the lost altitude once I arrived at the mountain range. I had no need to worry about wasting fuel. I had enough to make 900 miles and planned to travel only 342 that day. I always liked to keep as much fuel onboard as I could. Pilots have a proverb for every situation under the sun, and I remembered the saying that "there are three things that are useless to a pilot: the runway behind you, the altitude above you, and the fuel left in the truck."

As I neared the mountain range, I circled, trying to gain altitude. But the ample fuel that, moments earlier, I felt so smart to be carrying quickly became a burden. Earlier that year, on my way back from Oklahoma, I stopped in Jennings, Louisiana, where I talked to some crop dusters about the trip.

"The Stearman's going to have a load on it," one of them said. "If that were me, I'd want some way to dump that fuel in case of emergency. It can get pretty ugly if you can't get rid of extra weight."

I had no way to dump fuel, but I did have a way to burn it. I circled the area, climbing bit by bit, burning off the fuel. The speed was down to sixty knots. I knew that if I went any slower, the plane would stall out and drop, but I kept circling and climbing until I reached 8,500 feet. At that point, I saw a path through the mountains—one I thought I could clear. I kept the nose up and barreled through, floating over the pass at 8,700 feet. To my surprise, the Stearman kept rising ("Damn! How about that!"), reaching 8,800 feet.

It is difficult to describe what I felt that day. I had an icy wind hammering at my face and a range of deathly gray-white mountains as high as the Rockies not far beneath me. Imagine what it was like for me to be alone at the top of the planet piloting an open airplane that is almost as old as my father would be if he were still among us.

I had learned a great deal about myself on that day and I was proud. What may seem to others as a fool's folly or a maniac's dream was for me the culmination of a quest that erased the uncertainties I had about myself as a pilot. That plane and I were doing what had never been done before. I had found the hawk, chased it to the mountaintops, and become one with it.

Over those mountains, with the nose of the Stearman still pointed upward, I began to think about myself in a new way. To establish myself as a pilot, to be taken seriously as a flyer, is important to me. But would these feats help me gain the respect I sought? In my mind, I had already accomplished what I set out to do. I was confident of my piloting skills. I could take the Stearman anywhere.

The journey I had set out to take was one that would connect me to the pilots of the golden age of aviation and in the process prove to myself that I was worthy of that tradition. I had achieved that. Even if I died that day over these mountains there would be no question in anyone's mind that I knew how to fly a plane with the best of them. But I discovered something else about myself, something unexpected and vulnerable that lay hidden just beneath the desire to be counted among the great.

I was in the Bahamas, on vacation with my family, the day before I heard that my father was dying. We had flown over to a small island just to look around. One of the local guides told us about a priest who built a one-eighth scale reproduction of the monastery in Spain that he had lived in. He built the reproduction on the top of a secluded rock in the middle of the island, well off the beaten path. It was perfect—every detail, even the chapel and the sleeping cells were in replica. On the wall of his cell, so that he could see it when he went to sleep and when he got up, there was inscribed in Latin, "In the Sanctity of my Solitude, I give my life to God." I was translating the prayer for Hera when I was overcome by a sense of enduring solitude so profound that I had to sit down. I covered my face with my hands and tried to recover from the experience. Hera put her hand on me and asked what was wrong. I could only repeat the quote. The others came over concerned that I had fainted from the heat. My son, thinking he understood, said, "This guy was really lonely." I tried, but could not explain why the prayer had affected me so deeply. I felt so incredibly alone, so separate from everyone. I suppose the terrors that affect us most deeply dwell as demons within us and do not appear to others as they do to ourselves.

As a child in Mississippi, society tried to teach me, in little ways and big, to see myself as it saw me. I learned that to be an American most often means to be a mixture of heritages and cultures. The mix, ever dynamic, helps to define the many and changing ways we see ourselves. But if part of that mix comes from Africa, the dynamics grind to a halt and self-definition is predetermined for life. As an American with African blood, I was expected to forget from whom I inherited my name and where my people—all my people—had come from. And when I did not forget, I was made to feel that I was a poser living a dream that is an insult to any self-respecting American of color. I knew all that long before I climbed into the Stearman and headed into the unknown. But what I did not know was that *I* had not yet come to terms with how I see myself, in spite of all that nonsense, and that until I did, society, willy-nilly, would be my mirror.

Alone over that vast and unforgiving landscape, Gustavus Arius McLeod and I first met eye to eye. He was as stubborn as the bull on the McLeod crest, holding fast against all odds. He had the soul of a Choctaw warrior seeking the test and learning from the journey. His spirit was African—he could endure the unendurable, bear the unbearable, and suffer the insufferable. But in heart and mind he was and is an American. His place is with his wife and family, and his duty is to respect himself for what he is and does, and others for what they do. There is an African saying, "It is not what you call me; it is what I answer to." I answer only to "American."

I am able now to laugh when I am taunted by those demons—my childish beasts. If my grandfather had been with me that day, he would have told me that if I had enough guts to get there I should have enough guts to tell anybody to go to hell if they were unwilling to see me for who I am. My grandmother would have said that I already know who I am and that I was the only person who needed to know. My mother would have told me what a "damn good pilot" I am and that I did not have to prove anything to anyone. And my father, I hope, would have been proud of me and sorry that he would not be able to help me stay the course. But I know they all were there—in me—and that all I had to do was listen.

11. A Death Poem

▼

I pushed the Stearman to its limits and cleared the peaks at 7,500 feet. The airspeed held at seventy miles per hour. Eureka lay cradled inside one of the many valleys before me. The only challenge was to find out which one. I caught sight of a fjord branching off a large valley that looked promising. It occurred to me to try to radio Eureka. If I made contact the airport had to be no more than ten miles away, probably in that very valley.

"Eureka station, this is 8 November Papa." No answer.

Over a second fjord, I tried again. Still no answer. I was sure I had remembered the charts correctly—Eureka was somewhere in that valley.

I kept the charts in the Stearman with my gear but I had no way to reach them. Even if I had been able to reach them there was not enough room to unfold them, and even if there had been room I could not possibly read them in a 100-mile-an-hour wind. I was beginning to think that I had passed the airport when I spotted what appeared to be a small—too small—valley off to my right. Because there are so few animals and trees in the Arctic and almost nothing man-made, it is difficult to find something of recognizable size against which to calculate the scale of the landscape. For the hell of it I radioed in as I passed over the small valley.

"Eureka station, this is 8 November Papa."

A thick French accent answered my call. "This is Eureka radio. Are you the biplane supposed to be coming here?"

"How many biplanes *ever* come to Eureka?" I wanted to say but did not. With a shade of sarcasm left over from the thought, I responded.

"Yes, I think that's me. Could you turn up your runway lights?"

"Yes, we have a runway," the answer came back.

What? "No, no. Could you turn up the runway lights?"

"Yes, the runway has lights."

"Could you turn up the intensity of the runway lights up?"

The conversation was beginning to irritate me.

"Yes, this is Eureka station, we read you loud and clear."

I peered into the small valley and by the edge of the water saw a dark speck with smoke slowly rising from it. A closer look revealed a bunch of specks, about eight in all. I put the Stearman into a full dive directly at the airport. The Stearman is so sturdily built that it is all but impossible to overstress the plane by going too fast. I can run full power straight toward the ground, and unless I hit something, the Stearman will be fine.

Eureka station came back onto the radio. "Yes, 8 November Papa. We hear you. Someone down here is waiting to see you."

Diving through 5,000 feet, I noticed that the specks were actually little huts. But I still could not find a sign of a runway. Then I saw what I thought was a narrow strip atop a mountain, with what appeared to be runway lights. I was not sure it was wide enough for me to land. I have to laugh at the muddle in my mind when I think back to that moment. I should have known that I had no reason to fear the width of the strip because I knew that the Air Force C-130 Hercules, a four-engine turbo-prop military cargo plane, lands at Eureka. The wingspan of the C-130 is 132 feet while the Stearman's span is only 32 feet. My sense of logic must have fallen overboard in the dive. To set up for the runway, I jetted over the fjord, came down over the base, and turned on final for Eureka. From that approach the strip started to look wider, as well as longer.

My team and easily fifteen other people were crowded together near the hilltop strip when I pulled in. Twelve of them, I found out, were tourists from New Jersey who were going to the North Pole for an anniversary. Two Twin Otters stood on the field—one of them for the Jersey group and the other for my crew. When I stepped from the cockpit onto the ground I tried to say something like "Eureka! Glad to be here." But my mouth was nearly frozen, and what came out was mumbled and strange. I burst out laughing when I heard myself. Those waiting to greet me must have thought I had gone round the bend. But I did not care: I was a different person than I was when I left Resolute, more comfortable with myself.

One of the tourists approached and asked which part of me felt the coldest. In an open cockpit with a slipstream of −38 degrees Fahrenheit slamming you in the face, no one part feels the cold, I told him, "You're just kind of cold all over."

"I want to shake your hand," he said. "Anyone who can bring this plane up to the North Pole gets my respect."

When I found out that the tourists themselves were all pilots, I asked one who owned his own jet why he had not come up in his own plane.

"What do you think I am? Crazy?"

We all loaded into a van for the ride down to the station. Eureka charges planes $250 for each takeoff and each landing, and $100 dollars to transport passengers and crew the half a mile down a hill to the main base. It is a hundred dollars you really have to pay, because a half-mile that far north in the Arctic is hard on truck and driver. That little jaunt from the plane to the base was the most per mile I have ever paid for a taxi ride.

I use the word "base" advisedly. The structure looked like a trailer with a freezer door on it.

"What are you laughing about?" the taxi driver asked.

"That looks like a freezer door."

"The freezer is outside. Inside, you're in the warmth. We just think of it as going into the freezer when you leave the building."

Just inside the main door there is a mudroom to leave your wet and dirty clothes in so that the inside of the base stays clean and dry. While the Arctic is still pristine, the natural mixture of snow, dust, and wet is not that clean. We pulled off our outer gear and entered a warm room. The station is efficiently heated by waste-heat from the base's generator—much the same way a car's waste-motor-heat heats a car.

Although I was skeptical of ever being able to find a good meal in the north, I was particularly looking forward to dinner that night because we had been told that the food in Eureka is the best in the Arctic. The best we had had thus far was at Terry's place in Resolute. I doubted that the food in this glorified trailer at the end the earth would be better. But the stories about Eureka proved to be true. Dinner that night was excellent. The cook really knew her stuff, and the base was well supplied with food and drink—Lori would not have to sell her soul to find us something to drink.

"If it's booze you want," said Jobie, the station engineer, "booze we've got. I make my own beer."

When I learned that Jobie was responsible for all the machinery on the station, I made arrangements with him for a tour. Jobie worked six weeks on and two weeks off. Normally, workers in the region were scheduled for three months on and three months off. The head of the station managed to get the best duty—three months on and six months off. Jobie was a private contractor rather than a government employee, which, I think, is the reason he pulled the worst duty of anyone at the base. But Jobie loved that station above all else. He had been there for ten years, and his duty had ruined his marriage. He did tell me he planned to remarry again soon—I wonder if he did. Jobie was an original; I liked him a lot. And we all thought that his beer and liquor stash was imminently drinkable.

After we settled in, my crew split up as they always did in the downtime. Steve stayed with me while Lori went through the tourists like grease through a goose. Within three hours of her arrival she knew all their personal histories. Dwayne and Robert, taking full advantage of the captive audience, entertained the tourists to their riotous humiliation.

That day, Dwayne played one of his most effective jokes. He told the tourists that he needed some background shots for the day's events and as he set up his camera asked if they would mind being in a few of the shots. Of course, they enthusiastically agreed—everyone always did. Robert, who played his assistant, told them to "just act normally" while Dwayne started shooting his empty camera. Those who thought of themselves as star material for a National Geographic special put on a big show, gesturing and laughing outrageously. It was very funny. The longer it went on the funnier it got. You can learn a lot about people by how they behave in front of a camera. The ruse was elegant in its simplicity and predictable in its effect. It worked every time. Even Steve went along with it because it was so much fun to watch. But, later on, when Dwayne spotted an Arctic fox outside the window, the professional in him took over from the prankster. For more than two hours he lay on his stomach filming the fox and for his patience was rewarded with some postcard-quality shots.

Eureka had one phone with an unreliable connection, and the line waiting to use it was always long. We were so far north that the satellites were too low on the horizon for our satellite phone to work well, especially from the deep valley. Steve, Lori, and I went outside to try anyway, and I did manage to get a brief call to Mary. I did not say much, prompting her to ask if anything was wrong.

"You sound different," she said.

"I'm fine, everything is great. I'm trying for the pole tomorrow. Other people are standing here waiting to use the phone and it's cold out here so let me go, love you," and I hung up.

The call threw Mary so much that she spent the next four hours trying to get through to the station. It was the "love you" that got her. It was out of character for me to say something that intimate within earshot of anyone. When she finally reached me at the station I had to spend some time explaining to her that I really was okay.

Later that night, Jobie treated me to a Eureka specialty—beer on ice.

"We've got 250,000-year-old ice dug out of glaciers," he told me. "That's what we use to make our beer."

We stayed up until the wee hours of the morning putting back drinks made from the glacial ice. It was the best brew I have ever tasted.

One reason I stayed up so late that night was that the sun never set. Another, more compelling, reason was my nerves. Jobie's brew and his easy, interesting conversation had a calming effect on me. Even so, when I finally did turn in at 2:00 A.M. I could not get to sleep.

If all went according to plan, in a little less than twenty-four hours and 1,200 miles I would be back from the pole, alive and kicking. On the other hand, if all did not go as expected, I could fail, maybe even die. Since so many things could go wrong the odds were that something would. As I lay in bed that nightless night I tried to make sense out of what was to come. I was afraid I was going to die. A reasonable fear, I thought. More unsettling though was a feeling of resignation, a kind of passive acceptance that I could not shake. Was I a dead man walking?

Hours later I heard a knock on the door. It was either Robert or Steve — I do not know which.

"It's six o'clock," the voice said, "time to get up. Launch at seven."

I got up slowly, anxiously. For along time, I just sat on the edge of the bed. Each day of the trip had been harder for me than the day before. Each time I climbed into the Stearman I was less certain I would be able to complete the journey. With each ascent my body was beaten down another notch. With each landing the longing to return home grew stronger. Just do it, I told myself, just one more time. All you have to do is put on your cold-weather suit and go. But that was not true. I needed more time to consider what to do. Would I be able to get the Stearman back up to 9,000 feet to clear the next mountain range? I was worried about the wind and the rocks. Without a GPS, how would I be able to find my way back from the ice pack? There would be no landmarks, no signposts pointing home. I did not know if I had the will to continue on. And more fearsome, I did not think I had the courage to say I would *not* continue on.

A death poem is a Native American tradition. When death is imminent, a warrior makes an attempt to put the sum of his life into words. I thought back to my grandmother and the Choctaw ways and how much they had come to mean to me. I began to weep. Why did the Choctaw ways appeal to me so much? Humans, I think, are spiritual by nature. The longing to understand the so-far unanswerable question of why we are here seems to lead most humans to a spiritual explanation. Some express that spirituality through a belief in god, most often in the language of their parents. For the first six years of my life, my grandmother's ways were my ways. Even after I returned to live with my parents, my grandmother's influence continued. When I am able to find a place of comfort and meaning within me, I am in the woods of Mississippi digging dirt for her flowers, fishing, or walking with her to hunt for berries while she tells me her stories. Her stories spoke of life and death and our relationship to them. As I sat on the edge of that bed in Eureka I found new meaning in those stories. And drawing on them, I composed my death poem.

Was I just being stubborn, or was it more complicated? I had involved a lot of people in the trip, a lot of their time, their money, and their emotions—all better spent in different ways if I did not try to finish the job. I had told people that I would make the pole or perish in the attempt. I was ashamed to stop short of the goal.

It was then that I remembered the letter Mary had given me the night before I left home. She told me then to read it before going on to the pole. I had all but forgotten it and had to riffle around in my pack to find it. Inside of the envelope there was a letter and a picture of her and each of our children.

Gustavus,

I love you and miss you. I am, and always will be, proud of you. You don't have to prove anything to me. To me you have always been a hero.

Always, Mary

The letter was Mary's way of telling me how important I am to her and the children, but its effect was to jolt me into an understanding of their importance to me. I did not want to continue on. I wanted to go home. I wanted to call the whole thing off and turn back. But I did not know how. My ego would not allow me to tell Lori, Steve, Robert, and the band of wealthy tourists that I—

"so sorry"—would not be heading to the pole that day because I was turning around and going home. What I needed was for *them* to tell me, in no uncertain terms, not to try for the pole. Then I had a brainstorm.

I had been nursing a third-degree burn that I got on the flight from Geraldton, when, after nearly freezing to death on the flight between Elliot Lake and Geraldton, I decided to try out an electric suit I had been given. It worked well on the flight. But when I undid the suit in Pickle Lake I found that the heat had badly burned my stomach. A boil developed and soon after turned into a deep, nasty-looking wound that continued to bleed and weep. I neither mentioned the burn nor used the electric suit again. In truth, the burn did not hurt that much because the cold numbed it. But Lori did not need to know that. I was certain that once she saw the bloody mess she would try her best to talk me out of going on. I could save face if National Geographic said I was too injured to continue. The wound was my ticket home.

I jumped up from the bed and in my long johns ran down the hall to Lori's room. She would be my patsy. My ego would never let me ask Robert or Steve to talk me out of the attempt. But Lori is woman, which made it easier for me. I knocked on her door, paused, and then, with concern—but not panic—in my voice, said, "I think I have a problem."

"What is it?" she said, opening the door.

Sheepishly, I showed her the ugly wound. At first she almost retched, but quickly gained her composure. Then with the calm authority of a good doctor, she said, "Come with me to the medicine cabinet. I'll find something to put on that."

That was not what I had wanted her to say. I expected her to shout, "You can't possibly go on with an injury like that!" Perhaps she would have responded differently if I had not drilled into everyone involved the notion that nothing would stop me from getting to the pole. Even if Lori had thought the burn was too serious for me to continue on, she would have put aside her concerns and come up with a way to get me where she was certain I wanted to go.

"This thing really hurts," I said, desperately.

"It looks vicious, but here's a bandage." She put Neosporin on the wound and wrapped my stomach.

"That oughta hold it," she said cheerily.

The night before Lori and Steve had told me they were going to work on the GPS problem. I thought Steve might come up with something, but wondered what Lori could contribute to the solution. As I rebuttoned my long johns (taking extra time to do so to give full theatrical justice to the pain I was pretending to experience), Lori told me that she, Steve, and Dwayne had come up with a way to keep the GPS warm and functioning.

"Follow me," she said, as she walked out into the hall and turned into the common area toward a small pile of medical warmers donated by the station chief that were lying on a table.

"Break them, and they get hot," she said, smiling. "We're going to put two or three of them in a bag with the GPS."

She explained that when I wanted to get a reading, I would break one of the warmers, let it warm up, and then take the reading. She concluded her show and tell by reading the label, guaranteeing the warmers to last three hours—long enough to get to the first fuel stop.

I did not care if the GPS worked. I just wanted to go home.

"How's the weather?" I asked, pathetically. "Is it going to be good enough?"

"I think it's fine," Lori answered, and then told me to go and find out for myself.

"This *is* a weather station, you know."

In the weather center, they brought up all their satellite images for me and showed me their equipment and photographs. It took about thirty-five minutes for them to explain that the winds were calm, the sky sunny, and the temperature cold. It was −42 degrees Fahrenheit on the airport hill; down at the station it was only −38.

"This is your best shot," one of the weathermen said. "I've never seen the pole so clear."

"With all that white on the photographs, how can you tell there's no cloud cover?" I asked, looking for any excuse not to go.

"See these cracks," he said, holding up a photo and pointing to lines along the surface. "They go for hundreds of miles. When you see them, it means there's no cloud cover."

Even now, even after all that would happen in the hours, days, and months to follow, I am ashamed of my behavior on that morning.

All I had left to do was to ride to the top of the hill and strap myself into the death cart.

"Sit up here where it's warm?" Robert said as we boarded the pickup truck.

"Yeah, right," I answered a bit too sarcastically.

It was not Robert's fault that I had only a few more moments of warmth. It appealed to my sense of the dramatic to ride in the back of the pickup truck like a man going to the hangman's noose. I could see the Stearman standing steady on the field. With its dipstick heater pointing outward like a spike, it looked to me like a medieval torture chamber—a rack, Iron Maiden, and gallows all rolled into one.

Robert swept dust, snow, and ice off the top wing. In the frenzy of my imagination the ice dust created a halo around his head, making him look like a holy executioner in a painting of the Inquisition. Even his clothes were torn and soiled. As I walked toward the plane, the crowd of rich American tourists stood silently watching. No one cheered or waved, they just watched and some took pictures. It struck me that they did not believe I was going to make it.

As I stepped onto the side of the Stearman wing, it seemed that I was the only one who felt a foreboding. Steve handed me the GPS covered by the taped on medical heaters—"Remember, don't crack the bags until you get airborne."

I heard Robert say "the plane's gassed up and ready to go," and felt him pat me on the back and help me adjust my headset. It was as though he had placed a vice on my head. What was I doing? This was madness.

As I sat down in the cockpit Steve's voice managed to slip through my panic.

"This isn't survivable. If you don't like it, turn back. There's no shame."

It was what I had wanted to hear. But then I heard my voice reply. "I'm not going to turn back," I said. And after a pause, added, "I don't think I can."

Then I heard Lori ask if I was sure I wanted to go. If she had asked me that thirty minutes earlier, I would have said "no" and backed out of the trip. But I was battened down and bolted in, committed to my fate. I had composed my death poem and read my Mary's letter.

"Clear prop!" I hollered, as I cranked up the engine. The engine coughed a few times then whirred to life. The oil temperature immediately rose—130 degrees Fahrenheit, perfect for the engine. The dipstick heater and Herman Nelson had done their job. As the engine ran, the oil temperature dropped to 90 degrees Fahrenheit then started to rise again.

In the din, I heard Poul shout, "We're going to leave about forty minutes after you. We'll pass you about mid-course."

The flight to the pole would have been much easier for me if the Twin Otter could have stayed with me all the way. But they could not, and fuel was the issue. The Otter's economy cruise is 160 knots, while the Stearman travels at ninety knots. To slow to the Stearman's speed for a sustained period would have been a drain on the Otter's fuel. Already burdened with the weight they were carrying—the National Geographic gear and the passengers—the First Air pilots did not think the Otter could carry enough fuel to stay with me.

To get the Twin Otter to the pole is a logistical feat in itself. First Air uses the same Otters for the charters going to the pole as it does to ferry fuel out to a fuel depot on the ice. The ferry planes leave Eureka carrying as much fuel as they can hold. When they arrive at the depot, they offload their remaining fuel into fuel drums situated on the ice, holding back only enough fuel for them to make the return flight to Eureka. The stockpiled fuel is then used by the charters on their way to and from the pole.

I gave Poul a salute and a thumbs-up for success—always a dramatic gesture for a pilot—and tried to put it out of my mind that to First World War pilots heading to battle the gesture meant "death to our enemies." Early filmmakers misinterpreted the pilots' meaning and Hollywood's meaning took hold.

With my crew waving goodbye with their hats and the tourists shouting luck, I rolled to the end of the runway, gave full throttle, and the Stearman leaped to life. The tail darted off the ground and I went airborne.

Off in the distance loomed the last peak I had to climb. It was 8,500 feet high. If I could not make that height, I would search for a lower pass through the range. There was little wind and the Stearman was operating beautifully. I soon needed a GPS reading. As instructed I hit one of the warmer packs and glanced at the GPS. It was frozen. I put it back in the warmer so the heat could soak through and planned to check it again in a few minutes. Ten minutes later, I raised the warmer pack. It was frozen solid, along with the GPS. My excuse in hand I turned back for Eureka.

When I landed the team was getting ready to board the Otter. Lori was the first to reach me.

"What's wrong?" she said, visibly concerned.

"The GPS isn't working. It's frozen through."

I took the GPS out, handed it to Lori, who gave it to Steve.

"Oh, man," Steve said, "that warmer thing isn't going to work."

"What do we do?" Lori asked.

"I don't know," answered Steve, disheartened. "This thing is frozen."

There is still a question of who said what at that point. At the time I was certain I heard Lori say, "Well, I guess it's over. We're going back to base." She has told me since then that she said, "We're going to go back to base and try something else." Who knows for sure? At least we are clear on what happened next. Lori left for the base and while I remained in the airplane, Steve looked over the GPS.

"I guess it's done—you can get out. Need any help?"

"I don't think I can."

"It would be suicide to continue on."

"Yeah, I know that."

"Get some grit in your craw, son. Shack it off, suck it up, pull up your pants and hit the field," I can hear my father saying to one of his downed players. My father coached football at one of the high schools at which he taught. He never coached me and would not let me play football. He thought I did not have the necessary team spirit. He was right. I was a loner even then and did not really like team sports. I had just wanted to play football because the girls liked the football players.

"What do you want to do?" Steve asked.

I wanted to go back in the game.

"You know, you won't survive this if you go."

"Probably not," I said. "But at least I'll go down trying."

Steve backed away from the plane and I fired it back up. I was 600 miles from the pole and I was not going to turn back until I had no choices left.

For some reason I felt more comfortable leaving Eureka with only Steve waving me off than I had earlier when every one else was there. Whenever I left my grandmother's home to go back with my parents, I would see her through the back window of my father's car waving goodbye as we pulled away. That morning Steve stood in for my grandmother.

As I applied full power to the Stearman, a cold blast of air roared into the cockpit, blinding me for a moment. I looked out to the side of the plane and everything seemed clear for takeoff. I released the brakes. Weighed down with fuel, the Stearman rolled slowly down the runway. With each revolution of the wheel, I talked to the plane the way a quarterback talks to his team—"We can do this. We can do this." Then I felt the wheels jump up from the earth and we were airborne again.

When I looked back, Steve was still waving me on. Then, just before he disappeared from my sight, I saw him slowly turn and walk off, his head lowered, just as my grandmother would do when I left her.

I realize now that what I was doing made no sense. I had set something in motion that I had no reasonable expectation of being able to complete, the consequences of which could result in my death and emotional expense to my family. I had no plan of escape, no back door built in. Like the sun dancer, I had hung myself on ropes of my own making. Earlier that morning I all but begged to be cut down, but my warrior's soul had prevailed. I knew then that I could not stop myself from continuing on and when the time came I accepted my fate.

12. To the North Pole

The Stearman's climb out of Eureka was strong, far better than out of Resolute. At 6,000 feet we were still gaining altitude at more than 150 feet a minute. Huge mountains towered in the distance. From their spiked peaks they dropped 7,500 feet straight down to the sea. Glaciers, like massive frozen rivers, flowed lavalike in broad turns down the mountains. There were no trees or vegetation anywhere in sight, only ice, snow, and rock.

The cold at 8,000 feet was the worst I had experienced. On my head and face I wore large goggles, my flying hat pulled down over my forehead, and my beard—my breath would freeze anything else I tried to put over my face, and I would end the day tearing out skin and hair as I removed the protection. I am fortunate that I carry a lot of fat in the face, like my grandmother, because the best protection I could come up with was to let my beard and a layer of skin freeze, like the Inuit men do. Every hole and opening on my suit was taped down with duct tape—around the arms and chest—but because my face was so exposed I was always numb from the cold. The cold was so bad that day that I forced myself to sit as low and as hunched over in the seat as I could get. I operated the rudder with my toes; with my fingertips I controlled the stick.

I checked the freezer thermometer Mary had given me. It registered at −52 degrees Fahrenheit. The cold was worse in the climbs. Unable to take much more, I leveled out at 9,500 feet. It was then that I saw the Twin Otter fly past me. I did not want to move my head much, because it would let the cold into my suit. Instead, I just turned my eyes to the left to see them. They had the flaps down, rocked back in a nose-up position, slowing down to see me. As I peered over at the plane, less than 100 feet away, I could see the faces of the team pressed against the windows to see me.

Dwayne was in the copilot's seat with his camera fixed on me. Lori was in the next window with Robert next to her. Both were laughing. Steve sat in the back, a serious, almost sad look on his face. The plane circled me two or three times. I wondered what they were talking about and hoped they were not expecting me to wave.

Earlier in the trip, Lori asked me to wave for the camera on one of Ali's midair passes. I took off my gloves and gave her a special wave that she did not appreciate. We had a discussion about it when I landed. I explained to her that every time I stuck my arm out of the plane into the slipstream, cold air rushed into my sleeve, pushing out all the warmer body-heated air. I was not going to wave at anyone that day and hoped she would not ask.

Poul radioed on the Otter's third pass.

"Eight November Papa, the fuel has moved four miles to the east. When you arrive at the coordinates, look to your right and you'll see it."

"Roger," I replied.

I did not know if he was aware that my GPS was not working; although, I did think it odd that he thought I would be able to even get close to the old coordinates. Either way, I did not care if he knew my GPS was or was not functioning. There was nothing he could do for me in his airplane. I was alone and on my own. He could not stay with me; he could not lead me to the cache. And if I did go down anywhere but on a flat piece of ice he could not even stop to help me. That was the stark reality of my situation.

First Air had placed a beacon at the fuel depot. The beacon would send a signal to a satellite that would relay the location to the base at Resolute. Every twelve hours or so the base would get the new satellite data and radio it to the aircraft on route to the cache. The aircraft would then put the new location data into their GPS to go to the beacon. Because the ice can move as much as twelve miles a day, without the beacon it would be impossible to find the cache. Before the beacon, a man with a dog remained at the cache for the six-week season and regularly radioed back the location of the cache.

The Twin Otter passed me at the edge of the continent, right where the topography changes from majestic mountains to a frozen sea. The change is dramatic. Where the mountains meet the shore, there are huge ridges of broken ice thrusting out to the sea for three or four miles. Farther on, where the ice settles into jigsaw shapes like one of Mary's puzzles scattered on the kitchen table, there are open water leads that crack open and freeze before your eyes. There are pressure ridges that go on for hundreds of miles. There is also black ice—ice less than three inches thick—and gray ice and all shades of white. Smooth sections, bumpy sections, sections that looked like frozen waves for as far as the eye could see. To me, and I suspect to many, it looks like a frozen desert, terrifying in size and solitude.

I had 180 miles to go to reach the fuel stop. At the rate I was traveling it would take me about two hours—a long time over an alien wasteland. I figured that I was on course because the Twin Otter had found me. It would have been easy for them to miss me: it is a huge area and the reflection of the sun off the white ice makes it doubly difficult to see a plane, even a big blue plane with yellow wings. While I was reasonably certain I was on course and probably heading straight for the original fuel spot, my problems were not over. How would I locate the fuel if I did not know the coordinates of original cache? How would I know to look four miles east of "where" if I did not know where "where" was? As I watched the Otter climb away from me, I decided to line up on them, gambling that Poul would head straight for the new cache. They were moving at 150 knots, I was doing ninety. At that rate I would be able to keep them in my sights for about twenty minutes. After that I would have an hour and a half to go on my own.

As the Otter sped off, I looked down and saw that I had finally made it over the tallest of the mountains, clearing it by about 500 feet. The ocean lay in front of me; the last mountain ridge was to my right. Like the others, it too dropped vertically from its peaks to the sea—an almost 8,000-foot drop. For a moment I allowed myself to daydream of climbing it, wondering if it was even possible to scale.

Then I put my full attention to the frozen ocean ahead. The weather was not my immediate concern, keeping to the course over a featureless plane was. Any drifting—caused either by wind or pilot error—would put me God knows where. With the mountains looming behind me, I calculated that I could go out over the ocean for an hour or so without danger of getting lost. Anytime within the hour, if I felt I had drifted and not held course I could turn 180 degrees to see the mountains and, if necessary, head back. Then I got the idea that as long as I could see the mountains I could line up on them, using them as a reference to my proper orientation to course.

But what would I do after I had traveled beyond the sight of the mountains? If I attempted to turn around without benefit of the mountains as reference, how would I know I had completed a 180 turn? If I used the sun as reference for the turn, I could head back with confidence to find the mountains. It was then that I had the real breakthrough: if I could rely on the sun to set a course back to the mountains, I should be able to use it to navigate ahead and stay on course to the cache.

In college I learned a field engineer's trick to estimate the degrees of an arch on the horizon. There are 360 degrees in a day, 15 in an hour. One fist held out to the side at arm's length measures seven and a half degrees of an arch. Since the sun is up twenty-four hours a day that far north, I calculated that if I held a straight course the sun would move around the Stearman seven and a half degrees every thirty minutes. The sun was on the forward tip of the Stearman's left wing when I lost sight of the Otter. If I were still on course thirty minutes after that, the sun should have moved off the wingtip toward the front of the plane by seven and a half degrees, or a full fist. Thirty minutes after that, if I was still on course, the sun should measure two fists, or fifteen degrees off the wing tip, and so on until, in theory, the next day at the same time the sun would be back at the forward tip of the left wing. By that calculation, it would take the sun six hours to move from my wing tip to directly in front of my face, a quarter of the way and twelve fists around the plane.

Since it is easier to steer toward an object than it is to attempt to hold course blindly, it helps to find something in the distance to steer toward until the fist shot is taken. I could not find a unique looking crack or lead far enough out on the route, so I fixed on something nearer and took the fix at fifteen-minute intervals by using half a fist of sun movement.

The fist shots were extremely painful because I had to put my hand out into the full force of the wind at an arm's length. At −52 degrees Fahrenheit, the wind felt like knives thrown up my sleeve aimed to cut out my heart. When the cold air hit my chest, I felt like I was having a heart attack. Once, while taking a fist shot, I flew over some light cloud cover, obscuring the ice below. Luckily, the cover lasted only a couple of miles—had it continued I would not have been able to spot the cache. The fear of cloud cover stayed with me.

To stay on course, all I had to do was to line up on something at least thirty minutes in the distance, fly toward it, and every fifteen or thirty minutes take a sun shot with my fist. It could work, I thought, and at the same time cautioned myself to keep an eye on the mountains over my shoulder for as long as I could. The bastards were so tall I was sure I would be able to see them for seventy or eighty miles. I put the control stick between my knees, lined up on a distant ice crack, and extended my fist straight out.

The engine temperature was good. The plane was performing well. And I was confident that if I stayed attentive to the fist shots the sun would take me all the way to the fuel cache. I settled into the plane. There was nothing more that I could do. Ahead I saw nothing but an endless stretch of cracked and scattered ice. I was frightened but I calmed myself by thinking of my childhood and of the people and things I loved—my wife, my family, flying, and life. The understanding that in my mind the more important personal quest had ended in the no-man's-land outside of Eureka complicated the extremes of emotion. Every so often, the bravado that is my nature kicked in and I would get cocky. In those brave moments I was excited, proud that I was able to adapt on the fly in ways that the early aviators had used. Frozen GPS, no problem, I used the sun. It was primitive but effective. The old pilots in Corinth used to say that a good pilot was part of the airplane. That was certainly true of me and the Stearman. I wanted to shout, "Look at me. I am a barnstormer, a bush pilot, and a pioneer of aviation. I'm all the things I've ever wanted to be." The cold was killing, but I felt more alive than I had in ages. Then reality would slowly rein me in, and I would return to being a lonely, frightened pilot just wanting to land safely in friendly territory.

The radio crackled.

"We are on the approach end of the runway."

Off to my right, no more than a half a mile away, I could see the Twin Otter sitting on the ice. I had made it. "Son of a gun, I made it." New energy surged through me. I felt a rush of adrenaline so sweet that it made me laugh like a little boy. I no longer felt the cold or the pain. I was so pumped up that my blood must have spiked ten degrees.

The runway had been marked with trash bags filled with snow. I could see people walking around. I shouted with joy again and again. I reached down to lift up the seat as high as possible and began the descent to meet the runway. I only had 800 feet in which to land—another small runway, just like the one at Baughers Orchard where I had flipped the Stearman. I had to be careful not to repeat that error.

I had never landed on the ice pack before. And as far as I knew no one had ever successfully landed on the pack with wheels. In the planning stage I decided against using skis. The only ones I could find that fit the plane were wood and had rotted. The only other ski option I had was to build skis of either metal or wood, but I had read about someone who had miss-rigged the skis. They came loose in flight and tore the plane apart, killing everyone on board. Finally, there were no qualified Stearman ski riggers still alive, so I gave up the idea as too risky to try.

I kept the approach smooth. I did not want to come in too fast and run out of runway before I could stop. To go in as slowly as I could, I needed to make a three-point landing, one in which all three tires hit the ground at once. The seat was jacked up so far that I was looking over the windshield. As I neared the landing spot I leaned out from one side to the other, just like the pilots I had seen on carrier landings in the old Second World War movies. In the cold, thick air the Stearman was flying as solid as a rock. I needed the entire runway, so I put the plane down at the beginning of the strip. I felt all the wheels touch all at once, then, after a slight bounce, the Stearman rolled out beautifully. In the loose snow the bird stopped in less than 400 feet.

A big grin spread over Steve's face when he saw the landing, and I could see him whooping and hollering. Everyone was. I was on cloud nine. I was so impressed with myself that I taxied right up to where the team was standing, shut down the engine, got out of the airplane, and swaggered up to them, cool as could be, just like a barnstormer would have. Before I left Resolute, Robert and I had decided that we would keep the engine running during the refueling on the ice, but in the excitement of the moment I forgot. Joy and pride surged through me. I felt invincible.

I walked up to Robert and yelled, "Textbook perfect! Right on the numbers!"

I wish every pilot in the world had seen that landing. I was prouder of it than any I had ever made—seconded by the landing I made as a kid when I accidentally lifted off in Telford Norman's plane at Roscoe Turner's field. Had we had the time that day on the ice, I would have pulled up a couple of chairs for a good session of hangar flying about that landing. But there would be time for that later. I was not yet out of danger—in fact I was deeper in.

We were all talking on top of each other—layer upon layer of praise, disbelief, and amazement—when Steve asked a question that jolted us back to reality and changed the tone of the moment.

"How did you find us?" he asked. "Did you get the GPS working?"

"No," I said and, still cocky, told him about my sun-shot routine.

"That's the dumbest thing I've ever heard," said Poul. "That's a good way to get lost in the Arctic."

"Well," I replied, "that's all I had to work with."

"If I had known you were going to try that I would have given you one of my sextants."

"How could I have held it with these gloves?"

His impatience growing, Poul asked how I hoped to get from the ice pack to the pole. I told him that I had devised a plan for that.

"If you all leave twenty minutes after me, I'll get a mid-course correction when you pass me. Then, I'll do the sun shot to get me to the pole. Where are we going to land to refuel on the return?"

He explained that the National Science Foundation (NSF) had a base on the 186th parallel, thirty-six miles from the pole (we were traveling up the 80th parallel) and had agreed to let us land there to refuel. A pilot who had put in at the NSF station that morning told Poul that the station would be easy to locate because it was the only flat spot that could be seen that day from the pole—"The ice at the pole is really torn up today."

"I can find that," I said. "You guys rendezvous with me midway to the pole. If the base is somewhere near the pole, I'll find it."

Then Lori stepped into the conversation and said bluntly, "We can't meet you halfway."

"Why not," I said. "It's only thirty-six miles from the pole to NSF. When I get to the base, I'll have already flown over the pole."

"No," she pressed, "we have to verify your arrival at the pole. The last two National Geographic pole outings [Peary's and Byrd's] are still in controversy. We'll wait for you at the pole."

Poul interjected. "We can't land at the pole. The ice is too jagged today."

"Well," Lori said, "we'll circle the pole and wait."

"We can't circle and wait if we meet him halfway for a navigational correction. We don't have the fuel."

Shrugging, I added, "It looks like the only thing to do is to meet at the NSF base."

"No. That's not acceptable," Lori said firmly. "If you do that, the film is off. That's a deal breaker."

Poul was growing impatient. "If we don't give this guy a correction halfway, there's no way in hell he'll find the pole!"

Lori sighed. "Then it's not going to happen. If we don't see him fly over the pole then I will have to say that he didn't make it and the film won't be about a polar flight."

While Lori and Poul argued, Steve walked off in disgust. Robert was hanging out on the other side of the plane with Dwayne, who was filming. It was time for me to get back into the argument.

"You guys just circle the pole and give me a target," I said. "You don't have to meet me halfway for a course correction."

"What about the HF radio you brought along?" Poul asked. "Is it working?"

"No."

"What's wrong with it?"

"The headset adapter fell into the plane's wishing well. It's down for the count. I didn't know how to use the thing that well anyway."

Legend has it that Amelia Earhart did not know how to use her radios very well either.

"I'll find the pole," I said. "Keep circling it, you'll be my fix when I get there."

Until the argument, I had not realized how stressful the expedition was for the First Air crew. They were not only concerned for my safety, they were also responsible for their plane and passengers. Poul put his hand on my shoulder and asked how much fuel I was carrying.

"Tank's almost full."

"How far can you go?"

"All the way to Siberia, if I have to."

"Don't do that. The pole's 240 miles out. How long will it take you to get there?"

"Probably about two and a half, three hours."

"Here's what you do," he calmly began.

Poul told me that if I could not hear or see them after three hours of flying I should pick a spot to land. Once I was on the ice, I should set off my emergency beacon and see if I could get my satellite phone working.

"Whatever you do," he warned, "do not go past three hours in the air."

He explained that every minute over three hours increases the search area by an hour, a half an hour over increases the search by three days. Then he added soberly, "I can tell you now that if they don't find you in a day they're going to quit looking, and there's nothing I can do about that."

"You should be able to find my emergency beacon, and I should be able to reach you on the satellite phone," I said, the chill of fear in my voice.

"You could lose all of that in a crash, and we'd never find you. So I want you to tell me right now that you're going to set it down after three hours."

He was looking directly into my eyes. This was not a game. He was absolutely serious. I think my safety concerned him more than it did me. Not that I was suicidal, but I was still getting used to the idea that I might actually make it to the pole. I was taking the journey one leg at a time. It was the only way I could emotionally handle it. At that point, I was simply glad to have made it to the fuel cache and had not yet thought beyond it. Poul's orders sobered me. I still had to get back into the Stearman and, with no landmarks to guide me, fly deeper into the Arctic, out across its cold, life-taking ocean.

"You've got to call your wife," I heard Lori say. Her voice was short, businesslike. I dialed my home on the satellite phone. Mary answered.

"I'm at 86 north, out on the Arctic Ocean," I told her.

"That's nice—sounds pretty neat," she said, her voice flat.

I had been married for twenty-three years and should have expected her response. But I did not. I had always been the dead fish, the one who kept a lock on emotions, not Mary. I wondered why she sounded so cold, so distant. Could this be the same Mary who wrote me the letter? It occurred to me that someone must be in the room with her, someone not part of the family. Had Lori arranged for a cameraman to be at my house for the call? That would explain everything. Mary always hates it when people pry into her private life. If she was on camera—which I later found to be true—I was lucky Mary said anything at all.

"I'll call you when I get to the pole."

"Okay."

I hung up the phone and shoved it back in my suit pocket. I wanted to say "I love you" or "wish me luck" but with the camera in my face I could not.

Steve had been fiddling with the GPS and claimed to have it warmed up. "You'll be able to get the first coordinates going north," he said optimistically.

"If this flight is anything like the last one," I told him, "the thing will freeze as soon as I take off."

"It's not as cold up here," he said.

He was right. It had warmed up to a blistering −18 degrees Fahrenheit.

"Anyway," Steve continued, "I'm going to stand out on the runway and point north for you as you leave."

It is funny but that cheered me up a bit.

Even though the Stearman had been turned off for about thirty minutes, it fired back up when I gave ignition. As I taxied to the end of the runway area, I could see Steve and the First Air pilots standing to the side, pointing north. The sight was as startling as it was humorous—three pilots standing on the Arctic ice pointing north—and I broke into laughter. Later on, when things got crazy, I wished that I could see them down on the ice pointing the way.

The Stearman came off the ice right over their heads. I looked over my right shoulder at them and then to the direction they were pointing, made the adjustment, and started flying north. It was two and one-half hours to the pole.

"Don't quit on me now," I told the Stearman.

Steve was right: the air did seem warmer. I was almost comfortable. I flipped back the collar tucked around my chin and let the air hit me. Sharp needles began piercing my skin, but they did not bother me. I started to feel myself drift into a daydream. I was dehydrated, tired—worse, I was sleepy. If I could take a little nap, I thought, just a little nap, I would feel so good.

In a flash my instincts warned me that sleep was a bad idea. If I slept I could die. Was I hypothermic? Maybe I was. I felt warm for the first time on the trip. Too warm, I thought. I sensed I was in trouble. I was fixating and could not keep focused. I remember staring ahead and realizing the scene before me had changed. I had to stay awake. I was losing blocks of time. I was confused about my sun shots. I was sure—or was I—that I was going straight ahead, tracking straight. The temperature was −34 degrees Fahrenhiet, and the altitude 6,000 feet. What the hell was I doing that high? There was no danger in flying lower, nothing I could run into. I fixated again and when I woke I was at 6,500 feet. It was as though the altimeter had a mind of its own. "Concentrate, concentrate," I said. If I could not, I knew I was just as good as dead. But it was too late. I had begun to hallucinate.

The way I remember it now, I was standing alone in a room without walls. A group of men were approaching. I thought I recognized some of them and began to introduce myself. I asked them why they were there and what was happening. They told me that I belonged with them and they had come to welcome me to their ranks. I recognized several in the group. There was George Mallory, the British climber lost on Everest in 1924 whose body was found on the mountain in 1995; Robert Peary and Mathew Henson, who accompanied Peary on his still controversial trip to the North Pole; and hanging back from the group, Ernest Shackleton, captain of the H.M.S. *Endurance* and leader of the failed expedition to the South Pole.

"Aren't you fellas dead?" I asked.

My voice was calm and courteous, registering little fear and even less confusion. They nodded and I heard one of them say, "You will be too." And with a wink and nod, he added, "Soon."

I was not afraid, and they were not unfriendly. They were jocular, treating me the way seasoned pilots treat the new recruit. They all laughed when one of them told me that most of them had died doing things not nearly as crazy as I was trying. I was not offended; rather, I was happy to be among them and apparently accepted.

We talked easily. They told me stories of their exploits and of others less well known who had also pushed the limits. Some had been successful, some failures, but all had pressed to do something no one else had ever done. They all had their different reasons for trying what they tried, but each of us understood that at our core we were driven by the same needs.

"We know what you're going through," one of them said. There was agreement all around.

I do not know how long I stayed with them, but I do know that it was the best session of hangar flying I had ever experienced or probably ever would.

Before leaving them I worked my way out of the group to the place on the periphery where Shackleton was standing.

Shackleton's story is the greatest survival story of all times. From 1907 to

1909, he led an expedition to Antarctica where he lost his ship in the ice. After surviving with his men on the ice for two years, he and his team walked out, dragging their lifeboats behind them. But that was not the end of it. After they reached land no one came to rescue them, so Shakleton and a few of his men left the rest of the crew behind and in an eighteen-foot lifeboat made an 800-mile open water run through the South Atlantic. When they finally reached land they crossed an uncharted mountain range on foot to get help. Shackleton did all this without losing one of his crew.

I told him that history calls him a hero and that much had been written about his bravery.

"But I didn't make it," he said, forlorn.

Hungry, dehydrated, and hypothermic, I drifted in and out of reality. When I finally came out of it I did not know how I had been able to keep the plane aloft and on course. I had developed keen instincts over thirty years of flying. But instincts have no memory, so I am still unsure of how I managed to navigate during that period. All I remember is the hallucination.

In the distance I heard my radio crackle to life. A message was coming through. But the noise was distracting me from the dream, so I took off four gloves from one hand and turned down the volume on the radio. Then something told me— perhaps a voice from the dream—to turn up the radio.

"Someone's trying to talk to you, you idiot."

Instantly, I snapped out of the dream. But I was disoriented, still confused, and it took a few minutes to get hold of where I was and what I was doing. I had no feeling in my right hand and could not figure out why I was not wearing a glove. I looked at it as though it was not a part of me. I flexed it but felt nothing. I noticed the hand was changing color and held it up to my face. To this day I have little feeling in it.

"Eight November Papa, do you read?" It was Kevin's voice.

"This is 8 November Papa, go ahead," I said slowly.

"Roger, we've got you. We're thirty-eight miles from the pole. What's your location?"

I did not know so I made something up.

"I'm eleven miles from the pole now."

I do not know why I said that. I was just talking. Words were coming out, but my brain was not dictating what was being said.

My altitude was 500 feet. The last time I had remembered looking at the altimeter it was at 6,500 feet. I had dropped thousands of feet and I did not remember how. I tried to reconstruct what had happened but was unable to.

The voice came back over the radio. "Roger, we're speeding up now. We'll meet you at the pole. Keep your present heading."

Right after the words came over the radio, I saw a shadow cross the front of the Stearman. Looking up, I saw a Twin Otter passing above me. My first thought was that it was another plane and there was a lot of traffic in the area. Then I realized that it was the chase plane and frantically, got back on the radio.

"You're overhead! Slow down! I'll follow you in." No answer came back. It flashed through my mind again that the plane atop might not have been my crew. Kevin's voice came back. "I read your carrier wave, but I can't hear you. We're speeding up to catch you."

I panicked, again. "No, don't speed up! Slow down! I've got to follow you!"

"Roger, still read your carrier wave. We'll rendezvous at the pole."

All I could think was that if they ran off I might never find them again. In truth, I probably could have seen them all the way to the destination, but my mind was still muddled. In a madness to connect with the Twin Otter, I shouted once more into the radio.

"This is 8 November Papa, do you read?"

"Roger, we've got your carrier wave. Press your mike once for yes, twice for no. Are you at the pole?"

I clicked the mike a bunch of times. But they obviously could not understand what the hell I was trying to say. I am not sure I did.

"Roger," Kevin said, "we'll look for you."

In a panic, I stuck the mike into my mouth to thaw it out. The microphone stuck to my tongue and the roof of my mouth. I tried to pull it out, but it hurt like hell. I tried again, but the harder I pulled, the worse the pain was. I was about to let go of it and rest before trying again when out it popped. A salty taste of blood soaked my tongue. A patch of skin from my lip clung to the mike. I felt a rush of adrenaline and my head cleared. ·

The radio came back to life. "Eight November Papa, we're circling the pole looking for you. We don't see you. If we don't see you in five minutes we will assume you're lost."

Way out in front of me I could see them circling above. They were at the pole, on top of the world. I would soon be under them. I had to find a way to give them my location, so I yanked the GPS off the panel and rubbed it with my ungloved right hand, trying to heat it up. Nothing. By that time the Otter was directly above me and I went into a circle beneath them. At the end of the first turn, I ran into a little bump. It was my own vortex. The wing tips of an aircraft generate a swirling column of air that settles behind the aircraft, like the wake of a boat. Pilots say that it takes a good pilot to hit his own wake. If Telford Norman could have seen me then! There I was hitting my own wake as I circled the North Pole in an open-cockpit plane, the first in history to do so. The Stearman's clock read 9:07 P.M. It was April 17, 2000.

The radio came to life, and I heard Poul say, "Gus, I've got you in sight out my window. Gus, from everybody in this aircraft, congratulations on reaching the North Pole."

Reaching the pole did not exhilarate me. It meant little to me. I just wanted to go home. I had gone to follow through on the promise I had made to Doug to make it or die trying and to give the record to all those who believed in me and my ability. I circled the pole and looked below at the chewed-up ice— nowhere to land, not a flat spot of more than fifty feet in any direction. So this is the top of the world.

Then I hit my vortex again. It was much rougher than the first time around. I had planned to circle the pole four times, but on the third time the Stearman inverted when I hit my vortex. I decided to forgo the fourth. Three times would be enough.

I reported in to the Twin Otter.

"GPS is barely readable. I may have to follow you in. Am I on the proper heading?"

"Roger, roger. You're on the correct heading. We'll lead you in."

I was circling, how could I possibly be on the right heading? I was not sure what was going on in the First Air aircraft. Maybe they were so relieved to find me they were not thinking very straight either.

When I stopped circling, the Otter came down alongside of me and then slowly pulled in front of me. The Stearman suddenly started into a slow roll. It inverted, doing a complete 360. The vortex of the Twin Otter was hitting the Stearman. I put the plane into a hard left bank and turned back on course about 200 yards to the left of the Otter and followed them to the NSF base.

I relaxed as they lead me in, and I started singing a happy little song made famous by Nat King Cole that my daughter, Lara, likes to sing:

The buzzard took the monkey for a ride in the air
The monkey thought that everything was on the square
The buzzard tried to throw the monkey off his back
The monkey grabbed his neck and said, "Now, listen, Jack,
Straighten up and fly right, straighten up and stay right,
Straighten up and fly right, cool down papa, don't you blow your top."

In so little time, in the space of a few minutes and three circles, I had met the goal. I did not feel a rush of triumph or thrill. There was no bridge to cross, no line in the ice, no markers of past successes at the spot. Our being there meant nothing to the pole. The Stearman and I had not changed it in any way. It was then that I fully understood that it was not the goal but the long journey that I would remember, not the goal but the journey itself that had changed me forever. I looked with gratitude at the ever-present sun. "Give me a stout ship and a star to guide her," says a sailor's prayer. I had been given both. The sun was off my right wing tip. I looked off my left wing toward home. If I put the sun behind me now and held course I could find my way back to my wife, my family, my home, and my country.

13. Return Home

I was trying to think of something important to say when we landed at the NSF base, but the pain in my bones and the hunger in my gut kept any memorable words from forming.

"You've done it," Robert said as he walked toward the plane.

"Yeah, I thought the engine was going to quit, but I guess I made it."

My brain ached from questions I could not answer. How had I managed to make it that far? How would I get back home? Would the sun shots work as well on the way back? All I really wanted to do was return to the hallucinations and stay there until I was safely home. I smiled to myself, thinking of what Mallory and the gang would say when they found out I had made it. What was wrong with me? I sensed that I still was not right in the head, but I did not know what was normal and what was not. When I think back on the strangeness of that day, it is the hallucinations that scare me most. I was clearly not rational.

As I lifted myself out of the plane, I asked Robert to retrieve the Gaithersburg flag I had entrusted to Lori. I had promised the mayor of Gaithersburg to fly the flag when I reached the pole. Lori set up the scene and was taking a picture of me standing beside the Stearman holding the flag when we heard someone shout for us to hurry up and pump fuel. Then Steve noticed that I was not wearing my right glove set.

"Put your damn glove on. Are you nuts? You're going to lose that hand if you don't put the glove on."

"Yeah, yeah, I hear you, but my hand's not cold. It feels perfectly fine."

"Like hell it is. It's swelling and red. Put the glove on."

I looked down at my hand. Steve was right. It was puffy and redder than my usual red undertone. But I did not want to make too much out of it.

"I'm always red, that's nothing new. Look, I can still move it."

But Steve was not hearing my protests.

"Put the glove on or I'll go ahead and cut it off."

It was not in Steve's nature to be violent so I took his exaggerated threat as real concern and slipped on the outer mitt, without bothering to put on the inner pairs. No one but Steve seemed to notice that I was not doing well.

"Are you sure you can go on with this? You're not acting right."

"I'm fine, never better," I lied. What else could I do?

As Robert took a picture of Lori holding the Canadian flag, Dwayne mooned him. They titled the photograph "High Moon." Steve thought they were being childish, and I was too out of it to get the joke. It was often difficult to believe that Steve and I were on the same team as Robert, Lori, and Dwayne.

The guys from NSF invited me into their tent to warm up but Lori would not allow it.

"You don't have time to warm up," she said. "You've got to get fueled up and get out of here."

Poul had told Lori that the stop at the cache would have to be quick—time and possible changes in the weather left little room for fooling around. Lori can be forceful when she needs to be. I wanted to get inside out of the cold but she would not bend. It was good luck for me that she did not give in. Had she, the warmth would have made the pain in my right hand so much worse that I would not have been able to fly the Stearman out.

Numb from the cold, I called my wife.

"Mary Alice," I said, "I made it to the pole."

I listened for her response and quickly said, "Yeah, yeah, bye."

I had not heard what she said or even if she had said anything. I could not concentrate. Mary later told me she thought the satellite phone lost its signal while we were talking, but I think I probably hung up on her.

I went back to the Stearman to gas up the plane and noticed that someone I did not recognize was standing on the Stearman's wing with a hose in the ferry tank. It may have been Poul or Robert or one of the NSF scientists, but I do not know. Steve had checked the oil was trying to warm up the GPS and set it so I could at least get one good fix out of it. Lori and Dwayne were huddled for warmth in the Twin Otter while its pilots checked the plane and gear. Robert and the NSF guys were taking pictures. I stood in a daze and pumped the handle of the fuel pump. The drum I was pumping from had a black strip painted across its middle. All the other drums were red.

With the plane fueled, Steve reminded me that I had promised to call Mike Ruane, a writer from the *Washington Post*, when I successfully reached the pole. I dialed the satellite phone. Mike answered.

"I made it to the pole," I told him.

"Wow! That's great! How can you verify it?"

"The people here say so, the GPS says we're there, and the NSF says so."

"Who else is there?"

After giving him the names of everyone there, he asked the number of the phone I was calling from. I gave it to him and then hung up. Three minutes later the satellite phone rang. It was the first time on the trip that I had heard it ring. I handed the telephone to Steve and climbed up into the cockpit of the Stearman.

"Yes," I heard Steve say, "we're at the North Pole, no question. He can't talk right now, he's about to leave."

Steve gave me the warmed-up GPS and told me that it was set with the co-ordinates for the fuel cache, the same cache we had stopped at before crossing the pole. I wanted him to point me in the right direction on takeoff as he had done earlier, but he did not know for sure in which direction to send me.

"The thing should work at least to the end of the runway," he said. "At the very least you'll start out in the right direction."

On takeoff, I ran over a couple of snow banks. I was jolted a bit but the plane was undamaged. A quick glance at the GPS showed that it was working. I could make out the heading and turned onto the course Steve had set.

The course did not feel right. I wanted to go south, but the GPS course was sending me farther north. With twenty years of flying in instrument conditions, I had learned one rule: when in doubt, go with the instrument instead of your instincts. It took all the willpower I possessed not to turn that plane 180 degrees and head the other way. I needed to find out why the GPS was sending me north. I radioed the Twin Otter but there was no answer. Then I remembered that they had planned to eat something with the NSF team before starting back. It went through my mind that if Steve had sent me in the wrong direction I would be either on my way to Russia or heading out toward the North Atlantic. Russia was the more attractive scenario. Of course I could hit Greenland, I thought, or a smaller landmass before heading into the Atlantic. The Arctic Ocean is surrounded by land except in a few spots where it is possible to squeeze through into the Atlantic. My chances of hitting one of those spots were slim. As long as I kept on the GPS course I was confident I would sight land sometime, somewhere.

Shortly thereafter the GPS froze. With it out of commission I had to return to using sun shots. I checked the position of the sun in relation to the wing, as I had done earlier. The sun was one and a half fists forward of the left wing. Odd, I thought. That is the same wing I used going north. I checked the time; it was 11:05 P.M. I looked out straight ahead to see if I could spot something unique to fly toward. There was a distinctive lead about ten miles out. I flew to it. By 11:20, the sun was two fists forward of the left wing, and by 11:35 it was two and a half fists forward of the left wing. But I was not as careful with my measurements as I had been on the way to the pole.

About an hour into the flight, my radio crackled and I heard Kevin's voice.

"Eight November Papa, do you read?"

"This is 8 November Papa, I read you."

"We can't understand you. Reading your carrier wave."

My microphone was still frozen. Most of the time the mike would dry out and start working on its own. After about fifteen minutes in the dry cold air, the ice would go from a solid to a gaseous state and escape from the mike. When I was not using the mike I would pull it away from my mouth so sublimation could occur. But on that leg I had left the mike next to my mouth, and my breath had kept it frozen. I was not about to try to remedy the situation by putting the mike back in my mouth, so I clicked the mike three times.

"Roger. Click once for no, twice for yes. Are you on course for the fuel cache?"

I had to sit back and think about that for a moment. They asked again. I knew I was on the course Steve had set for me, but I was not certain that course would lead me to the cache. But I decided to trust Steve and the GPS and clicked twice.

"Understood, you're on course to fuel. What's your estimated time of arrival?"

What in the hell? How was I supposed to tell them my ETA in one or two clicks? I sent a series of five or six clicks, trying to spell out the time in Morse code.

"Sorry, sorry," the Kevin said, responding either to the Morse code or to my frustration. "Are you thirty minutes out from fuel?"

I clicked no. After a series of questions and responding clicks, I got across the message that I was about an hour and a half out of the fuel cache. They continued on and out of my radio range.

If I can hear them, I reasoned, I must be going in the right direction and they have to be within thirty miles of me. I took a good look at the position of the sun. I was not sure if I had drifted off since the GPS had stopped working. It was then that I understood why Steve had set the GPS heading north instead of south. The path we took to the pole was along the 80th parallel; the NSF camp was on the 185th parallel. Since we had flown over the pole to get to the NSF camp, to return to the First Air fuel cache from the NSF camp we had to fly approximately twenty miles north at an angle toward the pole, missing it by only five miles. As soon as I passed the pole, I headed almost due south.

I had made it to the geographic North Pole in an open-cockpit aircraft, and I was beginning to believe I would actually live to tell about it. I was pleased with myself and was glad that the end to the suffering was nearing. I was confident I would make it to the cache and from there on to home.

"Come on old girl, we're going home."

I imagined the Stearman hanging from the ceiling of an aircraft museum and showing it to my grandkids.

"Look, kids," I would say. "Your grandpa flew that thing over the North Pole."

"No," they would say. "You couldn't have done that."

"Oh, yes I did. I flew it all the way there and back."

It was a good dream. I hoped it would lead to others. I was getting colder and would have liked to return to the hallucinations to keep my mind off the pain. Perhaps this time I could play some cards with the guys, poker or something. Anything to pass the time. But the hallucinations did not return.

I looked at the fuel gauge; it registered a quarter tank. I did not want to risk running low on fuel so I decided to pump some from the auxiliary tanks up to the mains. With force, I hit the pump button. About four seconds into pumping, the engine sputtered and coughed. Immediately, I turned off the pump. There is an old flying adage that says, "If you do something and it doesn't work, don't do it again." As soon as I shut off the pump, the engine smoothed back out. I thought that maybe a little water had gotten into the tank. Stearmans can eat a bunch of water, so I was not really worried about that. I decided to pump a little more gas up top. Once again, the engine ran rough, quit, and then coughed. When I turned off the pump, the plane kept on spitting and coughing. Could I be running out of gas, I wondered. I decided to try the pump one more time.

On the next pump, the engine coughed and died. Nearly frantic, I turned off the fuel pump for the last time and looked toward the ice for a place to put down. When I had landed at the NSF base, they were in the midst of experiments on the various colors and the corresponding thickness of ice.

"Whatever you do," one of the guys had told me, "don't land on black ice." He thought the Stearman was too heavy to hold on black ice.

"If you can land on gray ice, that might be okay, but do so real gingerly. If the ice is bowl white, it's good to go, if it's smooth."

I remembered the conversation and a similar one that I had had with an Inuit the year before and concluded that I could survive a landing if I picked the right color of ice.

The engine had stopped and started a dozen times when I decided to put the plane down on the first suitable ice I could find. I was just about to make an emergency landing when I heard a voice say, "Turn right," followed by a voice that kept repeating, "Add power, you're too low. You're going to hit the ice ridge, you're too low." I obeyed without questioning and in a split second saw the fuel cache and my team standing around the Twin Otter on the ice in front of me. The Stearman missed the ice ridge but hit the ice very hard, hard enough to knock the breath out of me. It could not have rolled for more than 100 feet after that landing. I taxied up to the group, and as I got out of the plane I told them about the gas, the engine quitting, and how I had set up for an emergency landing.

"I thought I heard your engine sputtering and quitting for the last two minutes," Poul said. "Was that you?"

"Yeah, it was me. Who else would be out here?"

"We got worried. You're very late."

Poul told me that when he heard the engine sputter he thought I was clowning around and then added, "If you weren't you've got a real problem."

"Under the circumstances," I told him, "if I had been clowning around I really would have real problems—head problems."

He asked what I wanted to do, and from the tone of his voice I could tell that I had to make a decision and I had to make it quickly.

I ran over to Lori and asked her advice.

"I don't know," she answered. "It's your airplane. I'm not going to tell you what to do with your plane."

Steve and I were talking about what had gone wrong, when Robert joined in to say that no matter what had happened this was not the time or place to tear down the engine. Then Steve told me that bad weather was moving into Eureka and that Poul wanted to get back into the air.

"We don't have the tools or the time to work on the plane."

I knew the First Air pilots had already blown the hell out of their sixteen-hour duty day and did not want to take a chance getting caught in bad weather.

"We can leave the fuel here with you," Poul said, "and you can pump it yourself. We're leaving in five minutes."

Although Steve would not tell me what to do, he clearly did not want me to risk staying behind. My options, as he laid them out, gave me little choice.

"As I see it, you've got two choices. You can climb back in that plane and fly it the way it is or get in this airplane with us and leave. But if you leave it, I doubt you'll ever see it again."

I did not need to second-guess my decision. "Okay, I'm coming with you."

"Thank God," Poul said. "By every rule of Arctic flying you should be dead now. You're a walking miracle."

Steve reported that neither of them had thought I would make it out alive. Poul bet that I would get hypothermic and crash, and Steve was sure I would get lost and never be found. I asked them who won and they both laughed. I thought it was a legitimate question. For all I knew I was already dead. My hallucinations were just as real to me as Steve and Poul were.

When I heard Poul say that we had to leave in three minutes, I remembered Doug's ashes and my promise to his mother to bury him at pole. I told Poul about Doug and he agreed to the delay. While Lori ran off to the Twin Otter to retrieve the canister containing Doug's ashes, Poul asked me what I wanted to do about the Stearman. But I did not know what to do and looked to him for a solution. He told me that First Air would be using the cache for another couple of weeks.

"You can push it over into a snowdrift. We'll put a beacon on it, and you can find it later."

There was no more discussion. I had run out of options and was too exhausted to do more than give him a resigned nod.

Lori handed Doug's ashes to me. I took them, not knowing what to do next. In desperation I looked to Poul.

"You're the captain now, my ship's gone."

Poul declined and I turned to Robert.

"Sorry, no," he answered.

I did not have the energy to speak for Doug; nor did I have the heart to say nothing for him. We had been good friends. We had flown together. We had seen rainbows and sunbeams that day over Pennsylvania. If life had happened differently he would have piloted the chase plane. I owed him a farewell.

We had assembled by the side of the Twin Otter. There was a snowdrift in front of us about knee deep. My father had always wanted me to be a preacher, and I had always rejected the idea. But there I stood, my team gathered around me, in the middle of the Arctic Ocean holding a section of PVC pipe containing the ashes of my friend. The Stearman stood apart from us. The air was heavy in my lungs. I paused trying to gather my thoughts.

"I'm here to bury two friends. Doug," I said, holding up the pipe. Then I paused and lowered my head and said, "And my airplane. Maybe you can keep each other company."

I placed the canister into the snowdrift.

"You belong to the ages now, Doug. Eternity is yours."

Lori was visibly shaken, almost in tears.

Poul and Kevin boarded the Twin Otter and soon after the rest of us followed. I sat in one of the backseats of the plane, not bothering to buckle my seat belt. We were in the air before I knew it. As we flew off, I looked back at the Stearman sitting alone on the ice. I was having trouble keeping my emotions in check. While the others shared a sense of relief, I had not yet sorted out my thoughts. Steve expressed his sympathy about the Stearman and his happiness that I was alive and safely with them. They all told me that I had made the right choice in leaving the Stearman behind.

"There's nothing you could have done," Lori said, trying to console me. "I'm just glad we didn't have to bring you back in a body bag." To lighten the moment, she added, "I think they have one on board if you want to try it on for size."

We both laughed. Dwayne's humor was rubbing off on her.

Halfway into the two and a half hour trip, I went up into the cockpit to visit with the boys at the office. We talked about the day's events. I had relieved them of a great burden by abandoning the Stearman. I asked them about going over their duty day. Kevin said that Kelvin Williamson, the Transport Canada inspector, who had ridden with them from Resolute to Eureka and was scheduled to accompany them to the ice but had not because of weight concerns, would be waiting in Eureka to write them up. I asked Poul how they could have made it back within the duty date. He told me that originally they had no intention of waiting for me at the cache. Their original plan was to get me to the NSF base and from there direct me to the drifting fuel cache and then leave. They would have made it back in time had they followed that plan. Their responsibility to me was essentially over once they verified that I had made it to the pole and made certain I had enough fuel to get back to Resolute. But at the pole they thought I looked and acted unstable and did not have a prayer of getting back on my own. When I was late in getting to the fuel cache, Poul said he was certain that I was gone.

"Next thing I know, I hear an engine sputtering in the distance. Turned out to be you. Boy what a shock."

"Well, I'm glad you guys waited."

Kevin told me that they could not leave me once I had told them about the sun shot technique.

"Damn. Can I do anything to help?" I said, feeling guilty.

"Sure," Poul said, then chuckled. "Pay the fine."

"I don't think I can do that. . . . Hey, maybe you can call this a rescue mission—the plane's on the ice and I'm riding back with you."

They liked the idea, and we shared a laugh. Then I went to the back to my seat and tried to rest and enjoy the ride to Eureka.

When we arrived in Eureka, the Transport Canada inspector was standing by the runway. I walked up to him and started to explain what had happened and why Poul and Kevin should not be fined.

"It's okay," he said. "I already know what happened. They radioed everything in. They couldn't very well have left you out there with your plane going bad."

We landed at four in the morning on April 18. Jobie, the station engineer, was waiting for us in a pickup. He offered to taxi us down the hill free of charge because of my success. When we reached the station we entered the dayroom. The station employees and several of the American tourists were gathered to greet us with cheers and a standing ovation. They had waited up all night to welcome us back. I was deeply touched and choked back tears. It was the best and most sincere public celebration of the trip. Perhaps I remember it that way because it was the first to follow my victory. Afterward, we all had Jobie's 250,000-year-old cocktails.

Hours later, my right hand started to thaw out. The pain was so intense that I actually considered chopping it off. Jobie saw my distress and talked me down. He also plied me with the stiffest drinks he could make. He was not a doctor, but his remedy was right and in time.

Terry was waiting for us at the airport when we arrived in Resolute later that night. She offered her congratulations for my success and sympathy for the Stearman. She talked about the loss the way one talked about a death in the family. We did not return to the hotel, instead Terry kindly offered us a house. It was in town but away from questions and a crush of well-wishers. I guess that house was reserved for the successes of the "silly season."

Steve planned to head for home quickly and asked me if I wanted to fly with him in his 182 because Robert had decided to go back on a commercial flight. I felt bad letting him go on alone, but I still was physically and emotionally drained from the trip and did not feel up to climbing back into another small, cold aircraft. The First Air management had given me a complimentary ticket home—home, how wonderful that sounded—and I decided to accept.

The week I spent in Resolute was pure hell. The team was falling apart. Steve left on the nineteenth. I had little in common with the others and had formed few bonds with them. In a very real way the Stearman was all that had held us together. The breach began when we left the ice and by the time we returned to Resolute we were no longer a real team. Once Steve left, Robert and Dwayne's practical jokes started getting on my nerves—particularly since after the pole I was fair game to them. Lori was under pressure from National Geographic to produce the film quickly. She worked all day long on her computer writing the script for the documentary. She was short-tempered and nasty. We argued over the most insignificant details of the trip. She tried to interview me time after time for the voice-over on the film but I was being difficult too. Press people were also calling every five minutes, but I did not want to do those interviews either. I was still trying to figure out what to do about the Stearman and was still in pain.

My injuries from the trip were more painful than serious. My right hand hurt constantly and sometimes severely. Because I had not worn a face shield, my face was sore and the bottom of my chin was sporting large blisters that wept constantly. My knees were so stiff that bending them took a great deal of effort. The third-degree burn on my stomach was the size of a silver dollar and had become a gaping mess. And I was still in a haze, a residual of the hallucinations. All I wanted to do was go home. But Lori was relentless. One evening, she plied me with a six-pack of beer she convinced the local drunk to give her from his secret stash and got her interview. Dwayne called it the interview in a can.

That week, two First Air pilots contacted me with an offer to fix the airplane and fly it off the ice.

"How much?"

"We'll do it for $20,000 U.S. We think we know what's wrong with it."

I thought that was odd since even I did not know what ailed it. When I asked them how they knew, they hedged. I insisted, saying that if they wanted the job they better tell me what they knew. They had learned from someone in Eureka that by accident the fuel used to refuel the Stearman at the NSF base was retrograde-cargo. The retrograde-cargo consisted of old gas, used oil, and anything else that could not be dumped in the Arctic, which had been put into a barrel and set aside on the ice to be burned.

I told them if they could fly the plane off the ice, I would come and pick it up the next spring. Since I did not have the $20,000, the pilots said they would hold the plane as collateral until I came up with the money. I did not have any idea how I would get hold of that kind of money, but hoped that the insurance would pay for the whole thing.

And I was wallowing in self-pity. Terry introduced me to a couple of guys who had just been rescued off the ice cap. As they hobbled over to me, I noticed that one of them had a bandage on his nose and the other could not walk correctly. They had been walking toward the pole as I flew over it. One guy had lost his nose, and the other, a few fingers and toes. After meeting them I no longer felt sorry for myself. The two men wanted to know what kind of equipment I had used on my face to protect it so well.

"Fat!" I cheerily replied. "I'm a good hundred pounds heavier than you guys."

Word travels fast in the Arctic. After that, everywhere I went I was introduced as "the guy the Inuit call the Walrus." The children would laugh and say, "Walruses don't get frostbite because they're fat!"

When we got on the aircraft to leave Resolute, Dwayne put a HEAVY LOAD sticker on my back without me knowing it.

I wish I had been in better shape to fly back with Steve. On the trip back home, he almost killed himself in an ice storm over Hudson Bay—the same place where I had almost lost my life. The wings of his plane iced up during a storm, and the plane started to go down. It could not hold altitude, even at full power. He bottomed out of the clouds at 3,500 feet. The ice on the wings soon melted, and he was able to keep the plane aloft.

I have asked Steve if he prayed that day over Hudson Bay. It is the same question I am often asked. Unlike me, Steve is a religious person. So I was taken back when he said that he had not prayed. He told me that he had prayed hard for his family, but figured he was getting what he bought.

"I just asked to get it over quickly," he said, "because I didn't want to go down in that water and suffer."

At Rankin Inlet, Steve had stopped in to see Steven Fredland, the mechanic at Kewantin Air, and stayed the night in his home. In Churchill, Steve palled around with Tim Cameron, whom he still keeps in touch with. In Pickle Lake,

Bernie and Lynn Cox hosted him. I envy him for that trip. I would have liked to have had the chance to share my victory with many of the people I met in the north—Mayor Lyles of Taloyoak, Studly and Johnnie in Rankin Inlet, Tim Cameron, Cameron Doll, Whisky Jack, Wade, the Polar Bear man, and others in Churchill. They were part of my journey.

Steve and I have talked a lot about our trip north. We have become close friends and visit each other often. I still feel guilty about letting him return home alone. But he puts it best when he says, "I was too tired to stay, and you were too tired to leave." If I had known that after he left I would be fair game for Dwayne and Robert, I would have ridden back on the wing of Steve's airplane.

My crew was a strange team. Robert kept a keen eye on the plane. Steve, to the best of his ability, kept me out of trouble. Lori and Dwayne were involved in the documentary, which meant that they participated by mostly remaining at a distance. Their work paid off. The half-hour documentary Lori produced for National Geographic Television captured the trip better than I imagined. And when the film aired on June 4, 2000, on MSNBC, it was well received. But Lori did not understand the core experience of my journey. The distance I had come personally was staggering. We were on the same trip but not the same journey.

14. I Can't Leave Her

▼

On Easter Sunday, April 23, 2000, I arrived in Baltimore. Jay Rosenburg had arranged for a private jet to take me back to Gaithersburg. It was a kind but extravagant gesture. The jet probably used more fuel to fly from its base in eastern Maryland to my home and back than I burned on my entire flight to the North Pole.

When the jet landed in Gaithersburg, I was immediately swamped by reporters and camera crews. The only people I recognized in the entire crowd were Mary and Lara. I did not have much to say to the media. All that was on my mind was to take my family home and then, after a good rest, figure out how to retrieve the Stearman. Mary and Lara each gave me a small embrace. There were no tears or kisses for the cameras.

When we got back to the house there was no fanfare. The older children did not even come home from school early. It was as though I had left that morning for work and had returned in the afternoon. The family thought that except for leaving the Stearman behind everything had gone off without a hitch. I had learned my lesson from the first trip and kept the bad stuff to myself. Mary saw that I was limping when I got off the aircraft but thought nothing of it. Lara was sad about the plane but happy as a clam that I was home for good. I used to tease her that the Stearman belonged to her. I had hoped that one day she would fly it. She is the only one of the children who shows any interest in aviation.

Later there was hugging and crying when Mary saw my wounds and heard about the trip. She was worried that some of the damage might be permanent. The next few days were tough. In the warm Washington springtime, I felt hot all the time, no matter what I would do. I was still having trouble with my knees, and I had little feeling in my right hand. The sore on my stomach had not healed and would leave an ugly scar. And soon after I arrived home I became depressed. I do not know what caused it, perhaps an imbalance in my metabolism, maybe leaving the Stearman, or any one of a number of other things. I do not know.

A couple of days after I arrived, I got a call from Environment Canada, Canada's equivalent of the U.S. Environmental Protection Agency (EPA). They had heard about the Stearman going down on the ice and wanted to know if I planned to move it. When I told them I would like to get it back if I could, they said, "Good. Because that's Canadian territory."

"But it's 300 miles offshore!"

"We claim a wedge of the ice cap all the way to the North Pole. Leaving a plane on the ice is considered ocean dumping."

When I asked what would happen if I were unable to get it out, they told me that I probably did not want to consider that as an option because they could fine me as much as $150,000 a day.

The situation had the potential to get ugly. I called my insurance company and told them about my plan to have a couple of First Air pilots fly the plane off the ice. The insurance agent told me that if I wanted to fly it out I had to fly it out myself.

"You're the only qualified Arctic Stearman pilot, and if you don't move the plane we can't pay for it."

I laughed to myself wondering who exactly had qualified me.

After a little investigation, my insurance agent called me back and told me not to worry about the Canadian fines.

"Nobody ever acknowledges Canada's claim to that wedge to the North Pole. The U.S. government doesn't recognize the claim. They can't really claim the fine unless you go back to Canada."

The news did not make me feel any better. If I did not remove the plane, I would become a fugitive in Canada for the rest of my life. I did not want that to happen. It was getting clearer and clearer that I had no choice but to get back to the pole and retrieve my airplane. So I told the insurance company that I planned to bring a team to the ice cap to help me fix the Stearman and they agreed to cover the costs.

Mary was angry when she heard I planned to go back for the plane.

"I didn't hear about your test flight to the Arctic until five days before you left."

"I think I told you about it before that."

"It's an airplane for godsakes," Mary said.

She was right. It was just an airplane and there were other planes to be had. But I still could not abandon the Stearman, not if I had half a chance to get her back.

"To hell with that plane, the Canadians, and the insurance company!" There was anger and fear in her voice. "If the Canadians think a wooden airplane is going to pollute their ice, they can have it. If it had not been for those bastards selling you bad gas at $650 a barrel it wouldn't be there."

She was difficult to reason with because she was right. The year before Bruce had unwittingly helped me talk Mary into the polar attempt by his insistence that I not try it. But this time I was flying solo, and it was not going well. Mary knew that I would do whatever I wanted to do, but whenever I go on my walkabouts I always like to leave her in good spirits. I explained to her the simplicity and relative safety of my plan. I would try to fix the plane on the ice and then fly it out to Resolute, where I would take it apart and have it shipped back home. First Air had agreed to give me a good rate because their planes from Resolute come back empty.

Then I told her my contingency plan.

"If that doesn't work, I'll burn the wings on the ice and bring back what I can in the support plane. It won't be that hard. I'm not going to fly it that far,"

I assured her lamely. She was quiet, listening. I could tell a plan was brewing inside her brain.

"If you go I'm going with you," she said. The tone of her voice was preemptive. "You missed our anniversary last year because of your test flight. If you're in the Arctic for this anniversary I'm going to be there too."

Two days later, on May 9, we spent our twenty-fourth wedding anniversary together on route to Resolute.

Northern Outfitters shipped Mary a cold-weather suit overnight. I told them to make it special because it was our anniversary. They had come out with a new line of gear and they sent a pair of silky white snow boots with a flower pattern on the top that were the envy of every Inuit woman she met.

Frank Johnson, a friend of mine from Montgomery Airpark offered to fly us to Ottawa to get the First Air flight to Resolute. We got as far as Syracuse, New York, when a thunderstorm put us down. Frank was not an instrument-rated pilot so he had to turn back before flying into instrument conditions. Mary and I rented a car and drove the rest of the way to Ottawa.

Don Sanders, who had done wonders rebuilding the engine for the pole trip, agreed to come along to help with the repair. Don met us in Ottawa, where we picked up four cases of beer, and from there we all took a flight to Resolute. I needed one more person to make the trip to the ice. Shawn, one of the First Air mechanics, volunteered for the job when we chartered a Twin Otter from First Air to find and retrieve the abandoned Stearman.

Before we boarded the plane for Eureka, Don and I picked up 100 gallons of fresh auto gas to flush the tanks of the Stearman.

The flight from Resolute to Eureka was an eye-opener for Don and Mary. They were not prepared for the size and grandeur of the Arctic.

"I can't believe you flew over these mountains in the Stearman," said Don, amazed. "Look at the size of them. You have to be crazy!"

"They get worse," I said.

Mary was dumbstruck by the beauty of the landscape. I had often described the terrain to her, but the mind's eye is not up to the task of envisioning such wonders. Don looked out of the window, then back at me, and said, "Unbelievable."

I had tried to prepare myself for the likelihood that Don and I would not be able to get the Stearman into good enough shape to fly it off the ice and back to Eureka. I did not have the heart to cut up the plane and set fire to the parts that would burn. I felt like I was preparing to shoot my best friend. Mary did not care how the Stearman came out. Dead or alive made no difference to her.

We spent the night in Eureka, where we saw Jobie and drank martinis chilled with 250,000-year-old ice. Early the next morning, we boarded the Otter and set off to find the Stearman. The satellite beacon was still functioning since First Air still had fifteen barrels of jet fuel on the pack and was scheduled to use the stop for another week, which gave us a breathing space. The flight was long and I was impatient, but finally the pilot honed in on the cache. As we circled the area I looked down on the seeming endless expanse of ice and saw the blue and yellow biplane sitting on the ice like a long-lost friend waiting for me to return.

When we landed, the pilot told us that the ice was unstable and that they planned to stay in the plane with the engine idling.

"At the first sign of trouble, we're leaving."

"How do we get back in the plane?" I asked.

"You don't. When you get out, we're taxiing to the end of this runway. Any sign of trouble we're going to hit the throttle and get out of here."

He told us they would then fly back to Eureka, and when they returned they would find somewhere nearby to land.

"So just realize that if you hear those engines go full power, step out of the way, because we're leaving."

I could tell Mary was unnerved by the threat. She asked them how long we would have to stay on the ice before they returned. When their answer was noncommittal I tried to rally the troops. Don still looked worried and asked what we should do if the ice cracks.

"Get on another piece of ice." Both pilots were laughing.

"What if it cracks up so fast you go under?"

"It never happens that quickly. It'll start slowly, and you'll hear it going. You'll notice the ice start to tilt."

As we started working on the Stearman, I noticed something that made my heart sink. The plane had suffered some damage sitting out on the ice. There were rectangular holes in the fuselage and the wings. And when I looked into the cockpit, I saw nothing. No radio, no instruments, no clock, nothing. It had been stripped clean. I was enraged.

"Look at this!"

"Damn," Don said. "Looks like someone took a knife and cut out some holes in your wing."

I went to the First Air pilot and told him to get out of the plane and look at the damage. He did, and when he saw the Stearman he said it looked like it had been sitting on the streets of New York for a week.

Incensed, I said, "Don't blame this on an American city. This is supposed to be Canadian territory, remember? You guys aren't supposed to do this kind of thing!"

Mary showed me a hole on the side of the plane where it looked like someone had kicked it in. I felt like someone had ripped out my gut.

"Well," Don said, "what do you think?"

"I guess I don't need instruments to fly the thing back. If we can get it running, I'm flying it out."

For the next ten hours Don, Shawn, and I drained and flushed the fuel tanks, rebuilt the carburetor, and checked the engine. We put a big tarp over the engine compartment and fired up a portable gas-powered heater with a blower. I told Don that he was head mechanic at the world's northernmost airplane repair station.

"North, hell," he said. "I bet it's the world's most remote repair station."

Mary spent the time absorbing the incredible beauty of the place, taking pictures, and shuttling equipment back and forth from the Twin Otter to us. About ten yards from where we were working there was a pressure ridge where twenty-foot columns of ice were sticking straight up, like the columns in the ruins of an ancient building. On one side, the columns were brilliant turquoise and on the other side they were bright, blinding white. Whenever Don wandered over to this formation to have a smoke I heard him say, "Wow. Wow." It was an appropriate response.

After Don had checked all he could check without doing a complete tear down of the engine, he gave me his diagnoses.

"I think your engine was starved for fuel due to ice blocking the filter and fuel contamination. Either one would cause it to sputter and quit the way it did."

I found that hard to believe because the Stearman has a filter for particulate matter that would catch anything like dust, grit, or ice.

"Did you filter the fuel you got at the pole?"

I told him that normally we filtered all the fuel through a screen. I was reasonably, but not absolutely, certain that we had followed the same procedure at the pole because I remembered passing the filter up to whoever was holding the hose in the tank.

"Whatever you had in that tank wasn't fuel. Aviation gas is blue, car gas is orange or yellow tinted, this stuff is milky white. I don't know what it is, but it ain't gasoline. There was no way this plane would have made it back in this condition," he added soberly.

"I made it this far on something," I said. "Let's put some clean fuel in her and see if she'll fire up."

We put new gas in the Stearman, took down the makeshift tent we had put around the engine, and Don pulled the prop through twenty or thirty times. Shawn put in a battery, and I climbed into the cockpit. After sitting on a chunk of ice in the Arctic Ocean for four weeks and drifting more than eighty miles, the Stearman fired up within one blade. We were all stunned, all except Don, who was laughing. Don had built a hell of an engine.

"Now there's an airplane that wants to get out of here," Don said.

I ran the engine for five minutes—it was running smooth as silk—then I jumped out of the plane to help dig the wheels out of the ice.

When the First Air pilot heard the engine fire up, he ran over to see what was going on and if we were ready to go. The copilot stayed in the airplane with the engine running.

"If you take off out of here today and go down on the ice, I'm not going to be able to pick you up. I'll have to come back and get you."

Mary jumped on this before I had the chance to say anything. "You have skis on your plane. Why can't you land and get him today?"

He told her that company policy prohibited landings on virgin ice when it is overcast because it is hard to tell the difference between an eight-inch and an eight-foot depression in the shadows.

"When it's overcast we can't determine how many cracks are in the ice or how smooth the ice is."

When I challenged him that the day was overcast and we had landed, he responded that they knew the ice at the stash and had landed there before.

"We can come back and get you, or you can leave the plane here for now and come back tomorrow or the next day when the skies clear."

I had no intention of going out without the option of getting help. But even if I had thought to, I could tell from the look in Mary's eyes that she would have hit me if I had taken one step toward the cockpit of that airplane. We all agreed that to return the next day was the most prudent course of action.

That night we talked about the plans for the next day. Mary expressed her concerns about flying over the mountains in a plane that had been repaired on the ice. Don thought the engine would perform well but would not vouch for "any of the stuff they have been calling gas around here."

Then we talked about the route. I could avoid the mountains by following the fjords back to Eureka. The route would add eighty or ninety miles onto the trip. I had a GPS that would work in the cold, and I had a spare part for anything that could go wrong with it. I did not mind going the extra miles because the scenery would be spectacular. But I was concerned about getting lost if my GPS failed and I tried following the fjords. If it did fail, I did not think I could rely on my memory of the charts to navigate through the maze of fjords. The First Air pilot told me that he could carry enough fuel to slow the Twin Otter and stay with me if I took the direct route back to Eureka.

"But if you take the long way, you're on your own."

There was that phrase again, "on your own." I did not like it as much as I used to. There had to be another way.

"What about landing at Alert," I asked.

Alert is roughly 210 miles from where the Stearman was parked, while Eureka is 350 miles from the spot. Alert is on the coast, which meant that I would not have to fly over the mountains to get to it. If any problems developed along the way I could put down on the ice. Everyone agreed that that was the best option under the circumstances.

The Stearman had no instruments, and the holes in its wings had been duct-taped over. The Otter could slow down and stay with me the entire trip. In Alert, we could check the plane to see if it was fit to go over the mountains to Eureka. If it measured up, we would leave it overnight in Alert and return the next day fresh and ready to fly the 314 miles from Alert to Eureka. If it were not in good enough condition to fly over the mountains, at the very least it would be off the ice and safe.

The only problem with the plan was that we needed permission to land at Alert. Alert is a secret base operated by the Canadian military. It is fairly easy to find out what they do in Alert, but I am not at liberty to say. Because of the security concerns it is restricted. If a plane landed without permission it would likely be impounded.

Mary got on the phone to Washington to get help. The First Air pilots called their sources and the people at the weather station called theirs.

The next morning we woke to the sun. We were still waiting to hear if we had permission to land at Alert. But I thought we should take advantage of the weather and go with or without permission. I figured that it was better to just land there and apologize than to wait for, and possibly be denied, permission. Given the Stearman's condition, I was determined to get the plane out without going over the mountains to Eureka. The First Air copilot warned me that if Alert saw me coming in they might pull trucks out onto the runway.

"That runway is 5,000 feet long," I said. "I only need 400 feet of it. They had better have a lot of trucks."

When we got back to the Stearman, we took an ice drill and drilled two holes in the ice about one foot apart. It was an odd feeling to hit water a foot and a half down. We ran a chain through one hole and out the other and tied both ends to the tail of the Stearman.

Don stood beside me on the wing, and we started the engine. He signaled me to bring up power to what sounded like cruise power. As it was running in cruise power, I got out of the Stearman to help pack up all our tools and heaters. We decided to let it run for an hour. We figured that if it could run sitting on the ice for an hour it could run for that long in the air.

As we were loading the Otter, we could hear and feel the ice rumbling beneath our feet. Since we were packing to leave we did not pay much attention to it. When we finished the loading, I asked the others if they would come with me over to the place where I had buried Doug. I could see the pipe I had placed in a snow bank on the other side of our landing area. The wind had removed the snowdrift and had left the package standing perfectly straight on the smooth ice. I walked over to pay my respects alone. I told Doug that I was taking the Stearman back home but that I thought he should stay. It was a good place to be buried. The snowdrifts were reminiscent of clouds, and the endless expanse reminded me of flying VFR "on top," a term used to explain flying in clear weather above the clouds. It is a nice place for a pilot. And then I said goodbye to him for the last time.

After the Stearman had been running for about ninety minutes, we shut it down, untied it, and checked it again. Don declared it as fit as it would ever be under the circumstances. I hugged Mary and climbed in the Stearman. The First Air pilot came up to me and said, " We just got permission to fly into Alert."

The plan called for the Twin Otter to follow me to within twenty miles of Alert at which time they would take the lead and do all the radio work—the Stearman's radio had gone with the vandals—as I followed them in.

"Roger that. You follow me, then I follow you."

Everyone stepped back, and I gave the Stearman full power. It did not move. I rocked the tail, wagged the wings but still it would not budge. Don and Shawn came up and each grabbed hold of a wing tip and pushed with all their might. Nothing. I shut down the plane and Don went to work. His diagnosis was that the brakes had frozen. That upset me because I was the one who had put his arm down in that cold water to pull the chain through to secure the plane.

"Damn Don, if we had checked the brakes I wouldn't have had to tie it down for the test run-up."

That was true he said and then went on to remind me that if the brakes had let loose during the run up we would be looking at a trashed airplane.

It took a half-hour to unload the heaters again and thaw out the brakes. Meanwhile I got into a discussion with the pilot on polar navigation and other issues. He thought I was crazy for heading out without taking the plane out for a test. I disagreed.

"No way," I said. "I'm heading to Alert with every turn of the prop. If the wheels get off this ice, they ain't coming back."

After the brakes were thawed, I got in and tried again. This time the old girl started to roll. I was pumped up and excited. I may save her yet, I thought. While I was doing a check out, the Otter started rolling and pulled up behind me. We taxied in tandem to the far side of the smooth ice. On the way, the Stearman's tire fell into a crack that took me five minutes of jockeying power to free. On my takeoff roll, I again hit the crack hard but the Stearman bumped over it into the air. I circled once over the spot to line up on Alert, gave a hand salute to Doug, and was out of there.

I learned later that six hours after we left the fuel cache, First Air tried to use it to rescue pilots from a downed aircraft near the pole. A large pressure ridge had formed in the middle of the landing area, effectively putting the fuel cache out of business. The Stearman had gotten off the ice just in time. On more day and it would have been out of reach forever.

On the way to Alert, the Twin Otter pulled up alongside me. I saw Mary and Don in the windows. There was my wife looking out at me as I flew alone in this, the most desolate of places. I was not worried about Mary and how she was getting along. I knew she was safe and warm where she was, although later she told me that she would have preferred to be with me in the Stearman. Mary always says that she would rather fly with me than fly with anyone else.

"Believe me that was the one time you didn't want to be there," I told her. "No matter how cold it looked, it was ten time worse."

As I flew back toward shore I knew that with each mile the odds for saving the Stearman increased. If I could get within 100 miles of shore, a helicopter might be able to come and get it.

"Yea, baby, we can make it. I'm going to get you home."

There on the horizon, still more than 100 miles from Alert I saw the austere Arctic mountains off to my right. I saw the big one, the one I had barely been able to clear on the way to the pole. I was glad I was not heading for them and was seeing them only at a distance. But I was also excited to see them because it meant we were in sight of land. Another hour and I would see the Stearman safely off the ice. I wondered if in its sixty-one years of service, the Stearman had been through anything like what it had been through with me. The boys who trained in it during the Second World War sat in this very seat and had been yelled at by the instructor who sat up front. The instructor talked to the student through a tube, but the student had no way of talking back. How many cadets had you washed out? How many had you sent on to faster machines? How many had you sent into combat, glory, and death at the hand of our nation's enemies? How many hard landings had you suffered to be repaired and put back in service? How many times did a frightened cadet fly you for his first time aloft? This seat had cushioned a lot of fear. But you brought all your frightened masters home to fly again. All the fields you dusted in your twenty years as a crop duster. Overloaded, undermaintained, always on the brink of disaster, flying to help feed a nation. You survived all that. You deserve to go home, to rest, and never to be put in harm's way again.

It struck me as ironic that in my quest to connect with the ghosts of aviation's glorious past, my plane and I had become part of that history. I was seeing the world as the aviation pioneers had seen it in the very aircraft that some of them had flown. I smiled to myself and I was happy.

Over Alert I set up the plane to come into the airport, and before I knew it I was on the ground, rolling in a three-point position. It was done so effortlessly that it felt as though the Stearman had landed itself.

When I told Don about the landing, he said that he had not wanted to say it before but he had worked on a lot of old airplanes and "this one's got a soul." I asked him what he meant. He told me that at the cache the plane had fired up quickly, "like it was glad to finally get off the ice."

"This thing has a soul!" he said. "Think about how much it's seen—much more than you or I. It could tell you stories. Can you imagine—"

"Yes," I said, "I can."

We left the Stearman in Alert for the night, with plans to return the next day with fuel to fly it back to Eureka and then on to Resolute.

The next day, May 17, 2000, Mary decided to stay in Eureka instead of going back with us to Alert. Some of the military personnel who had been temporarily stationed at Eureka for communications maintenance were taking an excursion into the mountains and invited her to come with them. Mary loves to hike, and she accepted straight away.

When we arrived back in Alert, the base was out in force to meet us and take pictures. When we had landed on the previous day not a soul had been on the strip. We assumed that the base was so secret that they did not want us to know who was stationed there. But we found out that the reason no one met us was that the base is two miles away from the landing strip, and they did not have the time to get there before we departed.

After the meetings and greetings, and doing a final check of the Stearman, I started her up and took off with the Otter close behind. The winds that day were fifty- to sixty-miles an hour coming out of the northwest over those mountains with a vengeance. I have flown through some rough stuff before but nothing on a scale equal to that. The sharp edges of the mountains exaggerated the turbulence. I was tossed about so severely that I thought I was going to lose the plane. I knew that if I could climb above the tops of the mountains, I could get out of the most severe turbulence. I climbed for all I was worth when I hit an air pocket that started rolling the Stearman. There was nothing I could do but hold on and let the airplane complete the roll.

Caught in another gust of wind that was bent on taking me straight into the mountain, I turned as fast and as hard as I could. My efforts were to no avail. I was still heading toward that rock. At less than 1,000 feet from impact the plane shook violently and I was caught in an updraft that pinned me to the seat. If I could ride the updraft, I thought, I could gain enough altitude to turn around and fly back to Alert. When I got there I could circle over the beach until I gained enough altitude to play with these big mountains on a much fairer basis. On the way up in the updraft I started my turn. I could see the Otter above me at what I thought looked to be 2,000 feet. The Arctic air is so clear it was actually 8,000 feet above me. I hope he sees me turning around, I thought. As soon as I had finished my turn a downdraft hit the plane so hard I accidentally bit my lip. I knew that pulling up in a downdraft is the surest way to stay in the downdraft—which I did not want to do. To get out of the downdraft I would have to keep the plane straight, level, and ride it out. That way I would fly out of the downdraft sooner than if I tried to climb out of it. I was going down and fast. There was a small peak in front of me, 500 feet down, and a peak rising above me to either side. I was in a box canyon—the worst of all situations in mountain flying. I grabbed hold of the stick with both hands and braced for what I was sure would be an impact. Just before what seemed eminent, the downdraft was stopped by a violent updraft, and I cleared the ridge by what felt like inches. I saw Alert dead ahead at thirty miles. I had made it out of the mountains to the foothills around Alert.

On the way back toward the base, I started pumping fuel from the ferry tank up to the main. I left the pump running. But the main tank was not full by the time I reached the beach where I planned to start circling to gain the altitude necessary to play it a little safer in the mountains. It was soon evident that the fuel pump from the ferry tank could not keep up with the rate I was burning fuel. With that, I knew I could not make Eureka. With no other options I had to land at Alert.

The Twin Otter landed as I was rolling off the runway. The First Air pilot came up to tell me that they had seen me getting tossed around.

"It looked rough. What happened?"

"Fuel pumps are pumping too slow to keep up. One of my two fuel pumps is more than likely broken."

We all milled around the aircraft pondering what to do. Don and some of the mechanics at Alert told me that they could fix the fuel pump. The mechanics had some spare fuel pumps that they knew would work. I tried to come up with any reason I could to persuade them differently, but they always had an answer.

I finally had to come clean. I walked over to Don and said, "Don, there is nothing you could do to that airplane or say to me that would make me try to fly over those mountains again. I'm sorry, I just don't have it in me. I know my limits and I've reached them."

"Shoot, you don't have to tell me. We were up in the Otter watching you get thrown around. I sure as hell wouldn't fly it out. Then again, I wouldn't have flown it up here either."

I had achieved everything I wanted. I had reached my goal and had proven my skill as a pilot. One of the Tuskegee Airmen, Conway Jones, once asked me, "Who's the greatest person you ever met?"

As I tried to come up with something worthy to say to one of my heroes, he cut me off.

"You are. Every man who succeeds should be able to look in the mirror and say, 'That is the greatest person I've ever met.'"

The personal demons I had wrestled were not insignificant. I am relieved and happy to have jettisoned that heavy baggage. But I am sure there are other demons hiding within. No doubt, I will meet up with them on future adventures. It would be naive to think that a man has only one battle to fight and only one chance to win or lose.

There will be other quests, other frozen, desolate seas to cross. The journey and the quest are a life's endeavor. I was safe and the airplane was off the ice. The Stearman would stay in Alert until I could come up with a way to get it home. We had reached the goal together. We had been through many situations that could have killed me and destroyed it. It was time for both of us to rest.

When I arrived back in Eureka, Mary was still off trekking in the mountains. In a turn of events, I was now worried about her. She has a terrible sense of direction. What if she got lost before I could find her?

15. The Parting of Friends

▼

We spent another three days in Resolute waiting for the next flight out. They were wonderful days, the first since the expedition began that I did not have to worry about or plan for the next day and the next ordeal. Don and I had brought cases of beer with us from Ottawa and when we got back from Alert we had a hell of a party with the First Air group. The second day, Mary and I went seal hunting with one of the locals. When it came time for the traditional liver eating on the ice Mary declined. Not to offend our host I reluctantly put my vegetarian preferences aside and partook. Mary had arranged for one of the Inuit to take us out to investigate the frozen bay later that day. I told her that I was perfectly capable of taking us out on the ice on our own. She was skeptical and asked the guide if he thought it was safe for us to go alone.

"Sure," he said, "he's the Walrus."

I was proud that he said it in front of my wife. It meant that I had earned the respect of a people that I had learned to admire.

We went so far out on the ice that we lost sight of the shore. Mary grew concerned and asked if I could find the way back. I laughed at her lack of faith and showed her how the Inuit had taught me to read the snow and find which way was north. I showed her how to decipher the secrets of the ice by its thickness and color. I explained and demonstrated how I had found the pole by taking sun shots with my fist. It was as though I had not talked to her for a year. I was giddy to tell her everything about the expedition and how the flying connected me with Roscoe, Shorty Cramer, Byrd, Eddie Rickenbacker, and all the others who pitted their skills against the forces of nature in small fragile aircraft. I told her about the extremes of the trip—the expected and the unimagined—and the exhilaration and pride I felt in doing what no human had ever done. I also told her how in the vast loneliness of the Arctic I had caught sight of my soul, both its majesty and its frailty. And how in the process I came to know myself for who I am and what I value. I told her that in the harshness of the ice desert I learned that nature has no values and that nature does not care. Its indifference is its strength and its terror. But I told her how I had also learned that the way to fight the terrible impassivity is to care—to care deeply and passionately and constantly. I was wacky with enthusiasm and had difficulty containing my happiness. I could not stop talking and wanted to tell her everything. Her knowing smile told me that I did not have to say any more. But I did, I needed to tell her that I loved her and appreciated her more than I ever had. And so I told her. We stayed out on the ice beneath the bright Arctic sun until three the next morning. I was with the woman I love in a place I had grown to love. What more could I ask for?

In Resolute I met Dick Rutan, the pilot and balloonist who flew around the world nonstop without refueling. He and some friends broke through the ice near the pole when they tried to land with wheels. The team that carried us to retrieve the Stearman had rescued them. Rutan and his friends were staying at the same hotel we were. They had a good laugh when I told them that if they wanted to land on the ice they should have looked me up first.

"According to Lloyds of London, I'm the only pilot qualified to land an aircraft on the ice with wheels."

On May 19, 2000, a week after we arrived back from Resolute, the Smithsonian Institution invited me to a fund-raiser luncheon for their new National

Air and Space Museum addition to open at Dulles Airport in December 2003. At the luncheon, I met Don Lopez, deputy director of the National Air and Space Museum, and Tom Allison, director of the Paul E. Garber Preservation, Restoration, and Storage Facility in Suitland, Maryland. The planes that hang in the National Air and Space Museum are restored at the Garber Facility. They wanted to know what had happened to the Stearman. They were intrigued by the story of the rescue attempt. I told them I would donate the Stearman to the College Park Airpark Museum if I ever got it back from the north. Don told me that he might be able to help and that he would let me know what, if anything, the Smithsonian would be able to do.

In the meantime, I received another call from the Canadian government. This time the government official told me that the Stearman had to be removed from Alert before winter. They agreed to fly me to Alert for just that purpose. The ride they offered ended up costing me $1,300.

I arrived back in Alert on July 18. It was late in the season. By then the freezing rain of the late summer was a daily occurrence, making it impossible to fly the Stearman out even if it *could* still fly—which it probably could not. The Stearman was beaten up from the looting it had received on the ice at the First Air fuel cache. From what I gathered, First Air had taken a load of tourists to the pole between the time I had left the Stearman and the time I returned to retrieve it. When they stopped at the cache for fuel, the tourists helped themselves to some North Pole souvenirs while the pilots attended to the refueling. It was the only plausible explanation. I had heard that bush pilots had looted her, but that did not make sense. The First Air beacon was the only way to find the plane. It was the only cache First Air had on the ice cap at the time and any First Air flight going to the pole would have to stop there. The pilots would not have harmed her, but tourists probably would.

The base commander told me I had to leave within two days. I was running out of time and options, when members of a helicopter squadron on a temporary mission to Alert to survey power lines told me they had had a hard time flying in with aircraft built to withstand the conditions of the Arctic. One of the mechanics came up with the idea to declare the Stearman as unsafe to fly.

"If it's unsafe, the commander can't make you leave."

Sure enough, when the base commander heard that the plane was not airworthy, I was told to disassemble the plane and put it in a shed.

"We'll send it back with retro-cargo."

Retro-cargo consists of trash and other things that cannot be burned or dumped in the Arctic. Once felled by retro-cargo, the Stearman would now be saved by it. It was a final irony that only I seemed to get.

With the help of the helicopter squadron, I took the Stearman apart and stored it. When the job was finished, I was loaded onto a C-130 Hercules and headed home.

Not long after, the Canadian government called to make me a deal on the shipment of the Stearman. I was told it would cost $500 for every 100 pounds. I agreed. But shortly after that arrangement was made, they called back to tell me that they would need to put the plane on a pallet and that I would have to pay for the weight of the pallet. The pallet weighed 1,200 pounds. Another $6,000 would be needed.

Before I could figure out how to raise the money, I got yet another call from them saying that they needed another pallet because the Stearman would not fit on one. It too was a 1,200-pound pallet. That added up to a total load of 5,800 pounds at a cost of $29,000—well beyond my fund-raising capacity.

I called Don Lopez and told him the situation. He talked to Tom Allison, and when he called me back he said that they thought they could use the influence of the Smithsonian to get the plane back. It was a long shot, but they would do their best.

"That plane deserves to be home," Don said.

On August 19, 2000, I was in San Antonio, Texas, to receive an award from the Tuskegee Airmen when Tom called and told me that a U.S. Air National Guard outfit out of New York was doing exercises in Alert.

"Maybe they can pick up the Stearman and bring it back."

This was the break I had been hoping for. I told Tom where the plane was stored, and he promised to get back to me as soon as he knew anything.

The very next day, Don called me and said that the plane had been retrieved and was sitting at the U.S. Air Force base in Tuele, Greenland. The plane was back on U.S. soil. I felt like cheering. The Air Force then picked it up and brought it to McGuire Air Force Base in New Jersey. From McGuire, the plan was for the U.S. Navy to load it onto a C-130 and fly it back to Andrews Air Force Base in Maryland, just outside of Washington, D.C. Tom Allison, Cathy Allen, the director of the College Park Aviation Museum, and I traveled to McGuire to accompany the Stearman home.

I could hardly believe it when I saw the Stearman. It looked like a fallen hero returning from the war, the proud old soldier coming home to rest. The wings and tail had been carefully crated in five crates. The fuselage sat on its own wheels, and even without the wings and tail, it still looked strong. As the loader moved to the plane and the troops lifted the Stearman into the C-130, I almost wept. The symbolism of the moment was not lost on those who had come with me to retrieve her. We stood ramrod straight as the Stearman—a symbol of American aviation—disappeared into the hold of the huge C-130. Designed in the 1920s, born in the '30s, the Stearman had trained for world war, dusted crops and fields for twenty years, performed at air shows for the next ten years. And now it held two world records. Everyone on board felt a respect for the airplane, and the flight back was passed mostly in appropriate silence.

As I compared the Stearman to the monstrous C-130, it was hard for me to believe that I had flown the small and fragile airplane all the way to the end of the earth. The two planes were built less than fifty years apart, but in size, speed, and comfort they seemed light years apart.

Tom Allison asked me to get inside the disassembled plane as it sat in the back of the C-130.

"We're at 20,000 feet. You'll never get a better chance to fly a Stearman at this altitude."

In his military days, Tom had been the director of the SR-71 Blackbird high-altitude reconnaissance program for the Air Force. In 1990 an SR-71 set the U.S. coast-to-coast record of sixty-eight minutes, averaging 2,124 miles per hour. Here was a man who had flown an airplane that could have flown from my home to the pole and back—my entire trip—in less than two and one-half hours. That fact astonished me. I could hear Roscoe saying, "I'd love to get my paws on that stick for a go."

It felt good but disorienting to sit in the Stearman at 20,000 feet. It would have been wonderful to be this comfortable on the trip to the pole. But that was another world away, disconnected and so different that I did not feel I was in the Stearman I knew so well. But when I looked down at the panel, I saw the large Mack truck knob that Paul Thommesen had installed and I knew I was home.

The C-130 landed at Andrews, where the Smithsonian had a truck waiting to take the Stearman to their restoration facility at Silver Hill. I rode to Silver Hill in the truck with the Stearman. I know some of the guys who work at Silver Hill, and they were there waiting for us when we arrived. They unloaded the Stearman and took it to be stored with some of the greatest aircraft in the history of American aviation.

I officially gave the aircraft to College Park Aviation Museum. It seemed a natural fit. College Park is the oldest continuously operated airport in the world. It dates back to 1909 when Wilbur Wright set up a facility there to train Army aviators. It has been in operation ever since. I did some of my pilot training at College Park, and Maryland is now my home state. But the most important reason for giving it to the museum was as a small tribute to Mary. Mary's first flight was out of College Park, and I was her pilot. In more ways than I can name she has been with me on every flight I have ever flown in the Stearman.

The Stearman remained in the Silver Hill facility for a month, then it was trucked to College Park in mid-September 2000. I told the museum that my sole request of them was to be allowed to fly the Stearman one last time before it went into the museum. I did not want the flight into Alert to be my last flight in the Stearman. I wanted desperately to fly it one last time. Everyone was very concerned that I might damage the plane and were reluctant to let me fly it. I owe a debt of gratitude to Cathy Allen for understanding and granting my request.

Don Sanders and his son came up from Oklahoma to help me reassemble the airplane for its last flight. On September 23, 2000, at the College Park air show I stepped into the cockpit and sat down in the pilot's seat. I was wearing the red jacket the Tuskegee Airmen had presented to me. I wore the medal the Air Force Association had given me. I had on 1930s style aviator boots that Mary had given me years before. My best leather flying helmet and a pair of First World War goggles that Bruce had given me rounded out the look. A rush of excitement went through my body as I felt the touch of the rudders against my boots for the final time.

The day was overcast but it did not bother me in the least. I had been to the North Pole—of what concern was a low ceiling? I started the engine, taxied to the end of the runway, and took off, shooting up into the gray air.

For forty minutes we wheeled and soared and remembered our adventures together. So many memories: from the time the engine quit, putting me and Mary in the field, to the day I almost ground looped with my son, to the flip-over in Baughers Orchard, and to all our solo afternoons when the air was perfect and the flying sweet. We had flown as one to the top of the world and chased caribou across the frozen tundra. For one last time the Stearman was the body and I was the soul, and together we were the hawk.

I buzzed down over some trees near the airport and landed back at College Park. The crowd came up to the airplane as the sound of engines firing up and planes buzzing overhead filled my ears. After the crowds had gone and I was alone with the Stearman, I said "Goodbye ol' girl."

As I walked back to my car and drove home I allowed a new adventure to begin to take shape in my mind. Next time I want to fly around the world the hard way—pole to pole.

The journey continues just off the wing, over a hill, on the far side of a lake, above the cloud for as far as the mind can dream. Life and the quest go on. The goal lies over the next horizon.